TRANSFORMING
WORK

OTHER BOOKS BY JOHN D. ADAMS

Transforming Leadership

Life Changes: Growing Through Personal Transitions
with Sabina A. Spencer

Transition: Understanding and Managing
Personal Changes
with John Hayes and Barrie Hopson

Understanding and Managing Stress:
A Workbook in Changing Life Styles:
Facilitator's Guide, Workbook, Book of Readings

Organization Development in Health Care Organizations
with Newton Margulies

New Technologies in Organization Development

TRANSFORMING
WORK

2nd Edition

JOHN D. ADAMS
General Editor

A Miles River Press  **Professional Book**

Transforming Work

First Edition, 1984, Miles River Press
        Second Printing, 1988
        Third Printing, 1990
        Fourth Printing, 1993
Second Edition, 1998, Miles River Press

Miles River Press Team

    Publisher, Peg Paul
    Editorial, Peg Paul, Diane Reukauf, Sheila Gibson, Sandra Bisbey
    Cover Design, Grace Design
    Production, ME Graphics

Ordering Information

Orders by U.S. trade bookstores and wholesalers:
    Midpoint Trade Books
    27 West 20th Street, #1102
    New York, New York 10011
    Telephone: (212) 727-0190   Fax: (212) 727-0195

Orders for individuals, organizations, quantity sales
and college adoption:
    Miles River Press
    400 Madison Street, #1309
    Alexandria, Virginia 22314
    Telephone: (703) 683-1500   Fax: (703) 683-0827
    Toll-Free: (800) 767-1501

Library of Congress Cataloging-in-Publication Data:

Transforming work / John D. Adams, general editor. — 2nd ed.
      p. cm.
    Includes bibliographical references.
    ISBN 0-917917-12-X (alk. paper)
    1. Organizational change. 2. Management. I. Adams, John D.,
  1942–
    HD58.8T72   1988   98-4765
    658.4'06—dc21   CIP

For permission to reprint copyrighted materials, grateful acknowledgment is given to the following sources:
    Chapter 3: Adapted by Robert F. Allen and Charlotte Craft from their book *The Organizational
    Unconscious, published 1982 by Prentice-Hall.
    Chapter 5: ©1984 Kiefer and Stroh
    Chapter 7: ©1982 by Roger Harrison
    Chapter 10: ©1984 Kiefer and Senge

10 9 8 7 6 5 4 3 2

DEDICATION

For Pierre Teilhard de Chardin,
a man of vision,
who devoted his life to integrating science and spirituality

Contents

Acknowledgments — First Edition

Organization Transformation (OT) appears to be a new thrust, perhaps even the beginnings of a new field, for working with performance in the workplace. Such an initial book of readings can capture the initial excitement and activities from the perspectives of those who are carrying out the explorations. I think a book of readings is an appropriate format for introducing OT at this point in time.

One problem with books of readings is that they often are terribly disjointed. The chapters don't seem to build on each other, and there are tremendous variations in writing styles. I have attempted to select chapters, most of which were written specifically for this book, that reflect a coherence while portraying the diversity in OT today. Where I felt there were gaps initially, I have asked specific people for specific papers. I wish to thank all of the authors for their timely delivery of manuscripts, and for their patience with the editorial process we have used to enhance the flow of the book.

One thing we have all learned is that we have a tendency to write to please ourselves rather than our audience. Sometimes we write without being clear who the audience is! Three people are responsible for making this book considerably more readable than it might have been: Peg Paul, Dan Zincus, and Dave Keckler. Peg, founder and president of Miles River Press, spent patient hours teaching me how to publish a book of readings. In any one of those hours, I learned more about how to do this than I had learned from the entire process of editing three previous books of readings. Dan and Dave offered many helpful suggestions on the manuscript.

Peg also deserves special mention for her overall support of the project. The book represents a new venture for her firm — a risky thing to undertake in the publications world during a recession. Her personal commitment to transformation and to transforming her organization are most heartening. Without her guidance, we would not have been able to produce this book at the time we did.

I also want to acknowledge my colleagues in the Center for Excellence in Organizations for their moral support of the project, as well as for their contributions of chapters. The book is but one rallying point for our exciting new ventures together!

— John D. Adams

Preface — First Edition

S ince 1975, my consulting practice has been almost exclusively devoted to health promotion and stress-management programs. As I became involved with the broad range of knowledge and techniques needed to cover these topics comprehensively, it became progressively clearer that in order to protect health and to manage stress effectively, fundamental personal changes — transformations — are necessary.

Many people view themselves as hapless victims in a hostile universe, a viewpoint which makes self-responsible initiatives take responsibility for their own health — their psychological outlooks and their daily lifestyle choices about eating, drinking, smoking, exercising, and so on. Stimulating this transformational process in individuals has been the most challenging and most rewarding aspect of my work.

However, a new set of collective beliefs — a new paradigm — that is emerging in human consciousness has made me aware that transformations also must be examined at the organizational level, as well as at the global level, in order for us to live our lives more effectively. This new paradigm emphasizes, among other things, an expanded sense of personal identity and an awareness of the interconnectedness of people in their organizational cultures, and of organizational cultures to each other in the larger environment. Scientists at the leading edge of every discipline are making discoveries and putting forth theories that are dovetailing with several views of evolution, spirituality, and integrated consciousness which have been put forth over the centuries. Even our basic style of thinking is moving away from a Cartesian, reductionist/mechanistic base to include more expansionist and systemic thinking.

We clearly have all we need to create any kind of future we would like — a world that works for everyone. We also have all we need to destroy the world several times over. We will certainly decide between these outcomes within a generation. To paraphrase the late futurist, Buckminster Fuller, "the World is now taking its final exam."

I am concerned that only a relatively small group of people is seriously discussing these ideas, and that this group contains few decision-makers. In a sense, seminars on these topics "preach to the choir," in that those who attend are, by and large, already "believers." These ideas have a great deal of applicability to the organizations we work in, and these organizations must provide the vehicle for personal and global transformations. The complex nature of the problems faced today by major organizations makes them unsolvable unless the organizations *themselves* undergo major transformations.

For example, if present worldwide trends continue, by the year 2000 there will be: 50 percent more people; 33 percent less topsoil; 1.3 billion people experiencing severe malnutrition; a drastic shortage of clean water; as many as a million more species extinct; sufficient damage to the upper atmosphere to cause polar melts and radical climate changes; a 50-percent reduction in the forests of Asia, Africa, and Latin America; and 40 nations with nuclear weapons. Furthermore, massive shifts and strains are developing in the global economy. The organizations of the world, whether or not they are direct contributors to problems such as these, will have to be part of the solutions. The predominant modes of operating — focusing primarily on profit and return on investment — will have to give way to more global purposes if we are to survive.

And, especially in organizations in the United States, people are coming to work with more education and different values than was the case a few short decades ago. Many organizations still do little strategic planning and pay little attention to external environmental factors, which increasingly reflect a global sense of competition and interdependency.

On the positive side, technological advances and a spiritual reawakening are fostering a growing sense of a global community and the awareness that we have become the creators of our own future. Worldwide communications networks and the rapid flow of information around the globe provide organizations with incredible opportunities.

In 1982, I became committed to working on the problems and potentialities hinted at in the preceding paragraphs, as in the context of work and organizations. I began referring tò this work as *Organizational Transformation* (OT) in contrast to *Organizational Development* (OD) (in which I had been trained in graduate school in the 1960s). OD emerged from applied Social Psychology and adult education in the early 1960s as a process for helping organizations solve problems and more fully realize their potentials. Reflecting its academic roots, OD efforts have always been based on theories and the collection and analysis of data. I do not view OT as rejecting theory and data by any means, but it does somewhat shift the focus to establishing a vision of what is desired and working to create that vision from the perspective of a clearly articulated set of humanistic values. OD would not reject vision and values either — it's a matter of shifting the emphasis slightly towards a larger, more proactive perspective.

In my view, OT encompasses OD much in the same manner that Einstein's Theory of Relativity encompassed Newtonian physics. We should avoid getting into OT versus OD debates, since they do not represent an either/or polarity. OD is useful for helping a given organization (or unit within an organization) operate as effectively as it can, within the parameters of its charter. OT will help a given organization explore its purpose and charter in relation to the larger environment and facilitate the necessary fundamental realignments. Where OD has focused on form and function, OT will focus on energy and flow. Organizations need both.

While OD develops or enhances what is, there is a sense of discontinuity and irreversibility about OT. Ken Wilber, in *A Sociable God**, provides a useful metaphor. He likens translation (development) to moving the furniture around on the floor and transformation to moving the furniture to a new floor. Clearly, many of our organizations urgently need to "move their furniture to a new floor," both for their own good and for the good of the planet. Simultaneously, they will have to continue operating effectively while these transformations take place, and they will need at least as much developmental work as ever.

It didn't take long for me to learn two things. The first discovery was that many professionals were simultaneously arriving at the same conclusions I had about the need for the transformation of organizations — and also calling it OT — a phenomenon Carl Jung called *synchronicity*. Second, I learned that many organizations are already transforming themselves, and that our role is to facilitate these processes rather than to create them.

With all of this in mind, I felt that the time had come to produce a book about the emergence of OT. Rather than attempting to write the first book about this new field alone, it seemed appropriate that I should capture the emerging practice in the words of the practitioners. There is so much happening under the new rubric of "Organizational Transformation" all around the United States, and in some parts of Europe, that a single author couldn't begin to capture the range of ideas and technologies that are emerging. The 17 chapters were written by a total of 23 different people representing a wide diversity of backgrounds and professional orientations.

OT is by no means a clear-cut discipline or set of techniques. In fact, it is still in the early stages of emergence. Since many of the concepts are quite new to people who manage organizations and to their consultants, they are often challenging to write about. In the chapters that follow, you will find quite a few new word usages and a great many concepts borrowed from diverse fields of study. Out of all this diversity, however, six themes are clearly present. While it is much too early to define OT, these six themes do sketch out an initial arena for our work and theorizing. While none of these six themes is new, they have never received as much emphasis, priority, and interconnection as in this volume.

These six themes may be depicted graphically:

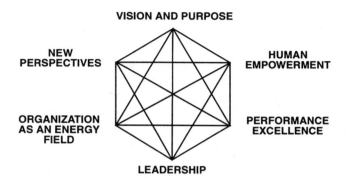

Vision implies the importance of establishing and clarifying the purposes, goals, directions, or focuses which the individual or system is working towards. Once this has been established, agreement with the vision and commitment to it are seen as being very important.

New Perspectives means questioning the basic assumptions and beliefs which are taken for granted in organizations. Following the lead of the physical sciences, new ways of knowing (new consciousnesses) are called for which are more holistic, expansive, and relativistic.

Organization as an Energy Field suggests the necessity of managing organizational *processes* in addition to managing organizational *positions*. It focuses on momentum and on the power of collective beliefs, myths, and traditions — the culture of the organization.

Leadership is seen as needing additional focuses on creating and sustaining the vision; catalyzing alignment with the vision; and encouraging learning, exploration, and creativity. Leaders will need to adopt the *new perspectives* first, especially the perspective of the organization as an energy field.

Performance Excellence, the highly competent execution and completion of required or desired tasks, is a component that is often missing in organizations on individual, group, and organization-wide levels. It is viewed by many of the authors as being of utmost importance in today's complex world. Many conditions and techniques for fostering performance excellence on these three levels are presented.

Human Empowerment involves the creation of environmental conditions in which people are encouraged to work toward achieving their potentials. In order to tap the true human potential and empower people to become what they can be, we must focus more on individual well-being; on encouraging individual self-responsibility and the alteration of self-limiting beliefs; and on encouraging the development of the spiritual self.

The 17 chapters in the book are divided into four parts. Part I provides a rationale for developing the field of OT and contains some preliminary frameworks for its practice. In Part II, the crucial role of the leader in transforming organizations is explored. Next, Part III discusses the facilitation of transformation in organizations and provides concepts and frameworks for the OT practitioner. Part IV provides a sample of OT technologies, to give the reader a taste of what to expect as OT develops over the next few years.

It is my hope that this book will stimulate much discussion and further development of ways and means to help organizations undergo the changes they need to make. I also hope that, ultimately, we will each contribute in our own way to creating a world that works for everyone.

— John D. Adams
Arlington, Virginia
February 1984

*K. Wilber, *A Sociable God.* (New York: New Press/McGraw-Hill, 1983).

The Brighter the Light, the Darker the Shadow?

T he selections in this collection were written during late 1983 and early 1984. As you will find as you read them, their messages are still very current today. The good news in this is that perhaps the concepts in the book are relatively timeless. On the other hand, perhaps they are still current because we haven't really accomplished the dreams embodied in our original writing. The contributors were asked to write a brief reflection on their original work for inclusion in this second edition of *Transforming Work*. These reflections seem to support both possibilities — that the ideas are still good ones, *and* that we have not realized what we had hoped for.

In the introduction to the first edition, I emphasized that the newly emerging field of Organization Transformation (OT) was not intended to be in competition with the already established field of Organization Development (OD) out of which it was being born. Rather, the intention was to cause the field of OD to enlarge itself to include the concepts of vision, purpose, and broader, more strategic perspectives. This, in fact, is what has happened, as supporting the creation and implementation of corporate visions has become standard operating practice in OD for several years now.

In 1983, I had trouble selling the original manuscript to a major publisher; "vision" work was seen as too much on the fringe to be saleable. Now Chrysler has had a car called Vision for several years, and almost every business has a vision of what it dreams to become. So instead of being a "visionary" anthology, this second edition stands to become a standard operating manual for building robust visions.

In the intervening years since the first edition, the Berlin Wall and Soviet Union have fallen, and capitalism and democracy are emerging with a flourish in Central and Eastern Europe. The late 80s brought us a spate of leveraged buyouts and hostile takeovers; in the early 90s, reengineering and downsizing became the vogue. None of these occurrences were anticipated by the authors when they wrote the selections in *Transforming Work*. While the globalization of business *was* in their writing, I doubt if any of them could have predicted the extent to which this has actually taken place. Even the smallest businesses in the most remote areas of the country are affected every day by the global nature of business.

In the arena of economics, the authors totally missed the impending massive growth in speculative markets as having a huge impact in the marketplace. In today's market, the equivalent of the GDP of the entire world passes through the Wall Street brokerages every three weeks. Nearly every business in the for-profit sector is now focused on protecting shareholder return as a primary part of its strategy planning. Issuing stock certificates to the public — once primarily a means to raise capital — is now itself a major focus of our attention, with the emphasis being on the value of the shares to the shareholder (and senior corporate executives hold vast numbers of shares in their own companies), rather than primarily on supplying capital for expansion.

While the environment was mentioned frequently in the first edition, we did not anticipate the rise of concerns for the very sustainability — the *survivability* of life as we know it — being strongly influenced by the practices of our enterprises. The very major concerns over global warming and holes in the ozone layer weren't yet on our "radar screens." Agricultural and fishing yields were at an all-time high, and little thought was being given to that situation changing. Today we are becoming aware that both agricultural and fishing yields have been declining each year since *Transforming Work* was first published. While we can still feed everyone, with nearly two billion additional people on the earth since the first edition, it is clear we cannot go on forever with declining food production and a global population that currently is doubling every 35 years.

Several hundred years ago, the church was the dominant institution in the West, and it took care of things within its sphere of influence. As Joseph Campbell pointed out, the church always had the tallest buildings. As the church's dominance gave way to the state, capital city skylines came to be dominated by government buildings, and governments took responsibility for their spheres of influence. In this century, and especially as the Cold War came to an end, businesses became the dominant institution on the planet, and their sphere of influence became the entire planet. For the evidence, just take a look at the skyline of any major city in the world. Today business is taking responsibility for its own bottom line and shareholder equity — but not for its total sphere of influence.

Business is clearly the institution best situated around the world to redefine our priorities and practices. It presently is also the primary generator of the pervasive ecological problems that are crying out for attention. It is clear that whatever future we do realize over the next thirty years or so will be strongly influenced by business practices, whether or not businesses are conscious of their influence. And our work with businesses will influence the outcomes, in some large or small way, whether or not we are conscious of our influence.

My fundamental view is that our future, in large part, will be strongly influenced by the images and expectations we are holding today. The prevailing mental models are short-term, local, reactive, and symptom-oriented in their focus. Therefore, if those of us who are OD or OT professionals demonstrate excellence in our practices, while operating with these presently prevailing mental models, we may actually be contributing to the collapse of a sustainable human presence on the planet. *The brighter the light, the darker the shadow!* If we help in making our businesses more effective, we are also improving their abilities to contribute to environmental degradation.

Marilyn Ferguson, author and speaker, often states:

If I continue to believe as I have always believed,
I will continue to act as I have always acted.
And if I continue to act as I have always acted,
I will continue to get what I have always gotten.

Relatedly, Ronald Laing points out that

The range of what we think and do
is limited by what we fail to notice.
And because we fail to notice
that we fail to notice,
there is little we can do to change,
until we notice how failing to notice
shapes our thoughts and deeds.*

I feel strongly that our profession is in an excellent position to lead the way in forging a vision for the future that can guide our enterprises, on the global level, through the difficult times that presumably lie ahead. In order to be truly successful in forging a viable vision for the future, we must collectively develop a trans-organizational, global mindset.

Mindsets operate outside of awareness most of the time, as Ronald Laing implies; and yet they tend to be self-fulfilling, as Marilyn Ferguson states. So one emerging role for professionals in Organization Transformation must include facilitation of what I call the "autopilot-to-choice" process. Unless we collectively learn to make these autopilot patterns conscious, and choose to change those that will not support us, we will not be able to overcome the complex challenges we are now realizing we must face up to. Many years ago, Einstein pointed out that we cannot resolve a complex problem by using the same mindset that caused the problem in the first place.

Autopilot-to-choice shifts will be along the dimensions illustrated below — from the mostly short term/local/reactive/symptom-treating position of the predominant mindset to a more long-term/global/co-creating/capacity-building mindset. Whenever the pressure builds up, as it seems to be doing in most organizations today, there is a natural tendency for the mindset to collapse even more severely towards the left ends of the dimensions above. As a result, much of our work, which requires a broader mindset to be effective, gets put on the "back burner" by our organizations.

```
┌─────────────────────────────────────────────────────────────┐
│              SOME KEY DIMENSIONS OF MINDSET                   │
│                                                              │
│   Short Term_____Long Term        │
│   Operational                              Strategic         │
│                     TIME DIMENSION                           │
│   Local_____Global            │
│   Reductionist                             Systemic          │
│                     SPACE DIMENSION                          │
│   Reactive_____Co-Creative        │
│   Responsive                               Initiating        │
│                  ATTITUDINAL DIMENSION                       │
│                                                              │
│   No Strategy_____Optimal Vitality   │
│   Treat Symptoms                           Build Capacity    │
│                    STRATEGY DIMENSION                        │
└─────────────────────────────────────────────────────────────┘
```

One essential feature of our thinking from now on must be to help the leadership of our organizations maintain broader mindsets in the face of pressure. Versatility in mindset does not preclude thinking locally, for example, but allows the person to consider simultaneously both the local and the global implications. In terms of the above dimensions, we must learn to maintain a wide zone of comfort along each of the dimensions, and help our organizations to do so also. We already know how to do this; we just have to overcome our *own* autopilot tendency to focus on the outer symptoms. We must learn to focus on the root causes of the symptoms.

If I could put forward a manifesto for the field of OT, it would focus on recasting at least part of our role on a more societal level, and on our becoming the custodians of a sustainable future. This would require reprogramming our own autopilots to encourage simultaneous and bi-level thinking on both the local and the global levels, in operational and in strategic time frames; being both proactively responsive to the environment and actively co-creating desired futures; and addressing the serious symptoms we come across as well as building system capacity for self-correction. This would mean taking an advocacy position more frequently. It would require long-term ethical involvement in major corporate policy decisions.

There are already moves in these directions. Networks have formed and inquiry processes are going on in many quarters. To be truly successful, we will have to seek out and work with cross-disciplinary, inter-organizational teams. Although our field was multi-disciplinary in its origins, it has tended to become a discipline unto itself. We need to open the doors again to some vigorous cross-disciplinary traffic.

I will close this introduction to the second edition with a series of questions for you to think about, and perhaps to use as stimuli for dialogues:

- How can we establish a community-wide forum to address sustainable business practices?
- How can the developed world and the developing world find common ground?
- How can we help our organizations identify true value from a systemic, long-term mindset?
- How can we involve the children more in our work?
- How can we influence our organizations to consider the questions of longer-range impact?
- What new methods and models do we need to develop or link with in order to connect ourselves and our organizations to the real issues of sustainability?
- What are we doing that perpetuates short-term, selfish mindsets?
- What do we want people to say about Organizational Transformation 30 years from now?

— John D. Adams

---

* R. Laing, in C. Zweig and J. Abrams, eds., *Meeting the Shadow: The Hidden Power of the Dark Side of Human Nature.* (Los Angeles: Jeremy P. Tarcher, Inc., 1991).

I.

SETTING THE STAGE:

THE REALM OF

ORGANIZATIONAL TRANSFORMATION

1

Grace Beyond the Rules: A New Paradigm for Lives on a Human Scale

DAVID NICOLL

Comments on the Second Edition

It seems another lifetime ago that I wrote this article. It was sometime during the summer of 1982, and I distinctly remember the halting, half-hearted beginnings I mustered in response to John's invitation to write. At that particular time, I had been "engaged" to the subject of paradigms and paradigm shifts for more than two years, thinking that these were phenomena of real importance. But the closer I came to committing my consulting practice to paradigmatic change, the more hesitant I became. When I started writing *Grace Beyond The Rules,* I recognized that being negative and skeptical about these subjects had been all too easy for me, and that if I were going to write the article, I would have to adopt the attitude and outlook necessary to both write and consult on this subject from a confident, upbeat perspective.

Today I'm pleased, even proud, of the confidence this article carries. Rereading it isn't at all embarrassing, as I thought it might be. And given the fears and hesitancies I felt that summer, it's a cleaner, more precise piece of work than I had a right to expect. It even says some useful things. Among these, what most stands out for me as an insightful comment is the statement:

> Another important proposition we need to think about is that this new paradigm, first and foremost, is challenging our common-sense views of the world . . . Our new paradigm is showing us that much of this common sense is really "junko-logic" — that is, words, phrases, and ideas strung together with connectors like "since," "because," and "so" that imply a causation that, given our new paradigmatic view, does not stand up . . . [These] propositions

point to the efficacy of feeling, thinking, and acting in "counter-intuitive" ways. That is, these propositions suggest we need to experiment with what our new paradigm shows us is effective, rather than to continue acting on what our common sense tells us.

Just last week I was making this point to a client who was lamenting the extent to which fear and blame were conditioning his organization, and how difficult it was for him and his colleagues to break the downward spiral that these poisonous pills produced. For him, it felt like those factors were way beyond his control and, like a whirlpool, were dragging them all down into disputes they didn't need to have. The "counter-intuitive" advice I offered him — accepting personal responsibility — did not make sense to him. Consequently, we were stuck, at least for the time being.

This vignette leads me to one other reflection that seems worth making at this place and point in time: I am quite surprised with how slowly this paradigm shift of ours is moving and, as a consequence, how slowly we as consultants are responding to it. Slow, slow, slow; to my mind we are barely creeping along — especially since way back in 1983 we "knew" that we were in the middle of this shift. I distinctly remember that during the summer I wrote this article I was quite confident that within a couple of years I would have learned all I needed to know to support my clients in their transformational efforts and that, at the least by 1990, I would have no problem finding clients who knew about paradigm shifts and who, as a consequence, would be easy to work with around this subject.

Surprise, Surprise. Today, I really know for sure very little more about effecting paradigmatic shifts within my client systems than I did fourteen years ago. Certainly, I have more experience; but I have far fewer tried-and-true interventions in my kit-bag than I thought I would have. Consequently, when talking with clients about the way our society's paradigm shift affects their businesses, I find myself telling them that, in doing our work, we are going to have to act more like Lewis and Clark trail-blazing their way to the Pacific, than a metropolitan bus driver following his well-worn route into downtown Los Angeles. Unfortunately, I also have to tell them that, in my opinion, we're going to have to wait at least a few decades before the consulting profession can offer them reframing interventions that carry the clarity and surety of OD's old stand-by interventions, role clarification and team-building.

— David Nicoll

We are developing a new story, and, in the process, altering much of what we think, feel, and do. What our grandchildren will accept as fact, we are in the process of discovering and creating. This chapter recognizes that transformation by providing fundamental perspective. It offers, in turn, some basic concepts about paradigms and paradigm shifts, and then a description of some of the characteristics of the emerging paradigm. All of this is offered in a straightforward way to give readers a clear reference point from which to do their own thinking about the new belief systems we are helping to build. It also provides an introduction to the theme of this book — the transformation of organizations.

The heart of the matter is this: We are in mid-stride between an old and a new era, and we have not yet found our way. We know the old no longer works; the new is not yet formed clearly enough to be believed. As many Indian tribes have suggested, it is all a question of story. Our story — the account of how the world came to be, and how and why we fit into it — has been around a long time. It has shaped our emotional attitudes, stimulated our actions, and provided us with perspective on life's problems. It has consecrated our suffering, integrated our knowledge, and offered us hope. Most of all, it has provided us a context in which our lives could function in a meaningful fashion. As Thomas Berry suggested,[1] we could awake in the morning and know where we were. We could answer the questions of our children. We could identify crime and punish criminals. Everything was taken care of, because the story was there. But now — between stories — we are confused.

We are developing a new story and, in the process, altering much of what we think, feel, and do. What our grandchildren will accept as fact, we are in the process of discovering and creating. In this context it is important for us to recognize that we are facing a change that matters. To do this we need some basic propositions that help us comprehend what is happening. That is what this chapter is about: recognizing the transformation by providing some fundamental perspective. In the next few pages I will attempt a first cut at this by offering, in turn, some basic concepts about paradigms and paradigm shifts, and then a description of some of the more apparent characteristics of our emerging paradigm. All of this I will offer in a straightforward way to provide readers a reference point from which to think about the new belief system we are helping to build.

BASIC PROPOSITIONS

A revolution has occurred, and our world has changed. This revolution has taken place in the beliefs, intentions, thoughts, and behavior of people. And this is the first concept we must recognize: the paradigm shift we all are talking about has occurred. We are not at the beginning of the revolution, but probably somewhere closer to the midpoint. The old order has been shattered, at least at the level of formal disciplines, by discoveries in the sciences and by new understandings in the humanities. Quantum mechanics powers NASA's space flights, and new biological discoveries make test tube babies possible. These changes, and many others like them, long ago began producing effects on our common understandings, and the impacts are becoming rapidly diffused. We are beginning to live this new paradigm day-to-day.

A second proposition worth considering is the idea of a paradigm itself. A paradigm is a civilization's fundamental view of things. It is the set of beliefs we hold, at the level of unquestioned and unexamined presuppositions about what is true and real. In a broad, metaphorical sense, it is the instrument through which we apprehend everything. It is our own internalized microscope, our own inescapable thermometer. In a philosophical sense, a paradigm is the set of answers we provide ourselves for these four questions:

1. What is reality?
2. How and why does this reality function?
3. How and why does reality change?
4. How do we know that what we believe about these questions is true?

These are ultimate questions. They demand answers because they come from our base presupposition, the assumption all humans everywhere make: there is order in disorder, a pattern in the chaos. If only we can find it, there is meaning somewhere.

The paradigm shift we currently are experiencing is different from any other the human race has experienced; it is the first one of which we are conscious while it is happening. In a startling way, we now truly understand that our presumptions — our paradigm — determines our experience. The shadows we see on the wall in front of us come from the flashlight we hold behind us.

This paradigm shift is not moving from one perspective to another. We often talk about it this way, implying something is replacing something else, that the new is supplanting the old. We should understand, however, that this is not the case. The new paradigm will not replace the old paradigm. Our new paradigm is emerging alongside the old. It is appearing inside and around the old paradigm. It is building on it, amplifying it and extending it. But it is not replacing it. Gravity is still a useful concept, as are cause-and-effect and friction.

The new paradigm is not bringing the millennium. This is so for many reasons: one of the most important is that it is not doing away with evil or with pain. These things will remain, and we will have to deal with them long after the new world view is in place.

Another important proposition we need to think about is that this new paradigm, first and foremost, is challenging our common-sense views of the world. This common sense of ours developed in prehistoric ages, when all we knew was that the sun came up in one place and set in another. We were the center of our experience, and our view of the physical world was the reality base around which our common sense grew. Our new paradigm is showing us that much of this common sense is really "junko logic" — words, phrases, and ideas strung together with connectors like "since," "because," and "so" that imply a causation which, given our new paradigmatic view, does not stand up. We *know* we are not the center of the universe, but in many ways we still act as if we were. Despite experience and knowledge to the contrary, we continue to say things like, "It's all downhill from here, so we can take it easy now" and, "If only we could get to the heart of this issue, we would know the answer." These examples show that much of our common sense is based on cause-and-effect metaphors that make sense at the level of primitive sensory experience, but are no longer grounded either in the way we know things are or in what we have learned is effective.

These are some of the basic concepts about paradigms and our current paradigm shift that I think need careful consideration. Before moving to the next issue — a description of the salient characteristics of our new paradigm — let me suggest that these propositions point to the efficacy of feeling, thinking, and acting in "counter-intuitive" ways. That is, these propositions suggest we need to experiment with what our new paradigm shows us is effective, rather than to continue acting on what our common sense tells us. For example, we all know that there are vicious circles in human affairs. If I blame you, you will reciprocate in turn, becoming angry with me and allowing yourself to be hurt. This prejudices the way you think about and feel toward me, generally causing you to exaggerate the very things in your behavior that caused me to blame you in the first place. We also know that we all project our attitudes onto others, and that this projection is probably the original source of most blaming behavior. What we don't like in others is what we don't like and have not come to terms with in ourselves. "Knowing" all this as we do, it makes "sense" for all of us to restrain ourselves from blaming others for anything. Indeed, as we are discovering in this and many other areas, our new paradigm is suggesting a fundamentally new perspective about what it means to be human. Our common sense is changing, and in this light we need to begin replacing our old behaviors with repertoires that our new precepts suggest are more effective.

CHARACTERISTICS OF THE EMERGENT PARADIGM

So far I have set the stage in general ways, talking about basic propositions that relate to this new paradigm of ours. This section attempts to crystallize the new paradigm by describing and probing the patterns underlying many of its disparate aspects. In particular, it outlines those presuppositional assumptions that answer the four fundamentally human questions outlined above.

Credit is due here to Peter Schwartz and James Ogilvy for their formation of this model and for their explication of it. All of what follows stems from my reading of their work,[2] and from conversations with James Ogilvy in the summer of 1983.

I divide my description of the emerging paradigm into three categories: Ordering, Causing, and Knowing. The Ordering category explores the questions "What is reality?" and "How does this reality function?" The Causing category describes what we are beginning to believe is true about how reality changes. The Knowing category describes presuppositions we are building that answer the question "How do we know what we believe is true?"

Ordering

There is an apparent order to things — or so it seems. By seeing our universe as ordered and understandable, we derive feelings of control and security. Consequently, we build our understanding of how this universe is ordered around three concerns:[3]

1. What kinds of structures are possible?
2. What kinds of relationships are possible among the elements of these structures?
3. What are the processes by which a structure interacts and changes?

Structure, relationship, and change. We build our presuppositions about order in the universe around these concepts. Assuming these concepts are real and building ideas around them allows us to be comfortable within our world.

The new paradigm alters our preconceptions about these concerns. At the risk of oversimplifying, our emerging view can be captured in a few words: Our world is complexly structured. In some instances, as we have thought for a long time, it is hierarchical. The basic structure is a pyramid, with a person, principle, or object sitting at the apex, transmitting orders down through the ranks. Through our parent-child, teacher-student, and boss-subordinate relationships, we have known this reality all of our lives. In other very important instances, we now are beginning to believe our world is also "heterarchically" structured.[4] That is, it is organized with multiple, overlapping hierarchies with no one controlling person, principle, or object at the top of everything. For the most part, we are finding that our political systems operate this way. In many respects we are finding that our organizations function this way as well. In other words, the world is both hierarchical and heterarchical.

In this context, two fundamental beliefs about the way our universe and our lives are structured are emerging from the physical and biological sciences. We are beginning to assume that:

1. There are multiple levels of reality.
2. Each of these different levels has its own laws, rules, principles of interaction, and patterns of activity.

These new beliefs come out of — and are resulting in — our letting go of our centuries-old drive to discover an "ultimate" reality. Universal laws, and a pristine objectivity from which to study them, are no longer our ideals. We previously believed in the possibility and desirability of objective knowledge, but now we are changing our minds — rapidly in the sciences and humanities, more slowly in everyday life.

Another important presupposition about the structure of reality is coming from brain research.[5] It suggests that both information and the use of that information are distributed throughout a system. Instead of using the computer as a common metaphor for how the brain works, researchers are taking up the hologram as a common metaphor, visualizing the human functions of thought and memory as distributed throughout the brain. In combination with cybernetics and systems theory, this distributed-function analogy — for this is what it is, at the level of knowledge and understanding at which most of us work — is shifting our presuppositions about the nature of reality. We now envision systems as complex networks of interdependent functions wherein the parts automatically contain knowledge of the whole.

These alterations in the way we see the basic structure of reality force collateral and compatible changes in the way we perceive the relationships between and among the various parts of a system. Where before we only saw top-down communications, we now hold a much more diverse set of presuppositional views. In addition to unilateral controls, we are beginning to believe in a complex set of communication and control processes spread among co-equal parts of a system. Interaction among the parts of a system is becoming critical.

Another important relationship perspective that is gaining currency is what Arthur Koestler called holarchy.[6] Here we imagine each element of a system as having both the independent properties of wholes, and the dependent properties of parts. That is, each system has its own characteristics, but its functioning in reality is an outcome of its membership in the larger system. The larger system or context frames behavior and determines meaning.

Neurologist Karl Pribram's work offers an additional relationship perspective that is important in our new paradigm.[7] In his research on brain functioning, he has identified a fine fiber network that links brain cells together in a parallel fashion. In explaining how this network functions, he suggests that a wave, like a light wave, is propagated inside the brain. This is a complex wave, carrying a great deal of information. It moves through these parallel networks, interacting with other waves in such a way that their joint movements result first in the distributed network of information described earlier, and second, in the creation of new information. This new metaphor of "wave-like functioning," where one wave interacts with other waves to create new patterns and structures, is a totally different way of picturing intra-system relationships. It suggests that patterns of interactions are important sources of information and definition. New structures can emerge from interaction patterns themselves.

The image of change that is emerging within this new paradigm is complex. We are conceptualizing several different approaches to change, several ways of understanding how systems, human and otherwise, alter themselves.

Continuous, quantitative change, known in common parlance as evolution, is still a viable model of change. Some systems change in a slow, smooth, uninterrupted fashion; plants are one example. But this model of change is being augmented. Beside it we also are developing faith in a process by which one form gives way to another in quick, qualitative ways. We are talking about discontinuities, treating change as a quick process where one structure suddenly gives way to another.

Ilya Prigogine, who won the 1977 Nobel Prize in chemistry for his theory of "dissipative structures," describes yet another of our new perspectives on change.[8] This model assumes that complex systems can and do evolve in an open environment from less order to more order, and from simpler to more complex structures. Fluctuations within a system interact with one another, and through this process they affect one another in qualitative ways, causing wholly new structures to arise. Prigogine called this morphogenesis.

A similar approach is that of C.S. Holling, who has developed an ecological model.[9] This approach replaces the concept of stability (which is fundamental to our old concept of change) with that of resilience. Resilience results from a combination of adequate diversity, mutually supportive relationships between elements of a system, and open subsystems capable of receiving input from the outside. In this context, the diversity among sets of the system, rather than any evolutionary process, acts to produce change.

In sum, our picture of how our universe is structured, relates, and changes is becoming quite complex. We are conceiving a world structured in both hierarchical and heterarchical terms. Relationships in these structures are holographic and holarchic; systems contain distributed information and functions, and promote interactions where the "whole" provides framing and definitional cues for its parts. We are postulating that systems change in multiple and manifold ways. They may shift in small and adaptive ways, by incremental additions and subtractions. They also may undergo quite dramatic and sudden alterations; change often appears out of chaos. Central to our new beliefs about change is our notion that difference produces change. We are beginning to believe that a small change, relying on mutual interaction and reciprocal causality with the surrounding environment, can amplify itself and produce even bigger change.

Causing

The issue of causality raises questions about how and why things happen the way they do. How do things change? Why do they change? And, in this instrumental era, how can we control and influence these processes? In considering such issues, creators of the new paradigm are proposing five distinct models by which system change occurs.

The first model of causality is the most ancient and familiar. It focuses on singular, external causes that produce change in a linear and mechanical sequence. Push a rock and it moves. Pushing it again produces the same result, every time.

The second model postulates that randomness and homogeneity are the ultimate condition of the universe and that things consequently tend to run down. (Most teenagers' rooms are classic examples of this model.) The world is basically entropic, and all cause comes from this tendency for things to deteriorate.

Cybernetics is the base of a third model. It suggests that information, fed back into the system, causes things to change. The thermostat is the classic model of a cybernetically-based causal system. If air cools below a given thermostatic setting, the thermostat fires up the heater. When the air warms above the desired temperature, the thermostat reacts by turning the heat off. Eventually, the heater and the thermostat together reach a range of off/on activity that is stabilized around the desired temperature. Given an explicit goal, a homeostatic condition is reached as a result of the negative information fed back into the system.

The fourth model, termed the "second cybernetics," also is based on information flow, but this time the emphasis is on positive feedback in an open system. In a mutually interactive system, positive information acts to amplify the effect. Human love and affection are good examples, encouraging babies and adults alike to walk, talk, and reach out for new challenges. In this case differences grow rather than diminish.

The fifth model assumes and postulates the power of conscious intent. Whereas in the fourth model change is caused by interaction within the system and between the system and environment, change in this model is based on a "conscious" intent to change — for example, an individual's interest in altering him- or herself. This kind of change presumably applies exclusively to human systems, which have the ability to change either internal circumstances (perspective) or external circumstances (context).

There is no doubt we are expanding our cause and effect presuppositions. From simple, linear, mechanical causality we are moving toward a complex, mutually-influencing and self-transcending causal belief structure. In addition, we are beginning to assume that change is a subtle issue that cannot be predetermined, regardless of the model of causality assumed. All of our simplistic notions in this regard were laid to rest by physicist Werner Heisenberg and his "Indeterminacy Principle," which tells us that at the subatomic level, the future state of a particle is in principle unknowable.[10] The implication we are building from this is not that there are no causal linkages, but rather that in complex systems possibilities can be known, but precise outcomes cannot be predicted.

This belief brings about some subtle shifts in our consciousness. For example, it invalidates the concept of "mistakes" and suggests that "outcomes" from systems changes are all that we get. Additionally, the indeterminacy principle suggests that ambiguity about the future is a fundamental condition of nature. Moreover, it suggests we acknowledge that not everything is possible, but that choice does affect actual outcome. Intention matters; it is not determinative.

These perspectives suggest confidence, expectation, and love as critical aspects of causality, at least in human affairs. For years we have known about the power of positive thinking. Only recently have we included what we know in this vein in the context of social-system causality. Now we are beginning to see that when we assume the world is benign and pursue our own intentions with confidence and love, good results come for everyone. Such a perspective goes a long way, for example, toward explaining how men like Mohandas K. Gandhi and Martin Luther King, Jr. could cause so much change: They knew how to replace fear with love. Rather than expecting suffering and loss, they had confidence that a useful response to their efforts would occur. This perspective produced outcomes for them that, with their sensitivity to positive feedback, could be appreciated and built upon. When we give up fear, we, too, can identify and reinforce the positive outcomes our efforts inevitably produce. Then it is possible to see how change can become a different subject: easy, appropriately timed and sized, self-sustaining, and stabilizing at the right point.

Knowing

This category encompasses those presuppositions and perspectives that explain how we know what we know. This is the arena of knowledge, learning, truth, and reality.

The presuppositions elaborated in the previous sections are producing a powerful meta-perspective for us and in us. That is, we are beginning to believe that there are many valid ways of seeing things, including ourselves. The old Sufi story of the blind fakirs and the elephant, with each fakir holding a different part of the elephant and claiming it as the whole, is true of all knowledge. There is more than one reality.

This perspective is becoming so acceptable that it is reflexing back on us, encouraging us to realize that all our knowledge is, in fact, partial. For example, our discoveries in the physical world are leading most physicists to believe that regardless of what they discover, they will never know the whole story. They have discovered molecules, atoms, protons, neutrons, neutrinos, and quarks, and still have not found the end. Physicists, of course, are not quitting, but they are concluding that they never will get it "right;" the basic particle will never be found. What is known will always be only part of what there is to discover. With this perspective comes an acceptance of the plurality of knowledge. We are accepting divergence, multiple perspectives, and incomplete truths. Having given up the search for universal laws, we are building a world on the premise of complementary knowledge.

"Knowing," consequently, is becoming a process of choice. In this new, divergent world nothing is a neutral act. To be useful, learning requires engagement. Knowing is an interpretive, dynamic act requiring the learner to decide what he or she wants to know, and to set about creating it, if possible.

All this suggests another emerging assumption. The meaning of knowledge comes from the context; all "facts" are relational and contextual. We are finding that what counts in a multiplex world is the willingness and ability to find those perspectives — social, psychological, historical, spatial, etc. — that provide the most functional interpretation of our situations. We are teaching ourselves to let go of our drive for the ideal form, and to find value and joy in a universe that is made up of multilayered, interpenetrating levels of diverse reality. A Zen phrase, "beginner's mind," catches the essence of this. It suggests that our emerging view about learning and knowing demands that we be able to receive unbiased feedback about our world and our activities. To learn, we need to continually see with fresh eyes. This means that we need to know how to cleanse the soul and attain a "beginner's mind" at will. This effort requires several subordinate presuppositions, all of which emerge in our new paradigm. They are the following:

1. Our universe, including the people in it, is benign. With respect to individual intention, the universe is neither malevolent nor benevolent; it is neutral.

2. The world is abundant.

3. Success in the world requires diversity and resilience.

4. Synergism, equifinality, and open-ended outcomes are the rule. There is more than one way to skin a cat — which may not be what needs skinning anyway.

5. Standing out of our own way is important. If we make our intentions clear, we can let the world act for us.

6. The feedback the world provides is and is not a function of our own acts. "It's me" and "it's not me" are important causal truisms that are simultaneously real.

Major change is occurring in how we know what we know. The human race is altering the way it tells itself that it "knows" something for certain. To this point, at least in the West, we have known that we know something because it had a personal-experience base. It was physical. For example, we thought the sun revolved around the earth because that is what our physical senses told us. Now, even though our physical senses still tell us this is so, we no longer believe it. Our logic and our science have shown us something different.

There are so many examples of this that there seems to be an irresistible momentum building in our psyches toward shifting the manner in which we tell ourselves we know something. We are moving toward multiple modes of conviction: a "logical" way, a "personal" way, and a "direct-knowing" way. The first emphasizes rational thought and problem solving, the second places heavy emphasis on experience, and the third looks to what we know through our connection to the collective unconscious of the human race. This is not to say that the old modes of knowing are disappearing, but in line with the shift toward meta-perspectives and many universes, we are developing multiple ways of knowing that include all of what we have created to date. The new paradigm is developing in such a way as to include three different, equally valid images of knowing and learning: the scientific, the exploratory, and the direct.

The scientific model describes learning as the process of getting the answers to specific questions. It accepts these questions as given, and as outside the learning activity. It makes individuals responsible for learning the answers to pre-formulated questions. In this effort, learners use special techniques that emphasize problem-definition and alternative explanations, before settling on the one best answer. Solutions developed in this way reduce uncertainty by providing predictability, "truth," and results.

The exploratory approach describes learning as the process of discovering both what questions to ask, and what constitutes useful answers. The vector of learning is outward, with learners participating not only in finding the answers but also in discovering the questions. Learners create their own techniques, and must accept the probability that this kind of inquiry will open up questions beyond the scope of the problem as initially defined. This model holds nothing constant, querying both the appropriateness of the questions asked and the relevancy of answers preferred. "Answers" developed in this way provide experiments instead of solutions, and require users to acknowledge and live with high levels of uncertainty.

The third model of learning, direct knowing, asserts that everything is already known. It suggests that if you don't know something, it is because you are not yet open to knowing it at the conscious level. All knowledge is implicative, with the conscious mind having the ability to know directly, if it is willing. In this model, there are no questions or answers. All is knowledge and faith. One can be aware of all there is to know. This model asserts that we can know without knowing how we know, or even why we know. It suggests that knowing and learning rest in living, and that living itself rests in acting from our highest thought.

In the Newtonian paradigm, learning and knowledge took us closer to the truth. In the new paradigm, learning and knowledge of the kind described above take us closer to effectiveness, happiness, satisfaction, calmness, and quietude. They move us toward a grace, a resonance with the universe.

Along with learning and knowledge, our concepts of reality and truth are undergoing change. Our current understanding of reality describes it as that state or quality of being, independent of the ideas concerning it. The current definition of truth is conformity with fact. Reality exists apart from, and transcends, perceived experience. The new paradigm is building a world with different definitions. In many cases these definitions are being reversed, for certainly we are coming to believe that reality is phenomenally-based, and that it is embedded in the ideas concerning it. We are also coming to believe that truth is not apart from or transcendent over experience, but very much a part of perceived experience. Truth and reality, not only beauty, are now "in the eye of the beholder."

The most important shift we are making in our beliefs about learning is toward seeing ourselves as infinitely malleable. We are developing a powerful meta-perspective of ourselves and our potential. With our conscious understanding of the impact of our paradigmatic beliefs on our own behavior, we are tentatively creating new human beings who are aware of their own hand in the formative process. "Existence precedes essence" is taking on solid, useful meaning as we come to understand that our acts and our achievements do more to determine our natures than do any indwelling essences.

Another related presupposition we are creating for ourselves is that all knowledge is ultimately "interested knowledge." Two perspectives play significant roles here: First, we are beginning to make a distinction between social knowledge (the perspective and source of wisdom that professional disciplines create and use) and personal knowledge (those self-discovered models people use to direct their lives). The former perspective enlivens our culture; the latter, individual activity. Second, we are beginning to assume that social knowledge, including what we heretofore have called sociology, biology, and physics, must become personal knowledge to be useful to individuals, small groups, or organizations.

For a long time, we have known that we can control and manipulate our world. We are learning also that we can surrender to and enjoy it. Most importantly, we are noticing that these activities are neither contradictory nor dichotomous. The new paradigm puts these two approaches together, combining instrumental and expressive activities in a way that integrates our need for control with our need for surrender and enjoyment. Aided by the insights of information theory and cybernetics, we are melding these two into a complementary process that leaves us free to pursue accomplishment without the drive and guilt previously associated with acknowledging our powerlessness to determine things. I call this new concept "receptive intention," to indicate that we are beginning to believe, for both survival and growth, that we can and must affect our world, and that we can relax in this effort. In fundamental ways, things work for us; however, if reality is going to match our intentions, we must try to influence things anyway.

We are beginning to believe in abundance. The new paradigm is teaching us that scarcity and poverty, lack and limitation, are not inevitable. This in no way suggests that scarcity and poverty do not exist in the world, nor does it suggest that everyone will become rich within the new paradigm. We can trust, given our capacity for synergistic creativity, that the world is replete with ability to reward us. Win-win models are being added to the pot, supporting an emerging ability to create rewards in different dimensions, which expands our ability to give everyone something for their efforts.

We are strengthening and refurbishing our understanding that there is truth in human affairs. The emerging assumption is that "we know what we know," and that "what we know we need to act on." We seem to be telling ourselves that, despite what we claim about our intentions, there is a clearly discernible correspondence between truth and our behavior. Each of us is responsible for our acts, because we indeed do know what will happen when we act.

This presumption is evident in many places, such as the environmental and nuclear-freeze movements. Nowhere is it more clearly evident than in the report issued by the Israeli Commission inquiring into the 1982 Beirut massacre. The authors of this report affirmed the idea of truth in human affairs, using the principle of "indirect responsibility" to judge the Israeli high command and its government. This concept is an old principle needing little clarification. Thomas Aquinas called it the sin of omission; in domestic law it is called negligence. The application is the same; if one does nothing to prevent a wrongful act, one shares a portion of the blame. If, however circuitously, you set in motion a train of events that lead to a calamity, you are culpable. Intention is mere detail; we are responsible for our acts. This old principle re-emerges in the new paradigm behind evidence from physics, cybernetics, and information theory. Strange bedfellows, but powerful nonetheless in building deep presuppositions.

The New Paradigm: Five Key Aspects

1. A meta-perspective about ourselves that includes knowledge both of our own consciousness and of this paradigm shift;

2. Limited arenas of knowledge where contingency perspectives and multiple realities are the rule;

3. Hierarchies, heterarchies, and distributed functions;

4. Multiple models of change and causality that emphasize interaction patterns, phenomenological intention, and love; and, by implication,

5. Conscious design of our new world.

CONCLUSION

In 1543, Nicholas Copernicus proposed changes in astronomical theory that he thought increased its accuracy and reliability. As we know, his idea involved transferring to the sun many of the astronomical functions previously attributed to the earth. Where before everyone believed the earth was the fixed center about which the stars and planets revolved, Copernicus proposed the sun as the center of the immediate physical world. This of course was a reform of fundamental proportion in the precepts of astronomy. It spawned a scientific revolution. During the seventeenth century, the reconciliation of other sciences with Copernican astronomy was an important cause of the ferment that eventually resulted in a transformation in people's conception of the universe and of their own relation to it.

Most large-scale upheavals in paradigmatic thought, as Thomas Kuhn suggested, produce similar disruptions.[11] Indeed, contemporary Western civilization is more exposed to these kinds of disruptive transformations, for our philosophy and our everyday existence are interdependent with our scientific concepts. Consequently, that we are today in the late stages of another scientific revolution is important. Many of us are already experiencing the turmoil and conflict associated with this transformation. Physicists' concepts like Max Bohr's atom and Albert Einstein's finite but unbounded space were introduced to solve pressing problems in a single scientific specialty. Despite their obvious conflict with common sense and some of the basic tenets of science, these concepts were used by scientists even though they seemed incredible. We now know that these ideas and concepts are highly credible. Their expansion and extended use have created wonderful — and horrible — results. The insights of these scientists have become basic tools for explaining and exploring our world. At this stage, their conceptions cannot be restricted to a single scientific specialty. As Kuhn suggested, every fundamental innovation in a scientific specialty inevitably transforms neighboring sciences and, more slowly, the worlds of the philosopher, the educator, and then everyone.

Because of this, we need to expect trouble ahead. The turmoil that we are already experiencing will get worse. However, this is not a prediction of gloom; our awareness of the disruptive nature of previous paradigm shifts, and our consciousness that we are in the midst of one, should enable us to deal with the confusion and travail that will be our common experience. If we understand what we are experiencing and where it comes from, we can make our paradigm transformation less painful, alienating, and disruptive. This understanding and awareness can lead us toward behavioral repertoires that will be, if not satisfying, at least effective. If we let it, it will also give us tolerance for ourselves as we experiment with new ways of believing and behaving. And perhaps, if we bring to our new encounters as much knowledge as we can about meta-perspectives, "beginner's mind," and love, we will have an ability both to live within the available rules, and, when necessary, to transcend old, outmoded ones. Being fully conscious of what we know, we will use the "rules" to our best advantage: where they work, we can use them; where they fall short, we can improvise, coming to the world and our fellow human beings in a way that gives us what we will need most — "grace beyond the rules."

Notes

[1] See T. Berry, "Comments on the Origin, Identification and Transmission of Values," *Anima* (Winter 1978).

[2] The material that follows is based on the original work of Peter Schwartz and Jay Ogilvy as reported in "The Emergent Paradigm: Changing Patterns of Thought and Belief," *Analytical Report: Values and Lifestyles Program*, SRI International (April 1979).

[3] See Jay Ogilvy, *Many Dimensional Man: Decentralizing Self, Society, and the Sacred* (New York: Harper & Row, 1979).

[4] Ibid.

[5] See Ken Wilber, *Eye to Eye: The Quest for the New Paradigm* (Boston: Shambhala Publications, 1982).

[6] Arthur Koestler, *Janus* (New York: Random House, 1978).

[7] Wilber.

[8] Ibid.

[9] Schwartz and Ogilvy.

[10] Wilber.

[11] Thomas S. Kuhn, *The Structure of Scientific Revolutions* (Chicago: The University of Chicago Press, 1970).

2

Process Wisdom for a New Age

PETER B. VAILL

Comments on the Second Edition

Re-reading "Process Wisdom for a New Age" nearly fifteen years later has a kind of time-capsule feel for me. The themes and the arguments of the essay continue to be my main preoccupations. I had considerable passion at the time to say as clearly as I could what I thought was wrong with the "facts-and-methods" approach to leadership and management development. That passion continues unabated; I am if anything more clear than ever that the applied-science approach is profoundly mistaken for understanding and developing leader-managers.

One point I would add today is that the facts-and-methods or applied science approach is wrong, regardless of the validity of the "science" being applied. I do not argue against validity in its technical sense; rather, I question its appropriateness to the nature of the phenomena of leading and managing.

The essay was not unique in its day. It belonged to a dawning genre of concerns that are much more sharply drawn today. More and more one hears the term "post-modernism" to refer to what my essay calls a "developed alternative." We are all much clearer today than before that a "new paradigm" is badly needed, and is slowly coalescing. In light of emerging trends, I think my essay's most distinctive contributions are the twin notions of "relationality" and "spirituality."

The idea of "process wisdom" is more and more salient, even though that phrase itself has not achieved currency. Since the essay was written I have concerned myself at length with the processes of what I call "permanent whitewater" — the collection of conditions in organizations that can be described as turbulent, chaotic, unstable, and unpredictable. I think the increasing instability of life in modern organizations is the central fact to be understood. Given this instability, an understanding of the process by which anything happens in an organizational context is all the more important. I have developed this idea in an essay titled "The Unspeakable Texture of Process Wisdom."*

In the original paper, there are several passing references to time. I have come to think that the temporal nature of all organizational action is vastly underrated in its importance. All processes occur in time. They occur in various rhythms and pacings, punctuated and interrupted in various ways. They may be understood temporally from a third-party point of view but, even more importantly, they are present in the consciousness of all involved actors. "Time pressure" is just one of the many manifestations of the temporality of all action. "Process wisdom," I would say today, is wisdom about pace and rhythm as much as about direction and objective.

All in all, Thomas Kuhn's call for a "developed objective" still calls to us. "Process wisdom" is more important than ever.

— Peter B. Vaill

* In S. Srivastva and David L. Cooperrider, eds., *Organizational Wisdom and Executive Courage* (San Francisco: Jossey-Bass, 1997).

Vaill's focus is on what the Organization Transformation (OT) movement means for the social sciences and what is involved in fundamental change in human systems. Drawing on a wide-ranging set of ideas and trends in the 20th century, he undertakes to contribute to a philosophical grounding for OT. His phrase "process wisdom" captures his sense of where the insights of OT genuinely derive. Of major significance in this chapter is Vaill's emphatic reminder of certain classic values about man and organization that have been present in prior work and in certain great thinkers and creators of change; these values which, he argues, are obscured in the welter of technical research findings and formal theories that flood the academic and managerial landscape. He considers these classic values to be of central importance to OT and to its process of development.

T he "process wisdom" of this chapter's title is displayed and discussed in two ways. First, I quote some of those whose consciousness of the nature of life is already transformed. While of course my choices are biased, I nevertheless suggest that in getting beyond the old positivist-objectivist world view, there is a remarkably consistent vision of the world as flow and as process in the thinking of those who seek to understand and repair the excesses of Western thought. Second, there is process wisdom *for* the process of understanding and repairing the excesses of Western thought, particularly as such thought appears in organizational conduct. I use various behavioral scientists whose work is memorable to working practitioners as exemplifying this process awareness. Positivist-objectivist facts and methods simply do not facilitate liberation. There are many men and women who are doing something other than merely communicating facts and methods. There is process wisdom in this something else.

This essay closes with a four-element theory of what human action in organizations might look like if it were transformed by process wisdom. To set the tone of this chapter, perhaps this remark of the British biologist J. Z. Young may capture the spirit of what is attempted here:

> Why must anyone seek for new ways of acting? The answer is that in the long run the continuity of life itself depends on the making of new experiments. . . . The continuous invention of new ways of observing is man's special secret of living.[1]

OT AND THE IDEA OF A DISCIPLINARY MATRIX

Organizational Transformation (OT) means change in thought and action, at a much more fundamental level than has been accomplished so far by most change agents. Since Kuhn's 1970 work *The Structure of Scientific Revolutions*,[2] we have used the word "paradigm" to refer to the deeper organizing principles that undergird everyday action. OT very probably *is* a paradigm shift for thinking about organizations and influencing them. But what does this mean?

In a "Postscript" written seven years after his original essay, Kuhn reconsidered the meaning of the idea of a "paradigm." He proposed disciplinary matrix as a better description of the phenomenon he had in mind. He suggested that a disciplinary matrix is composed of four basic elements:

1) *symbolic generalizations*, the way that problems within the paradigm are posed and solved (i.e., the formulations that are taken as sensible);

2) *metaphysical assumptions*, the taken-as-given beliefs about what shall be treated as real;

3) *values*, which embody the basic priorities and choices of what problems to pursue, and what social ends to serve; and

4) *exemplars*, those worked-out approaches and solutions that display the whole world-view as a coherent *gestalt*.[3]

Kuhn did not elaborate on his choice of "disciplinary matrix," but the phrase connotes the notion of a frame that makes possible the idea of *disciplined* (i.e., focused, connected, directed) thought and action. A disciplinary matrix — a paradigm — is present when the four elements are mutually complementary and reinforcing. Today, however, the disciplinary matrix of Western social thought and action is fragmented in virtually all directions: There is a major disconnection between symbolic generalizations and metaphysical assumptions on the one hand, and values and exemplars on the other. New Age people, in other words, have established new values and new classic demonstrations of these values (i.e., exemplars) quicker than they have spelled out the new symbolic generalizations and metaphysics that accompany their work. Furthermore, at a finer level of detail, enormous ferment exists in all four of Kuhn's categories. No discipline or school of thought is secure from the winds of revolution, due partly to new substantive discoveries about man, partly to the collapsing faith in positivistic objectivity, and partly to a refreshing, even thrilling new interest in ethics, morality, and the spiritual nature of man.

This chapter seeks to contribute to a disciplinary matrix for OT. The idea of "process wisdom" touches all four of Kuhn's categories. It suggests the fruitfulness of a new approach to social change (symbolic generalization); it relocates reality between the observer and observed, rather than in one or the other (a metaphysical assumption); in so doing, it calls attention to the value of *relationality* as a primary ingredient of effective action (values); and it illustrates all of this in the work of men and women who have been unusually effective in fostering OT (exemplars).

Much of what follows is not really new. These issues have been thoroughly explored in formal philosophy, particularly since Kant. But OT is not merely philosophy — and philosophers, with the exception of a few European existentialists and American pragmatists, have not distinguished themselves by their contributions to concrete change in institutions and people. OT does affect real institutions and real people: it wants *life* to change; it wants *society* to change; it wants people to more fully discover themselves in their lives, and in their thoughts and actions. OT is a many-dimensioned impulse cutting across existing institutions, roles, problem statements, and goal sets. This impulse is real for an exponentially growing number of men and women. This impulse makes OT something beyond a new label for old problems and methods.

OT is also not new in its interest in fostering change in society and organizational life. All leaders and managers are concerned with change, and leadership and management theory reflects this. More specifically, the quasi-profession known as Organizational Development (OD) has sought for 25 years to bring about change in organizations. However, much of this prior thinking is founded on a paradigm that is inappropriate to what we are beginning to learn about the process of change. This older paradigm is the one the social sciences inherited from the physical and biological sciences. It is an "applied science" approach: the belief is that truths about man and about organizations can be objectively established, and that these "findings" can be "applied" to various "problems" of change. Elsewhere, I have shown that perhaps OD teaches us something else entirely about the role that science plays in the process of change.[4] For the moment, however, let it simply be said that we are in the midst of a transition from the older, "applied science" paradigm to something else. This chapter gives voice to process wisdom as a major component of this new alternative. To be sure, there are far older schools and philosophies embodying process wisdom — for instance, the Chinese philosopher Lao Tsu[5], writing in the 6th century B.C. So far, though, few have put philosophies of process head-to-head with the gospel according to the typical American management school and corporate training department. This chapter seeks to do precisely that.

SAYING SOMETHING USEFUL

Recently a close colleague at another management school sent me an essay he had written about how managers make decisions. My friend asked me for feedback on the model he had developed. In reply, I reluctantly characterized his approach as a "negative phenomenology" of managerial decision-making — by which I meant that I thought he was 180 degrees off: his essay described precisely how managers don't think and don't decide. He had modeled the manager as a sophisticated information-processing "machine" who thinks in terms of decision trees, tracing out linear causes and effects, and optimizing her or his objectives from among the various alternative choices. The manager's mind, in this theory, could be portrayed as a wiring diagram with circuits that opened and closed. Everything was conscious; everything was calculated.

My friend's reaction to this was to understand and, somewhat ruefully, to agree with what I was saying. But then in a final paragraph of his acknowledgment, he uttered a genuine cry of the spirit. Perhaps to justify his quest for a model of how managers' minds work, he said "I would like to think that someone, someday, could say something useful to managers."

This was hardly the first time that I had heard, or said myself, that behavioral scientists ought to "say something useful" to managers. Utility, in fact has been a dominant value in the disciplinary matrix of the American behavioral sciences for the entire 20th century. Yet here we are in the 1980s, still trying to figure out how to be relevant. My colleague's statement, and the many like it one hears so often, are really utterances of an open secret: that as guides to action, the American behavioral sciences don't amount to much; that little of real value and import can be deduced from these sciences, and that little if anything is actually done as a consequence of the "knowledge" we claim to have of human behavior in organizations.

American behavioral science has been — we have been — saying the wrong thing. For decades we have tried to say the wrong thing better and better, for within our disciplinary matrix we have had trouble saying anything else. As long as we continue to say the wrong thing — no matter how well we say it, no matter how "reliably" and "validly," no matter how elegantly and mesmerically — it still will be the wrong thing. It will not feel right to the most honest ones among us, and it will not achieve any influence among practitioners.

Facts-and-Methods

This "wrong thing" that American behavioral science has been saying to practitioners is what I call "facts-and-methods." We have busily collected facts and invented methods, and then told manager-leaders that if they want to be effective they have to absorb our facts and learn our methods. In approaching our task this way, we persistently ignore three things:

1. History has seen legions of managers and leaders who were unaware of our facts and indifferent to our methods, but who nonetheless have been outstanding both in getting the job done and in attending to the needs of organization members.

2. The overwhelming majority of managers and leaders, even the most dutiful and dependent, find our facts-and-methods only marginally useful, and not very interesting. The most earnest and impressionable among them try to take the medicine we prescribe; the more skeptical among them think it's mostly crap. (And some of the daring ones even say so out loud.)

3. The best of the lot of behavioral scientists — the Maslows, Rogers, Lewins, Mayos, Roethlisbergers, McGregors, Tannenbaums, Trists, and so many others — are influential and memorable with managers and leaders for who they *are*, not for what they *know*. It is the way they are, the way their minds work, the way they express themselves in their protean passions, that we love and remember. One does not read Peter Drucker or Warren Bennis for "the facts," but rather for the song of possibility that sounds through their writings. They are people whom it is worth the trouble and expense to know personally. (Each of us has our own list of "giants." It need not be mine; the point is the same.)

The best among us are living proof that we have been saying the wrong thing, for the best among us have understood in our own ways, dim and acute, florid and dry, spare and prolix, what the enterprise is really about: The enterprise is really about what it means *to be in the world with responsibility*. In choosing this phrase to characterize the situation of manager or leader, I draw heavily on the European existentialist tradition, most notably on Heidegger,[6] who made *being-in-the-world* the fundamental fact of human existence. This concept captures formally what practicing managers and leaders have been saying to theorists and consultants for years: "My situation is more complex and unique than your theory allows for!" To be in an organizational world with responsibility for what happens there, to be grounded and rooted there — to be "thrown" there, as Heidegger would say — *is to be unable to select only those parts of one's world the theory deals with for attention*. This is why the facts-and-methods of so many well-intentioned behavioral scientists don't work; they are more selective than the person who is responsible for the situation can afford to be.

It is behavioral scientists' *own* ways of being in their worlds with their responsibilities that is the problem, and this problem derives from the strictures of the old paradigm that requires them to practice a model of scientific inquiry and change that separates them from the very managers, leaders, and others whom they are trying to influence. These behavioral scientists have turned their fascination with managers' and leaders' situations into something the latter can hardly recognize. This is why I called my friend's elegant decision tree a negative phenomenology of choice: To a real chooser, it would be unrecognizable as a map of the world in which the chooser lives.

Some of the material generated within the facts-and-methods paradigm has been marginally helpful when first articulated — for instance, ideas about participation, about the nature of power, or about group roles, norms, and the dynamics of social systems. But bold new formulations beget legions of adherents, markets for consultants, publication opportunities (and publish or perish systems!), new courses and fields of specialization. The great juggernaut of academic distinction-making grinds forward, increasingly without reference to the holistic, existential predicaments of practitioners, and ends in sterility. This is the history of OD, of participative management, of group dynamics, of Theory X and Theory Y, of leadership theory. Will it be the history of the quality of worklife movement, of the stress-management movement, of the women's movement, as these are applied in academic programs and in manager/leader training and development? I think it will be. The signs are already there. Those who seek distinction by making distinctions tend to forget that *being in the world with responsibility* is not well-captured in 2 X 2 diagrams and in lists of "key" factors. With tongue only partly in cheek, I recently predicted that if behavioral scientists were to try to write cookbooks, they would produce material that cooks could not read.[7]

Of course, it can be argued that these remarks are far too cavalier about the facts and methods of the behavioral sciences. A serious scientist who adhered to the objectivist paradigm would be obligated to argue this way. Yet, as Kuhn said, when the paradigm shifts, many things the old paradigm could deal with quite well are not addressed at all in the new paradigm.[8] A new paradigm's great power is that it deals with issues on what is experienced as the leading edge. It deals with the issues and anomalies that matter. The facts and methods of modern behavioral science don't deal with the things that matter to more and more people in action roles today. Ethics matter. Feelings matter. Community matters. The human spirit matters more and more as the terrible consequences of our century's fascination with technology, exploitation, and destruction become more crushingly manifest.

Toward a Developed Alternative

In his chapter "Revolutions as Changes of World View,"[9] Kuhn himself examines the adequacy of a purely objectivist science — i.e., a science that assumes its task is to uncover the laws that govern a world conceived as real, separate, and apart from man-the-perceiver. After puzzling for several pages over the meaning of all the psychological research showing the interconnectedness of observer and observed in all the sciences, Kuhn expresses doubt as to whether indeed there can be observer-independent truth; whether, in the language I have been using, there can be facts and methods that stand purely by themselves, as tools for use by practitioners. Then Kuhn comes to the nub of his problem — the problem of every scientist who pays close attention to the way a process of inquiry proceeds. On first reading, the statement sounds like a "remark," but the more I reflect on this thought of Kuhn's, the more it seems to be a cosmic cry:

> But is sensory experience fixed and neutral? Are theories simply man-made interpretations of given data? The epistemological viewpoint that has most often guided Western philosophy for three centuries dictates an immediate and unequivocal, Yes! In the absence of a developed alternative, I find it impossible to relinquish entirely that viewpoint, yet it no longer functions effectively, and the attempts to make it do so through the introduction of a neutral language of observations now seem to me hopeless .[10]

Now, over twenty years later, Kuhn's "developed alternative" still beckons to us. The OT movement is a profound impulse toward a developed alternative, toward ways of knowing and acting that do not misplace truth as "out there" in Kuhn's "fixed and neutral" facts and methods.

Writing at about the same time, the British philosopher Owen Barfield in 1961[11] captured epigrammatically the spirit of what Kuhn was looking for. The remarkable thing about Barfield's observation is that it embodies a truth known to every action-taker in the social world:

> Penetration to the meaning of a thing or a process, as distinct from the ability to describe it exactly, involves a participation by the knower in the known.[12]

The manager-leader is concerned with *meaning,* not just with pseudo-objective truth, for it is in meaning that one's *being in the world with responsibility* is discovered. (Significantly, too, a recent interpretation of the meaning of modern physics[13] makes substantial use of Barfield's philosophy.)

To talk of "transformation" is to attempt to talk of the new dilemmas, predicaments, challenges, and opportunities faced by practicing managers and leaders since World War II. Many writers have commented on the surprising emergence of these new challenges to action. One of the earliest and most penetrating of these was Eric Trist, who spoke of the "structural presence of post-industrial society,"[14] by which he meant all the conditions that have rendered obsolete the facts and methods of orthodox, old-paradigm behavioral science. The new patterns and ambiguities of post-industrial society are too messy for old-paradigm behavioral science.

Sometimes artists catch the texture of experience long in advance of more pedestrian thinkers. In *Lord Hornblower,* C.S. Forester had this to say about action in complex and turbulent systems:

> War was as unlike spherical trigonometry as anything could be, thought Hornblower, grinning at the inconsequence of his thoughts. Often one approached a problem in war without knowing what it was one wanted to achieve, to prove or construct, and without even knowing fully what means were available for doing it. War was generally a matter of slipshod, makeshift, hit-or-miss extemporization. Even if it were not murderous and wasteful it would still be no trade for a man who enjoyed logic.[15]

Although this statement flies in the face of all mainstream leadership and management theories, I think its content and spirit correctly capture the situation of the modern executive. It says, *"Goodnight, sweet paradigm of reason, which detaches observer from observed and makes of meaning a subjective whim."*

The "action trades" of organizational transformation are not for those who enjoy the mechanistic, hypothetico-deductive logic of the old paradigm. Leadership in social systems is not chess, and it is not programming. It is not PERT charting, and it is not systems analysis. It is not mapping contingencies, and it is not intellectualizing about the situational nature of one's "situation."

D.H. Lawrence, I believe, had it exactly right:

> If we think about it, we find that our life consists in this achieving of a pure relationship between ourselves and the living universe about us. This is how I 'save my soul' by accomplishing a pure relationship between me and another person, me and other people, me and a nation, me and a race of men, me and animals, me and the trees or flowers, me and the earth, me and the skies and sun and stars, me and the moon: an infinity of pure relationships, big and little. . . . This, if we knew it, is our life and our eternity: the subtle, perfected relation between me and the circumambient universe.[16]

To those who might observe that such a thought as Lawrence's is nothing but open systems thinking in lyrical clothes, I respond, "and that is all the difference." Yes, open systems ideas try to capture the dynamic nature of systems; but in scientizing the phenomenon, we have killed it.

Lawrence's lyricism is *part* of the idea, not just an appendage. Lawrence's thought talks about Barfield's knower-participating-in-the-known, and displays it at the same time.

The Blind Men and the Elephant in Motion

The relationality of all experience contains challenges to our understanding of organizations that we have barely begun to come to terms with. I can illustrate this by extending the metaphor of the blind men and the elephant. In its conventional telling, each blind man had a grip on a different part of the beast, and they were unable to agree on what it was really, *really* like — i.e., as one of Kuhn's "fixed and neutral experiences." But there is more; for the elephant isn't just standing there, but instead ambles through the forest and the veldt. The blind men are trying to understand the system as it evolves and as their experience of it unfolds. The blind man clinging to a leg experiences an elliptical forward motion. He who has the misfortune to have hold of the tail is jerked and whipped about in random fashion. A few feet forward, his colleague, in the crotch, is periodically flooded and/or pasted with output that seems to have nothing to do with the beast's motion or with the feel of the surface clung to. At the front end, another observer rides the probing trunk, jerked and whipped like the tail man but, it seems to him, in a somehow "purposeful" manner. Clinging high up on the massive haunch is another perceiver, subjected to none of the motions or indignities of his fellows and wondering what their gasps and protestations are all about.

And the observer who is astride the massive neck, an accidental mahout, finds that the flexing and shifting of his *own* body seem to correlate with the gait and momentum of the beast. This leads him to think he is *steering* it, and thus uniquely qualified to say what it really, *really* is. And we with sight — what of us? Is sight, in the metaphor, an analogue to science in real life? Is our experience different from each blind man's? Yes. Does it replace each blind man's? No. Are we the captives of our standpoint fully as much as each blind man? Yes.

What an instructive metaphor — the blind men and the elephant! One hundred years worth of organization theory has yet to declare the simple truth that every action-taker understands: an organization is a place where everybody is right and everybody is wrong. *Everybody.* The best among us whom I mentioned a moment ago have helped action-takers recognize this truth. They have done it in the way they are, in D.H. Lawrence's sense: not in their *findings,* but in their ways of *looking.*

If we want to help the action-taker, we have to talk about what the action-taker is interested in.[17] He or she is interested in effectively performing a set of relationships. What I have called *being in the world with responsibility* in fact provides a huge agenda of puzzling relationships for us all, theorists and practitioners alike, to think about and experiment with. We have to learn about Lawrence's relationality as it appears in thinking and feeling and judging and valuing and deciding and committing and perceiving; most of all in perceiving. Notice that I have phrased all of these as gerunds, processes of action. They are not the static categories of management and leadership and change, but instead are about managing, leading, changing.[18]

As open processes flowing in time, these phenomena do not obey the behavioral science theories and laws that derive from the old paradigm's search for Kuhn's "fixed and neutral" facts. Old-paradigm science is about the general case. Action and being in the world with responsibility are never about the general case. They are always about specific persons, specific issues, specific opportunities, and the practitioner has to *include* all the "other things being equal" that old-paradigm science must leave out in order to positively declare its theories and laws. Early apostles of transformation, with their insistence on coming to terms with the here-and-now, were right — perhaps more right than they knew. Their only error was to apply this insight only to face-to-face interpersonal relationships, when in fact it extends to everything the manager or leader is trying to deal with.

Media-Ease and Secret Paths

How much does our thinking have to change in order for us to better grasp, and help practitioners to better grasp, the nature of the transformations in which they are immersed? The answer, paradoxically, is that our thinking needs to change a *lot* — but, in another sense, not so much as we might think. It is a *shift* in thinking that is involved. The process has already started, if one considers all the yearnings and impulses and tentative forays toward ways of thinking about people and organizations that amplify and celebrate and enshrine the flowing, relational quality of existence. This new, relational thinking one finds in the OT movement is still on the margins of awareness, still not quite articulate as a world view, still not a "developed alternative."

The variety of our ways of knowing obscures these relational threads. Some of us know through four-square explication, some through parable and poetry. Many of us know through movement and through other nonverbal expressions of our awareness. In the OT movement, one finds more "media-ease" than in most other places in society, and this mirrors what always has been true of the best practitioners: "media-ease" is the capacity to absorb and express one's experience through a variety of media — media that involve both left and right hemispheres of the brain, and the limbic and reptilian levels as well as the neocortical. Media-ease is comfort and pleasure with the variety of windows with which we as persons are endowed. The old paradigm says that "knowledge" and "truth" are learned and expressed through the verbal, linear-logical windows alone. Everything else is "style," and as such is too unique for scientific laws to encompass. The new paradigm knows something different: the experience of being in the world with responsibility and actions on behalf of one's existence — "effectiveness," if you will — depend on media-ease. At the point of action, the artificial split between "true knowledge" and "style" dissolves.

These best thinkers among us who have touched managers and leaders with their lookings rather than their findings have media-ease, almost without exception. That is why practitioners find them so approachable and so interesting as persons, and so helpful in transforming understanding. These best among us walk what have been secret paths to meaning — secret, in the sense that the true nature of their paths of knowing and acting could not be displayed and discussed within the confines of the old objectivist paradigm of inquiry and knowledge. Even such geniuses as Carl Rogers and Abraham Maslow bowed to the prevailing world-view from time to time and tried to make systematic, objective statements of their theories and "findings." But their dominant modes have been much more undiscussable: Rogers' insistence on the to-me-ness of his patients' experience, and of his experience of his patients;[19] Lewin's realization that understanding something comes from entering into its flow and process;[20] Roethlisberger's emphasis on the skills of the practitioner as being relational, communicative skills, and what this means for the relational, communicative abilities of those who would be helpful to practitioners;[21] and Maslow's willingness, perhaps more than any other inquirer, to share his awareness of the phenomena without feeling that he must scientize himself.

I have said that perceiving is something we need to understand in relational terms. Here is Maslow's call on that subject:

> Perception is too much the study of mistakes, distortions, illusions, and the like. . . . Why not add to it the study of intuition, of subliminal perception, of unconscious perception? Why not the study of good taste enter here? Of the genuine, of the true, and the beautiful? How about aesthetic perception? Why do some people perceive beauty and others not? Under this same heading of perception we may also include the constructive manipulation of reality by hope, dreams, imagination, inventiveness, organizing, and ordering.[22]

The answer to all these questions, of course, has been that these phenomena are too esoteric and ethereal to be reduced to the investigatory strictures of the objectivist model of inquiry. Yet we know these phenomena — else how could we understand Maslow's questions? To those who walk the secret paths of meaning, there is nothing strange about any of these phenomena. Maslow continues:

> Unmotivated, disinterested, unselfish perception. Appreciation. Awe. Admiration. Plenty of studies of stereotypes, but practically no study of fresh, concrete, Bergsonian reality. Free-floating attention of the type Freud spoke about. What are the factors that make it possible for healthy people to perceive reality more efficiently, to predict the future more accurately, to perceive more easily what people are really like, that makes it possible for them to endure or to enjoy the unknown, the unstructured and ambiguous, and the mysterious? Why do the wishes and hopes of healthy people have so little power to distort their perceptions? The healthier people are, the more their capacities are interrelated.[23]

Here was a serious person talking what 1950s American psychology considered paradigmatic nonsense. Who could be interested in the study of, say, "awe"? Where is the intellectual and employment market for that focus? Never mind that any leader worth his or her salt would like to know more about it, would like to know how to excite it in others. It is just too loose an idea for disciplined inquiry. And to try to become disciplined about it in terms of the objectivist paradigm turns it into something else entirely — something that most practitioners find uninteresting and irrelevant. We may say the same of other phenomena that practitioners really care about — love, trust, power, leadership, change, goals and objectives, personality, motivation. Consciousness of being in the world with responsibility has these phenomena one way; objectivist science turns them into something else.

PROCESS WISDOM AND THE DEVELOPED ALTERNATIVE

In the Kuhn passage quoted earlier, he spoke of "the absence of a developed alternative." In this chapter I have been trying to show that we are closer, perhaps, to a developed alternative — for the behavioral sciences, at least — than is generally realized. There *are* symbolic generalizations, metaphysical assumptions, values, and exemplars available that constitute a new disciplinary matrix (paradigm), by Kuhn's definition. We *can* avoid turning the phenomena of our experience into something unrecognizable in the name of valid truth. We *can* stop invalidating our *selves*.

I do not know exactly what the developed alternative will be, but I suggest that we all have intuitions of its nature. There are truths beyond the mechanistic, empirical truths of the paradigm that has ruled our minds for Kuhn's three centuries. We phrase them differently, separating ourselves from each other with terminology, and we value them differently, seeking distinction with distinctions. But across the wider spectrum of experience, we know what some of these truths are. Those men and women who are trying to envision "transformation" have as good a chance as any of articulating these deeper themes.

The themes are at least four in number, which together are beginning to comprise a developed alternative. First, there is existence. Second, there is openness and relationality. Third, there is the nature of consciousness itself. And fourth, there is spirituality. The old paradigm of objectivist science ignores all four and, when their relevance is asserted, declares them specious. This is why the developed alternative will be a new fundamental paradigm, rather than just a slight modification or enrichment of the traditional view.

Existence

The difference I have in mind here was eloquently captured by Steinbeck:

> The Mexican sierra has 17 plus 15 plus 9 spines in the dorsal fin. These can be easily counted. But if the sierra strikes hard on the line so that our hands are burned, if the fish sounds and nearly escapes and finally comes in over the rail, his colors pulsing and his tail beating the air, a whole new relational externality has come into being — an entity which is more than the sum of the fish plus the fisherman. The only way to count the spines of the sierra unaffected by this second relational reality is to sit in a laboratory, open an evil smelling jar, remove a still colorless fish from the formalin solution, count the spines, and write the truth . . . . There you have recorded a reality which cannot be assailed — probably the least important reality concerning either the fish or yourself.
>
> It is good to know what you are doing. The man with his pickled fish has set down one truth and recorded in his experience many lies. The fish is not that color, that texture, that dead, nor does he smell that way.[24]

Managers and leaders are not fish, and theorists and facilitators are not fishermen. Each is infinitely more complex, as is their relationship. The developed alternative must face the *existence* of the practitioner. We must stop retreating into the "lab," whether the real lab of the controlled experiment, or the metaphorical lab of casual abstraction and categorization. We have been recording "least important truths" and we must stop.

Elsewhere, I have developed the idea that "management is a performing art."[25] This simple metaphor brings in many of the themes I have touched on already in this chapter: that we are talking about personal expressiveness; that we are talking about a dynamic, holistic phenomenon not easily or fruitfully broken into elements and lists of key factors; and that the process of understanding such a phenomenon and the process of improving the effectiveness of those who practice it cannot be a matter of objectivist science. One's *being in the world with responsibility* is performed expressively. With such a view one will not forget the textures and subtleties of the practitioner's existence.

Openness and Relationality

The developed alternative also will celebrate the openness that is so profoundly displayed in the preceding quote from D.H. Lawrence. That remark is truly an archetype of the new view discussed here. The statement has a crucial implication that I have never seen spelled out before. The "infinity of pure relationships" Lawrence would have us accomplish means that man is not and cannot be a finished phenomenon himself. Man is a creator of phenomena, not a repetitive enactor of gene-driven patterns or the "conditioned" subject of cultural "laws." The study of man cannot be the objectivist search for laws that presumably underlie the variety of human actions. What underlies human action is a variety *generator*— namely, man! The study of man and the process of helping specific persons to act effectively is more a process of discovery of the new, the unanticipated, and the unprecedented than it is the application of known "laws" to an already-explored territory. As S. Cox observed:

> What you mean is never what anyone else means exactly. And the only thing that makes you more than a drop in the common bucket, a particle of sand in the universal hourglass, is the interplay of your specialness with your commonness.[26]

This from an essay for aspiring writers, a point of view that masks as advice but is really a description of the way we *all* are anyway: interplay of specialness and commonness. How could anyone ever think that a "science" in its traditional, objectivist sense could be fashioned about such a creature? The facts and methods of American behavioral science deal only with commonness. What of specialness? That is what, in power and beauty, confronts every leader or manager who would "get things done through people." Perhaps, indeed, this is the nub of the difference: the objectivist scientist searches for laws that apply commonly. The practitioner, deeply aware of her or his own specialness, always confronts others who are deeply aware of their specialness. The cynic would say the sense of specialness is merely self-serving, that people are much more alike than they are different. But *sotto voce* with all such claims one hears, ". . . except, of course, for me."

Consciousness

The developed alternative also has to take consciousness into account. Human consciousness connects itself to the world outside it; that is its essence. The technical term is "intentionality," i.e., that consciousness is consciousness *of* something. Consciousness is not a biochemical characteristic of the brain, not a set of looping circuits that merely go round and round within the skull. Consciousness is out *there* in existence in the world. It is the bridge of the biochemistry of the brain to the phenomena outside it.

To deal consciously with consciousness, a developed alternative faces perhaps its greatest challenge. To be conscious of consciousness is to free oneself from stricture — from routines, from methodologies, and from (favorite term in the old paradigm) protocols. Those best among us who walk what I called a secret path have done this in their own ways. They have been able to let themselves be free enough to gaze at organizational life and at manager-leaders' efforts to influence it, relatively unconstrained by notions of right-theory, right-method, right-data, right-mode-of-expression of learnings, and — Eureka! Manager-leaders have responded enthusiastically: "Here at last is someone who is interested in my world." How can this freedom from stricture and dogma, this capacity to be conscious of one's inspection of other consciousnesses, be institutionalized in a developed alternative?

The answer lies partly in what has been called *humanism,* partly in what has been called the *artistic consciousness.* The answer also lies partly in new territory, because art and humanism, old and rich and gorgeous as they may be as modes of illuminating the human spirit, have not yet captured the idea of *being in the world with responsibility.* There is an edge or dimension that seems to elude even the richest representations of how things are for us in the world, whether a Russian novel or a Shakespearean play. Lest I be accused of suggesting archly that Shakespeare or Tolstoy did not have it quite right, this is not my intent. Rather, my point is that the manifestations of *being in the world with responsibility* are ever-new, and that were Shakespeare or Tolstoy alive today, neither would be concluding that there is nothing more to say. The trouble is that objectivist science is saying precisely that: the phenomena are known and fixed, and the task now is to proceed with the categorizing and the counting.

What is important about art and humanism is not what they have said, but what they have attempted. The specialness of myself right here, right now, is the sense that is most with each of us. Documentations of what this sense has been in the past are not this sense now. We frequently feel the uniqueness of the situation we are presently immersed in. But existentially, is this the unspeakable, the unnameable? Even if it is, the least the developed alternative can do is to declare the reality of this sense, and not banish it as metaphysical hogwash like its objectivist ancestor has been doing. The old paradigm is awash in reductionism: "This phenomenon is nothing but a case of. . ." The opposite of reductionism is what the developed alternative must embrace: "This phenomenon is more than I can possibly know." That is the essential starting assumption.

Spirituality

Finally, it seems to me that a developed alternative has to come to terms with the spiritual. Spirituality is an aspect of our existence that is truly undiscussable in objectivist science. But why do so many men and women in positions of responsibility go to church and otherwise ponder the depths of the circumstances in which they find themselves? The old paradigm does not permit them to talk about this. What goes on in their heads as they read the ancient texts, sing the ancient hymns, utter the ancient prayers?

Nearly a century and a half ago, Ralph Waldo Emerson spoke of the conflict between the material and the spiritual:

> You will hear everyday the maxims of a low prudence. You will hear that the first duty is to get land and money, place and name. "What is this Truth you seek? What is this Beauty?" men will ask, with derision. If, nevertheless, God has called any of you to explore truth and beauty, be bold, be firm, be true. When you shall say, "As others do, so will I. I renounce, I am sorry for it, my early visions; I must eat the good of the land, and let learning and romantic expectations go, until a more convenient season;"

— then dies the man in you; then once more perish the buds of art, and poetry, and science, as they have died already in a thousand thousand men.[27]

"Then dies the man [person] in you . . ." if you deny the spirit. "Then dies the man [person] in you . . ." if you let objectivist science control your thought and action. If you are called by something beyond what you know materially, whatever you call it and whatever you conceive it to be, respond.

Again we are in a realm that managers and leaders know almost instinctively. We are in the realm of the loneliness of command. We are in the realm of "you can't please everybody." We are in the realm of such ordinary qualities as patience, of giving another chance, of thanking, and of taking care of each other.

I think William Barrett was right. In *The Illusion of Technique*[28] he came, painfully and reluctantly, to the conclusion that every exercise of what he calls "the moral will" depends on a faith that is, at bottom, supernatural. Every time we say what ought to be, every time we value this over that, our choice traces back to an implicit vision of an order and a moral scheme that lies outside material existence. Somehow, we just know that what we are doing is the right thing to do.

Many of us skillfully evade this intuition. We would prefer to believe that our choices can be defended by referring to facts and validated theories right here on earth; that we do not need any "revelations" to anchor our truths. But Barrett, I think, is more profound. We cannot prove the rightness of our moral choices solely by appealing to the facts, methods, and theories of our material existence. We reach a point where we have run out of arguments for what we believe; they all have been refuted and shown to be shallow and ill-founded. Yet we still believe what we believe. We may change what we believe over time, but the process is one of reflection and development occurring outside the boundaries of purely rational analysis.

In an earlier work, Barrett said this:

Man is the measure of all things, runs an old humanist aphorism. But in fact men do not always like to assume this lonely and arrogant role of a measuring stick for all reality. Man is void and empty unless he finds something by which to measure his own Being.[29]

What we mean by spirituality is consciousness' attempt to get beyond the lonely and arrogant role that Barrett spoke of. It is our name for what is missing in us; it is the object of our faith, whether that faith be in terms of a well worked-out organized religion or in terms of something more personal and perhaps unique. This yearning we all feel, in one way or another, brings spirit back into the developed alternative. But how are we to deal with it and with the funny feelings many of us have, as products of a very secularized world, about taking it seriously once again? OT as practiced in the developed alternative will not be a secular science — that much is clear. But what will it be?

Once again, the seeds of an answer are already around us. Many of the best among us, whose ways of looking and ways of being have touched manager-leaders, are men and women of deep compassion and faith. They do not try to make their ideas the measure of all reality in Barrett's sense, and thus they are not seen by others as possessing the answer. We walk paths of understanding with them; their thinking and actions open a way for us, and that is why they speak so powerfully to those who are being in the world with responsibility.

SUMMARY

Organization Transformation is a set of ideas and actions that take us beyond the nature of our existing institutions and beyond ways of thinking which support them. There is little agreement on exactly what OT is, nor should there be. As a liberating spirit in American thought its essence is multi-directional and multi-disciplinary.

Major use has been made of Thomas Kuhn's phrase "a developed alternative" to refer to the fashioning of new ways of thinking about what organizations are, and about the roles and needs of the men and women who inhabit them. It has been suggested that the basic characteristic of managing and leading is what I call being in the world with responsibility. It is a phenomenon that is deeply experienced, but has been left almost wholly unaddressed by mainstream behavioral science, with its objectivist criteria for truth and relevance.

Still, there have been men and women in this century whose thought and being have touched men and women of action. In this occurrence lie some major clues to what the developed alternative of Organization Transformation might be like. Four such clues are briefly described: 1) a grounding in the actual existence that is life in organizations; 2) a comfort and enjoyment of the openness of the human spirit to D.H. Lawrence's "circumambient universe" and the absence of an impulse to close off, to limit, to categorize fixedly; 3) an understanding of human consciousness as our bridge to the world — not a radical subjectivity in which everything is relative, but a locating of awareness in the relationality of the human being to the people and the things around it; and 4) a new appreciation of the spiritual nature of man, and a determination to keep it in any new formulation of the nature of organizational life.

Notes

1 J.Z. Young, *Doubt and Certainty in Science* (New York: Galaxy Books of Oxford University Press, 1960).

2 Thomas S. Kuhn, *The Structure of Scientific Revolutions* (Chicago: The University of Chicago Press, 1970).

3 Ibid., pp. 182-187.

4 See Peter B. Vaill, "OD as a Scientific Revolution" in *Current Developments in Organization Development*, ed. D.D. Warrick (New York: Scott, Foresman, 1984).

5 Tsu Lao, *Tao Te Ching*, trans. Gia-Fu Feng and J. English (New York: Vintage Books, 1972; orginially published 6th century B.C.).

6 Martin Heidegger, *Being and Time*, trans. J. Macquarrie and E. Robinson (New York: Harper & Row, 1962; originally published 1927).

7 Peter B. Vaill, "Cookbooks, Auctions, and Claptrap Cocoons," *Exchange: The Organizational Behavior Teaching Journal* 4:1 (1979), pp. 3-6.

8 See Kuhn, pp. 109-110.

9 Ibid.

10 Kuhn, p. 126.

11 O. Barfield, "The Rediscovery of Meaning" in *Adventures of the Mind*, eds. R. Thruelsen and J. Kobler (New York: Vintage Books, 1961), p. 288.

12 Ibid., p. 126.

13 See R.S. Jones, *Physics as Metaphor* (New York: New American Library, 1983).

14 E.L. Trist, "Urban North America: The Challenge of the Next Thirty Years" in *Organizational Frontiers and Human Values*, ed. W. Schmidt (Belmont, California: Wadsworth, 1970), p. 78.

15 C.S. Forester, *The Indomitable Hornblower* [compendium of three novels, including *Lord Hornblower*] (Boston: Little, Brown and Co., undated).

16 D.H. Lawrence, "Morality and the Novel" in *Phoenix: The Posthumous Papers of D.H. Lawrence*, ed. E.D. McDonald (New York: The Viking Press, 1968; originally published 1925), p. 258.

17 See Vaill, "Cookbooks, Auctions, and Claptrap Cocoons."

18 Ibid., p. 3.

19 Carl Rogers, *On Becoming a Person* (Boston: Houghton-Mifflin, 1961), pp. 66-69.

20 See A. Marrow, *The Practical Theorist: The Life and Work of Kurt Lewin* (New York: Basic Books, 1969), p. 235.

21 F.J. Roethlisberger, *Man in Organization* (Cambridge, Massachusetts: Belknap Press of Harvard University Press, 1968), pp. 191-192; pp. 208-216.

22 Abraham H. Maslow, *Motivation and Personality* (New York: Harper & Row, 1954).

23 Ibid., pp. 365-366.

24 J. Steinbeck and E.F. Ricketts, *Sea of Cortez* (Mamaroneck, New York: P.O. Appeal Press, 1971), pp. 2-3.

25 Peter B. Vaill, Commencement Address, George Washington University, Washington, D.C., unpublished (May 1974).

26 S. Cox, *Indirections* (New York: Viking Press, Compass Books Edition, 1962), p. 19.

27 Ralph Waldo Emerson, "Literary Ethics" in *The Collected Works of Ralph Waldo Emerson*, Vol. 1, ed., R.E. Spiller (Cambridge, Massachusetts: Belknap Press of Harvard University Press, 1971), p. 99.

28 W. Barrett, *The Illusion of Technique* (New York: Anchor Books, 1978).

29 W. Barrett, *Time Of Need* (New York: Harper & Row, 1972), 137.

3

Transformations That Last: A Cultural Approach

ROBERT F. ALLEN, Ph.D.
CHARLOTTE KRAFT

Comments on the Second Edition

Robert Allen and Charlotte Kraft's vision of empowering people to create healthier and more productive cultural environments is as necessary today as it was more than a decade ago. Few practitioners would dispute their basic premise: cultural support largely determines our success as individuals, and the success of our communities and organizations. However, the technology of Normative Systems Culture Change advanced by Allen and Kraft has yet to be adopted by most training and development practitioners. Instead, individual, organizational and community change efforts are primarily directed at individual learning and motivation. These programs rarely focus on how people can systematically create cultural environments that support new practices. The few culture-change initiatives now underway tend to be organized around helping management to shape the behavior of employees. Such programs are inconsistent with Allen and Kraft's empowerment model.

Why has Normative Systems been passed over? Our community and organizational cultures do not embrace training and development practices that are consistent with the basic ideas of this model. Such changes only begin with the recognition that we must change the culture of our own profession.

Allen and Kraft believed that groups of like-minded people could create subcultures that embrace alternative practices. Actually, any organization or community can create a training and development subculture that enjoys such norms for systematic culture change and empowerment.

— Judd Robert Allen

*Change agents who are involved with the intentional devel-
opment of organizations want not only to improve them for
the moment, but also to facilitate a far-reaching and long-
lasting transformation of organizational life. For this to happen, our organizations must be seen and understood as
cultural entities — determined, to a considerable extent, by
behavioral norms that make up the "organizational unconscious." Once we are aware of the crucial norms, they can
be consciously and systematically changed and supported,
creating a long-lasting transformation that has ramifications
for the larger society.*

C learly, the seeds for transformation to a new and better level of
human existence are already planted in the organizational world.
Humanistic values, holistic approaches, and participative styles of
management are not only being increasingly discussed, they are also being
applied in the literature and tried by innovative leaders.

Will these positive elements create a fully developed paradigm that will
counteract the destructive forces operating in the world today? A new paradigm
must overcome the negative forces that rule our lives: international distrust,
divisive competition, growth for growth's sake, over-reliance on technology,
and an arms race that drains the economy and threatens us with extinction.

A true transformation, therefore, must reach the far-flung corners of
the world and affect many layers of human society. Our economic and social
plight cries for significant change, as does the imperative of our nuclear
knowledge. Since we can never return to the days before we knew how to
destroy the world, we must depend on the collective human consciousness to
find and carry out creative solutions.

Between the extremes of individual change and global transformation
lies a large middle ground, the organizations and institutions to which we
devote so many of our working hours. Although our organizations to some
extent reflect the world view of their surroundings, each one also creates its
own internal patterns. Our organizations are not only products, they are also
producers of our social environments.

Organizations are appropriate places to instigate change, because their
hierarchical structure makes it possible to institute change programs quickly;
they comprise great numbers of people, and are capable of grouping people
in smaller units in which the power of peer influence is a crucial force.

THE CULTURAL CLIMATE

The elements of the new paradigm must grow in a climate that will encourage, support, and cultivate them. Therefore, change occurs through a cultural approach.

The cultural approach involves looking beyond individual causes and solutions to the social factors that influence us and to make use of those factors to create change. It means seeing organizations as having cultural norms of their own that can either reflect the outer culture or not. The members of organizations, working together, can make profound and long-lasting changes not only in the organizational climate, but also in other aspects of the lives and the world.

This chapter presents both the theory and the methodology of cultural change. First it explains the key concepts of the organizational unconscious, of cultural norms, showing how awareness of underlying patterns can prepare us for transformation. Then it suggests some proven methods for putting the concepts into action, with guidelines for the change process. These ideas can be used by organizations of any type or size.

THE ORGANIZATIONAL UNCONSCIOUS

Why can't we have the kind of organization we really want? Why don't the changes we make last? Over and over again, efforts to improve are thwarted by invisible, unacknowledged forces. Each organization contains two organizations, one visible, articulated, expressed in stated goals, policy statements, and procedural manuals; the other invisible, lying quietly under the surface, but actually determining what will happen in the long run. We call this unseen but powerful force the organizational unconscious.

The idea of an individual unconscious has been with us since Sigmund Freud contributed his systematic analysis of unseen personal forces that work beneath the surface of our awareness, determining so much of our individual behavior. In dealing with organizations, we find it useful to envision another form of unconscious, one that exerts a powerful influence on group behavior. As we conceptualize it, the organizational unconscious represents those patterns of social behavior and normative expectations that become characteristic without its members consciously choosing them. These norms determine much of what people in organizations do, and even when the patterns of behavior have outlived their usefulness, people continue to respect them: "It's just the way things are around here."

We often see what happens when the organizational unconscious is not understood and dealt with. When a program is imposed upon an organization without dealing with its unconscious, the change may appear to succeed at first, but unseen forces gradually take over until finally the change has disappeared. We can achieve only temporary results until we deal effectively with the organizational unconscious, and remold the organization's culture into an atmosphere that will support the desired innovations.

Unfortunately, most efforts at change — even when we label them as "cooperation," or "teamwork," or "total organizational effort" — fall far short of treating the unconscious forces, and are destined to be short-lived. Our "results" often turn out to be merely temporary changes. We see this happen with social welfare and job programs, litter clean-up campaigns, the crackdown on nursing homes, and environmental standards, to name a few.

Once we recognize that this invisible, powerful force exists, we can design our change efforts more effectively. Then we will see that a weekend of training is not enough. We must devise some means to instill new behavior so that it becomes part of the fabric of the organization. Similarly, we must transform community-wide goals into neighborhood action, and in schools we must incorporate the good things planned in committee meetings into the daily norms of the classroom.

THE CULTURES OF ORGANIZATIONS

Seeing organizations as having unique cultures has wide ramifications, for it encourages us to treat their members not as roles but as full human beings. The approach can be contrasted with a narrower type of "system approach" or "systems analysis process," which starts with a model of the organization as a mechanical system, and proceeds to make stepwise analyses and development programs. A cultural approach treats people as multidimensional beings rather than as component parts of a mechanistic system.

Because cultures are complex, it is necessary to work on them systematically; but note the difference between a systems approach and a systematic cultural approach. In the latter, a model helps track where you are and where you are going in the change effort, and a checklist of influence areas and levels of implementation assures that you cover all important areas. Unlike the systems approach, however, people participate at each step. Decision makers listen to members of the organization and incorporate their ideas into the change process where possible.

Some change specialists fear that involving many people with a wide range of abilities and experience in the change process will lower the level of thinking and dilute the quality of the program. We can avoid that possibility by helping people understand the nature of "culture" and the cultural change process, and to identify the cultural norms affecting them. Various cultural change programs have proven that when people take "ownership" of a program, they are far more capable of understanding and dealing with change than change specialists may expect. It is crucial, therefore, to take the time needed at the outset of a change effort to help people clearly see the relationship between organizational cultures and cultural change influences.

Culture can be an elusive concept, because we are often oblivious to its effect on our own behavior and perceptions. The term "culture" is often used broadly: we refer to the American culture, the Japanese culture, and so on. In our organizational transformation work, culture refers to the shared goals and values of the cultural entity — any group of people who get together over a period of time. These shared goals and values are a more or less enduring constellation of forces within the group or organization, that causes its members to respond in specific ways. This use of the term encompasses the idea that cultures have a sustaining quality, but are not permanently fixed.

A corporation or a unit within a corporation may be a cultural entity. In this chapter, we are primarily concerned with the particular kind of culture we find in organizations, broadly encompassing businesses, schools, communities, and large institutions. The lessons learned in dealing with organizational cultures, however, can carry over into other cultures of family, neighborhood, social circles, and so forth.

Norms — Our Building Blocks

The building blocks of our cultures are the norms that develop — those expected, accepted, and supported ways of behaving that determine so much of what we do. Norms are universal phenomena. They are necessary, tenacious, but also extremely malleable. Because they can change so quickly and easily, they present a tremendous opportunity to people interested in change. Once it understands itself as a cultural entity, any group, regardless of its size, can create positive norms that will help it reach its goals, and can modify or discard the negative ones. The group can do this despite what the outer culture does.

Since we live in a sea of norms, we need to be selective as we embark upon a change program, finding the norm areas that will be crucial to our success. It won't make too much difference to us if the norm is to wear a necktie, but it will make a tremendous difference if the norm is for individuals or departments within the organization not to trust each other.

We generally find that organizations have a crucial need for norms in the following areas:

- *Rewards and Recognition.* What behavior do we reward? What are the rewards? Do we punish people when they behave contrary to the way we wish? Do we fail to give people permission to do the right thing?

- *Modeling Behavior.* What kind of behavior do people model? Do our leaders model the behavior we ask for in our goals? What do people perceive as being modeled?

- *Confrontation.* What kinds of things do we confront? How do we confront them? Do we use destructive win-lose tactics? Is the norm to place blame?

- *Communication and Information Systems.* What do we communicate? How do we communicate? Are there missed messages on one-way communications? Is there adequate information flow about the things that are important?

- *Interactions and Relationships.* Do people have adequate interaction with others who practice desirable norms? Do people trust each other and treat each other with dignity and respect?

- *Training.* What is the training supposed to produce? How do we conduct training? Who does the training? How do people respond to training? What skills do we need that we do not include in our training?

- *Orientation.* Who introduces new members into the group? What kinds of norms do we inculcate into new members?

- *Commitment and Allocation of Resources.* What is the level of commitment to change? What do we spend our money on? What do we devote our time to? What does assignment of personnel show about our real commitment?

Depending on the nature of the changes sought, other norm influence areas can be selected for examination. Whatever the key areas are, we need to clearly identify norms within them.

Roots of the Cultural Approach

Our particular approach to change is rooted in the work of many innovative thinkers, such as Kurt Lewin, Abraham Maslow, and Erich Fromm, who have helped open our eyes to the power of the culture and to the tremendous possibilities for people-controlled change.

Lewin[1] saw learning as a progressive discovery of structure, either in the material to be learned or in the areas of experience. For example, learning to get someplace means to learn the structure of the route. Learning to achieve an organizational goal means to discover patterns of relationships involving members of the organization. Lewin devised ways to analyze the life spaces of individuals and groups, and also contributed the concept of "barriers" — obstacles to behavior that keep us from doing what we want to do, whether we are aware of them or not.

Maslow's hierarchy of human needs[2] pointed the way to an understanding of motivations within the corporate world. The satisfaction of these needs — progressing from security and comfort, through self-respect, to self-actualization — and his emphasis on peak experiences and their importance as models for what we can be, have proved invaluable.

Fromm's insights into the social nature of human beings provided groundwork for understanding the power of cultural forces, and emphasized the necessity of coming to grips with them. "The social character," said Fromm, "results from the dynamic adaptation of human nature to the structure of society."[3]

In the psychological field, a number of social learning theorists have contributed to our understanding of how individuals interact with their environments. Albert Bandura, for example, explained psychological functioning in terms of continuing reciprocal interaction of personal and environmental determinants.[4] His social learning theory fostered an understanding of the importance of external factors in influencing individual behavior.

In the organizational development (OD) movement, a number of practitioners have paid homage to culture's power and pervasiveness, and pointed out the necessity of dealing with it.

Many similarities exist between our approach, which we call the Normative Systems Approach, and other OD efforts. The key difference lies in the emphasis we place on cultural considerations and on the practical, easily communicated methods we have developed to deal with them. The assumption that organizations have cultures has led us to the following beliefs:

- It is not enough for managers and other leaders to understand the influence of culture; it is also essential that everyone in the organization share this understanding.

- Culture is not a peripheral concern to be taken into account with a number of variables; it is a central concern that underlies all of the other variables which influence the success of the change effort. (Thus interpersonal and socio-technical change strategies are themselves culturally determined, and therefore cannot exist as variables.)

- Group norms and norm influence areas are important components to work with.

- Systematic, planned change requires a multivariable, cultural approach throughout, in which all crucial areas are accounted for, with special attention to their oft-neglected cultural base.

- Cultural objectives, cultural achievements, cultural results, and cultural evaluations must undergird the change effort if achievements are to be sustained.

- Participation in decision making by all the people affected is critical to planned cultural change; it heightens motivation and yields more lasting results.

- A basic framework for responsiveness to changing cultural problems and needs can help an organization to move its style from one of rigidity, to one of flexibility.

Our primary thesis is that if organizations think of themselves as having cultures, and focus on changing their cultural norms, the negative forces of the organizational unconscious can be dissipated, and meaningful change can be achieved and sustained.

One reason it has been so difficult to encourage a realistic focus on the extent of the culture's power is because Western society puts a strong emphasis on what we have come to call individuality. This focus on individual separateness has tended to result in higher levels of conformity. Because we have neglected to deal effectively with the power of group influences, they work on people without the people being aware of what is happening to them. Thus, people often feel they are "choosing" behavior when in fact they are merely conforming to the norms of the culture — outworn traditions that they have had little part in shaping.

As a result of this lack of awareness, people feel helpless in the grip of something outside themselves, without knowing what it is and without realizing that they can exercise a great deal of control over their behavior. As awareness of the culture is developed, and people are provided with tools for shaping their environments, they can achieve new and more profound levels of freedom and true individuality.

A PRESCRIPTION FOR CHANGE

The model we have developed for transforming organizational cultures, the Normative Systems Approach, consists of four phases: discovery, involving people, bringing about change, and evaluating and renewing. This model is shared with everyone affected by the change program. People need to know where they are and where they are going in the program, and their feeling of ownership depends a good deal on this. The conceptual framework we propose is a result of an interplay of many ideas and techniques.

FOUR PHASES: A BRIEF SUMMARY

Phase I: Discovery

This first phase focuses on discovering and understanding the organizational unconscious and its influences. We analyze the organizational culture, including identification of current cultural norms and a preliminary setting of objectives based on what the organization's members want it to be. This phase includes fact finding and study to assure that the change process is based on sound information. Norm instruments aid in identifying existing norms and establishing the gap between what is, and what is desired.

In this way we reveal the unconscious patterns. Levels of organizational support for certain behaviors are assessed. Key norm influences affecting the culture are discussed, choices are made, and goals are set. Objectives are set on three levels: performance, programmatic, and cultural. Once an analysis has been made and objectives have been set, the program can be tailored to the special needs and characteristics of the organization.

Phase II: Involving People

Here we introduce the cultural change system to those directly affected, involving them in the change process. In this phase there is a special emphasis on cultural norms and cultural objectives. Participants get a clear idea of what norms are, and what their normative objectives might be. They have an opportunity, usually in an experiential workshop, to try out the kind of culture they desire and to begin to create an environment in which change can take place.

The workshop is organized into three parts: understanding, identifying, and changing. People learn about culture and the process by which cultural change takes place. They look at each change area and think about what they would like it to be. They learn to identify the norms that are affecting them in relation to the problems at hand. They begin to map out plans for individual and organizational change. They have some direct experience with change as it affects their group's functioning. An important element in that experience is in the realm of human relationships and openness, because most organizations need help in interpersonal relations.

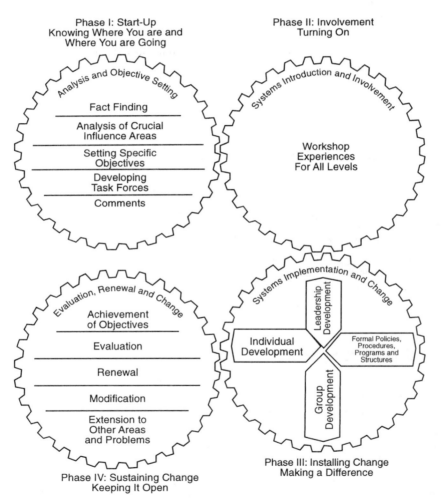

Phase I: Start-Up
Knowing Where You are and
Where You are Going

Analysis and Objective Setting

Fact Finding

Analysis of Crucial
Influence Areas

Setting Specific
Objectives

Developing
Task Forces

Comments

Phase II: Involvement
Turning On

Systems Introduction and Involvement

Workshop
Experiences
For All Levels

Evaluation, Renewal and Change

Achievement
of Objectives

Evaluation

Renewal

Modification

Extension to
Other Areas
and Problems

Phase IV: Sustaining Change
Keeping It Open

Systems Implementation and Change

Leadership
Development

Individual
Development

Formal Policies,
Procedures,
Programs and
Structures

Group
Development

Phase III: Installing Change
Making a Difference

The Normative Systems Cultural Change Model.

(Copyright 1976 by HRI Human Resources Institute)

Phase III: Bringing About Change

This is an implementation phase, during which the various elements of the organizational culture are systematically modified so that they can more effectively contribute to the achievement of objectives. During this stage, four key elements are emphasized: individual development; work team or peer group development; leadership development; and the development of the policies, programs, and procedures of the culture. Specific change programs are usually required in each of these four elements, with each program being directed toward modifying the norm influences that previously have been identified. All three levels of goals are emphasized, with the cultural level particularly stressed so that not only are problems solved, but new ways of handling problems are built into the culture. Members put norm changes into practice within the day-to-day activities of the group, and reinforce them with rewards and support systems.

Phase IV: Evaluating and Renewing

The fourth phase provides ongoing feedback on the effectiveness of the change program. It includes re-evaluation and renewal meetings that continue as long as the change program is in effect. These meetings provide a periodic opportunity for members of the organization to review the positive norms, either to strengthen them or to modify them according to the changing times, and to lend further support to the internalization of skills dealing with both human and technical problems. Results on all three goal levels are evaluated. Extension to other areas of the organization or to other concerns is now possible, and serves to strengthen achievement of the original project goals.

These four phases make up the basic process of any Normative Systems program. Whether the objective is to increase productivity on an assembly line, to achieve a more harmonious work force in an office, or to humanize a small committee or a whole community, the basic model is the same. Each step is important, and cannot be omitted if change is to be successful and continuing.

We have found it helpful for people in a change program to become familiar with this model early in the process, to have it available to them at all stages of the program. To see the process clearly conceptualized gives them greater confidence in their ability to change, and it is a motivational aid throughout the program for members to see where they are in the change process.

Installing a systematic, cultural change program begins a process that is ongoing, self-evaluative, and self-renewing. It is not a panacea, and it involves hard work. Our experience shows that when all parts of the system are accounted for and dealt with, meaningful change will come about, often at an amazing rate, and it will be sustained.

GUIDELINES THAT HUMANIZE

In successful cultural change programs, certain key principles undergird the total change process, helping the organizational unconscious to become an integrating, humanizing, force. By adhering to the following principles on all levels and in all situations, people can erase the destructive patterns that have impeded meaningful change:

- Involving people in the problems and programs affecting them
- Refraining from blaming people
- Having clarity of goals, objectives, purposes, and tasks
- Focusing on results, both short and long range
- Working from a sound data base
- Being systematic and using multilevel change strategies
- Emphasizing sustained cultural change

Guiding principles often appear in public reports and planning documents, only to be disregarded when the action begins. To avoid this, it is important that they receive the same cultural attention as the programmatic goals that are established, and that they become the norms or everyday way of doing things throughout the total change program.

This is particularly important because such principles frequently do not constitute the norm when the change program is introduced. If they are to become the norm, members will need to take specific steps from the outset. If, for example, win-win solutions are to be the watchword of the change program, the program leaders and consultants need to model that behavior in their own day-to-day interactions. If sound information is to be required as a program principle, the program leadership cannot violate this principle in its rush to get things done.

For the guiding principles to become the norms of the change project, supportive environments must be created for them; that is, people must receive praise and rewards for their use, rather than penalty or criticism. Similarly, with confrontation, it is important that negative norms be confronted creatively, so that blaming is avoided but the negative norm is identified. Rather than making the accusation that "John makes promises he can't deliver," members should look at the norms of the group: "Is this a place where it is expected and accepted to make promises, rather than working for results? If so, what can we do to change that norm?"

Norms that most often impede effective implementation of such principles are the following:

- Looking for simplistic, one-level solutions
- Blaming others, finding fault, and, particularly, blaming the victim
- Proceeding on the basis of inadequate information, wishful thinking, or well-intentioned myths
- Leaving it up to other people, especially the experts
- Trying to do it all by one's self without involving others
- Making promises and not delivering results
- Helplessness — believing that people can't really change, that "It's just human nature," and "You can't fight City Hall"
- False individualism, seeing difficulties and solutions only in individual terms

Applying the positive principles of the program can help dissipate these negative norms. Let us look more closely at the principles, with special attention to the first one, which deals with the involvement of people.

Involving People in Change

We hear a lot about people resisting change, but often this resistance is to change that others impose upon them without their participation in its development. Most of us are eager to participate in changes that we create ourselves, particularly when we share that creative activity with others.

A large, prestigious company gave its employees generous benefits: expensive, paid vacations; expanded insurance benefits; and a generous pension plan. Their buildings were beautiful, the equipment was the latest. No one was ever fired or laid off. Yet a routine survey showed that employee morale was low. The same corporation started a new division in another location. People on all levels, from top management to the lowest hourly employees, were, from the moment they joined the company, encouraged to help plan the kind of organization they would like. Their ideas and suggestions were listened to, and many were carried out. The term "associate" was used, rather than "employee," to reinforce the idea that "ownership" belonged to everyone who worked there. Morale was high and lasting, and the plant opened ahead of schedule, on a lower budget than had been anticipated.

The difference in the two divisions was largely a result of the involvement of people in the decisions that would affect their lives. All organizational members should be part of the analysis, the setting of goals, the making of plans, the executing of those plans, and the evaluation, renewal, and extension activities. Leaving them out in any of these phases can doom a program to failure. A large organization might involve people in analyzing its needs, for example, and may even have exciting goal-setting sessions where plans are made for change. But when the report is filed, people return to their desks and things go back to the old ways. The implementation of the plans is put back into the hands of a few, and the sense of excitement is lost. Participation, to be a valuable force, must be continual.

A Matter of Ownership

Participation also means that people "own" the program. This feeling of ownership is an important motivating force. The most successful organizations are those where all of the people own, and not just those at the top. This ownership only comes from people being involved in the development and implementation of the change program.

Involvement means intelligent involvement, based on people understanding what the change program is all about and being aware of the cultural norms that can help it succeed or drag it to defeat. If people are to participate in decision making, they need the skills and training to make intelligent decisions based on sound information. Participation must be informed.

The amount of authority, power, and responsibility that go with participation will depend on the situation and the basic structure of the organization. In hierarchical organizations, there is never total equality in these areas, but there can be equality in the areas of listening, feedback, and information flow. There can be communication in which people on lower levels of the hierarchy can offer their ideas to those above them, and people on the higher levels make decisions only after finding out what those below them think and feel about what is proposed.

PITFALLS OF THE PARTICIPATION IDEA

The idea of involving representatives from all levels as a management technique is not without its problems. In OD literature we find warnings about participative decision making. Chris Argyris[5] talks about the "misplaced emphasis" in the recent push toward participation by employees in organizations, by citizens in communities, and by students in schools. "The idea," he explains, "was to give these groups more power in the decision-making process." But he points out that

> [T]his policy overlooked the fact that such participation would probably increase the number of people with Model I assumptions (learning systems that inhibit the detection and correction of error), who in turn would create even more-complicated learning systems.[6]

This very real problem can, our experience indicates, be averted by simultaneous attention to other variables: sound information, proper skills, and results orientation. The question is not whether or not to have participation, but what is the quality and form of the participation. People need to understand the culture and to identify the cultural norms affecting the problem before they develop action programs for change.

No-Fault Approaches

Rather than trying to find out who's to blame for problems, the emphasis needs to be on finding solutions that will benefit everyone. In a well-conceived change program, problem-solving without blame is a constructive asset.

When all parties deal with problem behavior as it relates to norms, there is less risk of arousing personal defensiveness. It is easier to take the criticism, "It's the norm here to arrive fifteen minutes late to meetings. Can we change it?" than "You are always holding up the meeting because you're late."

Another no-fault approach is for each member to focus on what he or she can do to bring about change, rather than what others can do. Most problems require that each individual examine his/her own behavior in relation to the group's objectives. People are more likely to do this when the focus is on achieving results and modifying the culture, rather than on placing blame for what has occurred. This tends to free energy formerly wasted in win-lose confrontations, and to spark enthusiastic movement toward change. Therefore, it is productive to avoid creating environments in which people cannot succeed and then get blamed for failure, and to move toward creating environments that help people to succeed.

Clarity

Not only should goals, objectives, purposes, and tasks be clear, but they need to be stated in specific terms, with the group frequently checking to make sure members understand. Openness of communication can assure such clarity.

In successful cultures, goals and purposes are constantly kept in view as the change process develops and work gets underway in installing and sustaining positive norms. People in one department or one segment of the cultural entity share their objectives with other departments or segments and have an opportunity to receive help and feedback. In the course of this process, objectives may be modified or people's perception of them may be sharpened. And at all times people can refer to the change model to confirm their progress through the change programs.

Continuing emphasis on results not only replaces empty promises, it also replaces the negative norm of blaming. Finger-pointing is bypassed when the emphasis is on accomplishment and concrete results. The negative norm of helplessness is also undermined, for the realization that something is being accomplished spurs people on. At first many people don't think that change is possible, but their attitude changes when they see some results.

Successful change programs set specific, measurable short- and long-range goals that everyone agrees will constitute satisfactory cultural change. The short-range goals need to be goals that can be achieved reasonably quickly, and that lead to early visible results. In effective change programs, results are regularly and promptly reported in a manner that people throughout the organization can understand. Reports on results have the greatest impact when they are positioned in the larger framework of agreed-upon objectives and are seen as progress toward shared goals.

The long-range goals must be clearly defined as well, for mere "activities" that aren't framed in the larger context can be as disappointing as unfulfilled promises. Both immediate and continuing actions must be planned, since early success in modifying a culture motivates continued efforts.

A Sound Informational Base

Rather than relying on hunches, wishful thinking, or so-called common sense, we need to put the program on a sound data base, gathering whatever information is needed to do this. This information needs to be shared willingly throughout the organization. In many organizations, the negative norm of keeping information to oneself or within the department is the greatest obstacle to organizational harmony.

Three kinds of information are needed for developing target goals: hard data, i.e., factual, quantifiable data that can be used to measure progress; programmatic information, i.e., facts about the extent to which proposed actions are being carried out; and cultural information, covering what the norms are, their strengths, and what is actually happening in the organization, as contrasted with what is supposedly or officially happening.

Systematic, Multilevel Approaches

Even problems that seem relatively simple must be approached on several levels simultaneously rather than by simple, single-variable solutions. There are usually several key points in a change situation at which effective work can bring about the desired change. The way to success is to attack problems intelligently and systematically, working on the important pressure points in a coordinated way. Cultural problems are usually the result of complex variables, and their solution will require systematic and creative attention to a number of such variables if successful and sustained changes are to take place.

Sustained Cultural Change

Instead of treating symptoms, we need to deal with root causes and try to develop norms of support that will be long-lasting. If we really want to change, we must be willing to commit ourselves to an effort that will extend over a long time, for negative norms are often deeply rooted, and it is crucial to build support for positive ones.

Interlocking Principles and Norms

The norms of all these cultural change principles interlock and reinforce each other. Look, for example, at how the other six affect the first crucial principle of people involvement. Without mutually beneficial, no-fault approaches, many people will get "turned off." Without clarity of tasks, goals, and plans, increased involvement may only muddy the waters and impede progress. Without a focus on results, greater people involvement could result in a complexity of undirected and unconnected activities. Without a sound information base, involving more people might merely involve them in more wasted effort. Without a systematic, multilevel approach, important aspects would likely be forgotten. Without sustained commitment, follow-through, and deep cultural change, we would only have greater numbers of frustrated and disillusioned people.

Since the process itself is as important as the goal, these principles need to be included at the very beginning. If they are followed throughout all phases of the systematic program, the chances of making the transformation and sustaining it are very great indeed.

BUILDING SUPPORT THROUGH SMALL GROUPS

If our organizations and communities are going to achieve lasting transformation, the small subgroups within them will have to provide supportive environments. The small groups of which we are members — our work groups, families, the classroom, the office staff, the board, the faculty, and so on — have a tremendous influence upon us. Each one of our primary groups (the people we actually associate with each day) is a small culture, full of norms that profoundly affect our lives. Though every one of us has certain areas in which we confront or flaunt the norm, for the most part our lives are determined by the norms of our groups, especially our primary groups.

Members of our staff first began to realize the importance of the small group while working with delinquent youngsters in the inner city. We found that a small, newly formed group could set its own positive norms, and by adding people slowly and helping them to understand themselves in a cultural context, a supportive environment was built. This group, never more than fourteen teenage boys, gave the boys the support they needed to turn from their delinquent ways and carve new and better lifestyles for themselves.[7]

Later, the same principle of creating small, positive subcultures was used in successful cultural change programs with migrant workers,[8] communities, families, agencies, unions, churches, and businesses.[9] Without waiting for the whole company to change, or for the whole community to be more humanistic, the subgroups can get the process going. Today this principle is proving useful in building successful corporate and community health programs. For instance, people who are trying to change to healthier lifestyles find support in the small group. The sense of community that builds in such a group is a more powerful motivation than education or factual knowledge of the value of health practices.[10]

Power in the Primary Group

The face-to-face group is a powerful tool because it relates to a profound need in our lives. Robert Nisbet, in his book *The Quest for Community*,[11] addressed the question, "Where can we find relief from the sense of isolation and anxiety that haunts us in our age of abundance?" He said that relief lies *in the realm of the small, primary, personal relationships of society, relationships that mediate directly between man and his larger world of economic, moral, and political and religious values.*[12]

Small support groups create an opportunity to develop primary relationships. We can learn to share with and trust one another within a group that is small enough for everyone to be heard, and to get to know each other. Here the norms of "community" can be built and tried out, slowly and solidly. There is an opportunity to check back on these norms from time to time, to confront the negative norms when they creep back in, but confront them in a friendly, trusting way.

A support group, when properly developed, can become the very opposite of the closed "clique," for it radiates outward, often building norms strong enough to make it possible for its members to practice positive behaviors not only in the group, but in the outer world as well.

Types of Support Groups

There are many types of support groups. They include small groups already set up for other purposes, such as boards, committees, classes, work groups, and small departments that can be transformed into supportive environments for their members. While such groups would continue to devote their major effort to the tasks for which they were set up, they would also put aside time to view themselves as a cultural entity, to look at the kind of support they are giving to their members, and to work to develop more of the kind of norms they want. In a change program, time set aside for this has proved valuable and worthwhile. To solve chronic problems or accomplish meaningful and lasting change, we will save time in the long run if we first spend some time on developing support.

This phenomenon has occurred in corporate settings. A large retail company involved in an organization-wide cultural change program found out just how valuable a support group can be. Work groups already set up were helped to start the process of building good community norms. They quickly became support groups, creating the environment needed for sustained change. Within the first few months of the program, the difference was already remarkable. Even customers coming into the various stores noticed it. As the norms of caring began to take effect, the stores became places where customers felt that their needs were important.

Getting the Group Started

Leaders must commit themselves publicly to the idea of developing "community," thereby helping to set up the climatic conditions that will aid its growth. The actual work of building a supportive environment, however, is done on a person-to-person level, and the small support group is a powerful tool for making it happen.

You can start with small groups which already exist, or you can purposefully create a new group. It can be a small group; in fact, you can start with as few as one or two other people. Whoever it is, you have made a start when you first say to this person, "Let's talk about ways in which we can do things even better around here, ways in which we all can relate with more openness, ways we can take care of each other and our whole group's needs."

By your action you are already starting to develop a small subculture with different norms, norms of openness and caring. As you gradually add other people to your group, they can partake in the cooperative atmosphere you have created. Just getting a group together to achieve a common goal is not enough. There also needs to be conscious effort to build good relationships among the people in the group and to develop the supportive cultures that will undergird the task-oriented work of the group.

The support group approach is primarily one of democratic, participatory decision making and involvement. It is essentially self-led, although in some cases a support group leader, an OD practitioner, a chairperson, or a teacher may fulfill the leadership role. This person is primarily a facilitator and coordinator rather than a director. Decisions about what will be discussed and which skills will be learned rest with the group as a whole, although groups can often benefit from the experience of others.

Joining a support group is moste of an ongoing group, such as a board or a classroom, for support group activities, should be, to the extent possible, a group decision.

Ordinarily, "small group" means not more than a dozen people. In large corporations we often start with the executive committee, then work with whole departments that report to members of the executive committee. The departments are subdivided into small groups after the initial workshop.

Go from Special Interests to Human Interests

Whatever your reason for starting the group — to solve a civic problem, to start a new business, to promote good health practice, or to reduce absenteeism — avoid neglecting personal and human factors by doing the following:

- Give people a chance to get to know one another as people, beyond the framework of the particular task or purpose.
- Give each person a chance to share feelings about the kind of support and encouragement he or she gets, and wants to get, from the group.

Help People Understand and Work With Norms

Small groups can easily make a change, but the problem is to maintain it. People often start a project with great enthusiasm and cooperation, but the old norms take over and the group spirit evaporates when someone is left with the work or someone finds emotional needs unsatisfied. In the small group you can help people become aware of typical norms of handling change. The more we can be conscious of these norms and how they operate in our lives, the better we will be able to circumvent their destructive influence.

It Doesn't Have to Take a Lot of Time

A small group meeting can be short and simple, a quick report of any new achievement or obstacles. The meeting is not task-oriented and it is not used for solving large problems. It is time set aside for sharing concerns and celebrating successes. It is a time to check with each other on progress. The important work of changing behavior is taking place in day-to-day activities. "We live the program every day" is the slogan of one change program.

Include the Leaders

Many times, work groups create support groups but exclude the organizational leaders and supervisors. It is our judgment that in hierarchical organizations it is better to include the leaders. Many people feel that members will not feel free to speak when the leaders are there. This feeling in itself is something that should be dealt with, and dealing with it face-to-face in a supportive environment is the most beneficial way to solve the problem.

Don't Be Exclusive

The difference between a small support group and a clique is openness. To be open means not only mutual support within the group but openness to outsiders. Most of us can better maintain and strengthen our personal group transformations by reaching out to be helpful to other people.

Building a Community Without Walls

If supportive principles are at work in a small group within the larger organization, a positive culture can be built that can withstand the negative norms that may rule in the total organization. Even better is the spread of the positive norms from the small group to the total organization. If people can avoid placing blame within their support group, they often find they can also avoid placing blame in the next department meeting, within their family, or even in a political context.

If there are a number of support groups within the larger organization and they are developing good norms of relatedness and trust among their members, it is bound to affect the larger corporation. If the leadership of the organization has already committed itself to seeking a greater sense of community, then the change can take place rapidly and reach out far beyond the organization.

When people discover that their true identity can grow within the group and that they need not fear manipulation and control when there is an open exchange, then the sense of community can spread rapidly. It cannot be contained within any particular group because, fortunately, it is one of our most contagious human traits.

HOW A CHANGE AGENT GETS STARTED

The way that one person functions will vary according to his or her position in the organization or community. It's easier if you're president of the company or mayor of the town, but you don't have to be in the top position to initiate change.

People at other levels in the hierarchy also can get things started. The head of a company or of a community might make use of the system described. Other people within the company or community may first want to develop their own support networks and approach the management later.

How Fred Did It

Fred was manager of the sales division of a large manufacturing company. He had been an outstanding engineer, and had been promoted to a managerial position. Most of the managers he had worked under had come from the old school, and he, at first, tried to imitate their approaches. However, he was soon dissatisfied with the competitiveness, politics, and alienation he felt throughout the company.

Then Fred learned about the concept of the manager as a cultural change agent, and decided to try this new approach. "What do you think of how we're doing around here?" he asked some fellow managers. "Are there some improvements possible? Are there some things we could do better?"

The responses Fred met with ranged from deeply rooted negatives to full support. He listened carefully and made use of many of the ideas that were suggested. Most important, he built upon the positive responses. He used the four-phase change process as a framework and the principles of cultural change as a constant guide.

Fred's first step toward change was to focus on understanding cultures. He responded to the negatives with, "Why do we feel helpless? Not because we can't, but because it's the norm around here for people to say and think nothing will happen. If we accept that norm without changing it, we're defeated from the start. Instead, even a few of us can get together and say, 'Let's have a new norm in sted colleagues to dinner to discuss some norms that were getting in the way of organizational change. Together they planned some small but immediate steps:

"Let's get a few others together and discuss some possibilities."

"Let's put it on the board agenda to spend a few minutes brainstorming about what we'd really like to see happening around here."

"Let's use a support barometer and see what the picture is here."

Fred found that one of the most helpful ways to begin change was for people to stop using their energy to find fault. "Let's not spend time pointing our fingers at others. It doesn't matter so much who's to blame. The problem is, what do we do next? Let's focus our energy on that."

The change agent's role is to be constantly alert, aware that people can only too easily slip back into the old way of placing blame for problems. The leader needs to be constantly checking for this trend and reminding the group when they get off the track. "Aren't we falling into the old trap of blaming the victim here?" Fred found that such statements had to be repeated many times, and he also found that he too needed to reflect the new norms in his own daily behavior.

Fred and his associates set up a plan for evaluating how they were doing and met regularly to review progress and consider new possibilities and alternatives.

TOMORROW'S ORGANIZATIONS

Michael Maccoby pointed out a sad truth about today's corporate world when he said,

> Corporate work stimulates and rewards qualities of the head and not of the heart. Those [of 250 most-admired individuals within the best companies of the United States] who were active and interested in their work moved ahead in the modern corporation, while those who were the most compassionate were more likely to suffer severe emotional conflicts.[13]

We believe that the organizational world of tomorrow can have heart. It can provide a supportive environment where compassion is rewarded and qualities of the heart are stimulated, accepted, and encouraged. We believe that the most effective change agents will use both head and heart, and that the two aspects will not be in conflict, for both intelligence and compassion will be in the service of human freedom.

Notes:

[1] K. Lewin, *Field Theory and Social Science* (New York: Harper & Row, 1951).

[2] Abraham Maslow, "A Theory of Human Motivation," *Technological Review* 50 (1943), pp. 370-396.

[3] Erich Fromm, *Escape from Freedom* (New York: Farrar, Straus, Giroux, 1941), pp. 326-327.

[4] A. Bandura, *Social Learning Theory* (Englewood Cliffs, New Jersey: Prentice-Hall, 1977).

[5] Chris Argyris, "Double Look Learning in Organizations," *Harvard Business Review* 55:5 (1977), pp. 122-123.

[6] Ibid.

[7] R.F. Allen, H.N. Dubin, S. Pilnick, and A. Youtz, *Collegefields from Delinquency to Freedom* (Seattle: Special Child Publications, 1970).

[8] S. Harris and R.F. Allen, *The Quiet Revolution: How Florida Migrants Changed Their LIves* (New York: Rawson Associates, 1978).

[9] R.F. Allen and C. Kraft, *Beat the System* (New York: McGraw-Hill, 1980).

[10] R.F. Allen and S. Linde, *Lifegain* (New York: Appleton, Century, Crofts, 1981).

[11] R. Nisbet, *The Quest for Community* (New York: Oxford University Press, 1953).

[12] Ibid., pp. 48-49.

[13] Michael Maccoby, *The Gamesman: The New Corporate Leaders* (New York: Simon and Schuster, 1976), p. 43.

4

Managing the Complexity of Organizational Transformation

KAREN WILHELM BUCKLEY
DANI MONROE PERKINS

Comments on the Second Edition

The intervening years since *Transforming Work* was first published have been filled with grand efforts of self- and organizational transformation. We have learned a tremendous amount, including a profound humility about the unforeseen consequences of non-linear, not staying in the same endless spiral, truly jumping into a new pattern, *transformative* change. There is still much to learn, not only about the dynamics of guiding an organizational transformation but, perhaps most difficult, to develop in ourselves and those we serve the mindfulness and compassion sufficient to intelligently respond to the accompanying disruptions in people's work and home lives.

Change is necessary. Differentiating between minor, major, and transformative level changes, whether these are within an individual, non-profit institution, midsized company or multinational corporation, is critical to planning a successful transition. The dynamics and stages of transition articulated in this chapter have been applied countless times to all manner of changes. Hopefully this work can continue to remind us to be more sensitive to ourselves and others as we guide or undergo further experiments in organizational change.

The time of *unconsciousness* is the prelude: a readiness to accept change is building. The *awakening*, whether by internal or external catalysts, can be shocking, taking many folks by surprise. The key analysts, intuitive listeners, and synthesizers help by articulating possible benefits and predicting future instabilities. Intelligent planners provide for the internalizing process needed by both the formal and informal leaders. Once they understand the implications and potential advantages of the needed changes they become the ark, capable of riding the waters of change.

Soon the *reordering* begins — like our childhood playing with "tinker toys," the structure of our lives or organizations is dismantled, leaving a pile of parts and pieces. This is for some the scariest time; for others, the most exciting. The possibilities are endless, the boundaries insubstantial, and each step is without guideposts into an unknown land. Quicksand and solid ground rotate in a kaleidoscope of challenges. Grabbing for the seemingly secure past hijacks the change. Leaping too early for a potential ledge of safety can return us to the fertile ground of unconscious denials and attachments.

The transition team's task is to ride the storms of change, grounding lightning and diffusing thunder cells, while bringing the healing balms of information, courage, careful listening, reason and meaning. A coherent vision begins to form in a period of *translation*, providing momentum for those ready to jump on board. For those still unconscious or just awakening, this formulation of the future can provoke an "I will not!" stance, having less to do with the content of the vision and more to do with an as yet undeveloped internal capacity to accept the change.

Widespread *commitment* to the vision brings a solidity, a runway for launching. This is the time to bring everyone up to speed, because a full *embodiment* requires completed shifts in the three dimensions of *behavior, structure,* and *consciousness.* This *Triangle of Embodiment* has proven to be a useful tool in planning, diagnosing incongruities, and assessing progress during organization-wide changes. Emphasis on all three points culminates in a fuller change and the focused action of *integration.*

Transformational change is work — scary, exhilarating, and necessary work. We will not solve the world's problems without it. Yet the ethical ramifications of catalyzing such profound changes in organizations, in other people's lives, are vast and deserve careful consideration. Hopefully, through conscious reflection we will expand our own capacities for compassion, trust, and true caring.

— Karen Wilhelm Buckley
Dani Monroe Perkins

Managing the complexities of Organizational Transformation is one of the major challenges confronting organizations in the 1980s: how to successfully maintain high-level performance while experiencing transformative change. The authors have developed a seven-stage model that describes the transition cycle, which they use to diagnose and facilitate transformative processes. The model points out dilemmas and opportunities encountered by individuals and organizations experiencing transformation. The authors are finding that responsive organizations are realizing more of their potential as they understand the particular dynamics of transformative change.

T he changes affecting our world today are causing societal shifts as dramatic as those that occurred in the Renaissance and during the Industrial Revolution. During times of massive change, profound modifications of most forms of organizations, social relationships, and individual lifestyle accompany societal shifts. These changes challenge the major premises and underlying patterns of current society, and result in a transformation. Faced with depletion of natural resources, introduction of new technology, and changing consumer values, individuals and organizations are undergoing major overhauls of their basic assumptions and operating policies. This type of complex restructuring is viewed as transformative change.

In transformation, a transition occurs from the present state to an altered future state. During this transition, modification of structure, behavior, and consciousness occurs. In their work on organizational transitions, Beckhard and Harris[1] traditionally defined transition as "the period of time and state of affairs that exist between an identification of need and the achievement of a desired future state." However, within transformation a future state is not able to be predicted or designed. Therefore, *transition* is used here to identify a cycle contained within the transformation process.

This chapter presents a seven-stage transition cycle that an individual or an organization experiences in making a transformative change. In this transition cycle the stages are Unconsciousness, Awakening, Reordering, Translation, Commitment, Embodiment, and Integration. The authors developed these stages from their personal and professional experiences.

This seven-stage cycle of transition is described both for an organization in a transformation process, and for the individual affected by the organization's transformation. A fully integrated process requires movement through all seven stages of the transition cycle. The tempo and direction vary as the organization moves in a random manner, jumping backward and forward. Rhythm and timing are determined by the rate the transition can be managed. Progression through the cycle can be instantaneous or ponderously slow. Often a micro-cycle of the seven stages is encompassed within each stage.

Transition Cycle.
(Buckley & Perkins, January 1983 © *VISION/ACTION*)

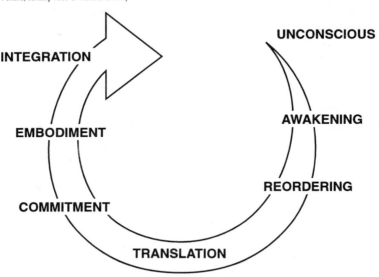

During a transition, great potential exists for innovation, growth, and positive development. This time can also be very confusing and filled with turmoil, pain, and destructive chaos. Whether the transition is initiated internally or imposed externally, individuals and organizations may find themselves experiencing the same type of turmoil.

The seven-stage transition cycle may provide a better understanding of the experience of individuals and organizations in transformation. Our intention is that this transition cycle provide individuals and organizations with a context in which to view themselves in the midst of today's transforming world. It is often difficult to grasp the multiplicity of factors involved in transformative changes. For the purposes of this chapter, the authors have found it helpful to delineate three levels of change: minor, major, and transformative.

A minor change entails the modification of mental attitudes and behaviors without a shift in perception. This type of change addresses the surface issues, and avoids threats to deep-seated beliefs. The individual or organization tries various options, while remaining stable and relatively unchanged.

A major change occurs when an individual or an organization develops a new perspective and truly begins acting in new ways. A high degree of ambiguity, turmoil, and chaos accompany this radical change. As old habits are discarded, new patterns are developed. This level of change involves a search for underlying causes in order to reorganize the whole system, rather than just some parts. Within a major change, a transformation may or may not occur, depending on the readiness and willingness of the individual or the organization.

Transformative change is accompanied by a fundamental shift in consciousness, values, or perceptions. This level of change entails a profound transmutation of the prevailing vision of reality. This shift in consciousness alters the basic ways an organization or individual responds to the environment. A transformation has occurred when new meaning is successfully established in relation to the organization's environment.

In a rapidly changing world, the limitations of minor and major change become obvious to individuals and organizations as they strive to survive and grow. For example, the surface alterations of minor and major change often will not meet the challenges of automation, or the desire for greater meaning in the workplace. New technological and social innovations bring with them a need to shift the basic ways of responding. A transformative shift in perception allows us to find workable alternatives and to deepen the connection to "right purpose" when organization life feels empty.

Evidence of transformative change is all around us. For instance, to compete with foreign manufacturers, the American automotive industry has had to redesign not only the product but the process of production. Not just surface changes, but all aspects of the system have been affected. In 1983 *Leading Edge Bulletin* reported that a General Motors plant near Detroit "has made a major overhaul of its basic operating philosophy and has undergone a complete renewal of every procedure as it affects that philosophy . . . from quality control to who eats in which cafeteria."[2] The complexity of their problems required a transformation to an entirely new way of viewing work and business.

Fritjof Capra, a well-known physicist, offered a perceptual way of organizing or viewing the current experience of societal, organizational, or individual transformation. Capra pointed out, "The world is approaching a turning point. A massive shift in the perception of reality is underway, with thinkers in many disciplines beginning to move away from the traditional reductionist, mechanical world view to a holistic, ecological, systems paradigm."[3] Capra characterized the traditional world view as the classical mechanistic-Cartesian paradigm that developed throughout the 16th and 17th centuries. This paradigm includes belief in the scientific method as the only valid approach to knowledge, and the notion of the universe as a mechanical system composed of elementary material building blocks. The mechanistic view presents units as having closed boundaries. Change is seen as the replacement of a defective unit by a new unit, with the change having little impact on the larger machine or system. In the restructuring of one division, the impact on another division is not considered.

A new perspective is emerging to deal adequately with the complexities of technological and social innovations. In acquiring a new perspective, one experiences a paradigm shift: a profound change that occurs in the thoughts, perceptions, and values that form a particular vision of reality. Capra viewed the emerging new paradigm as a holistic-ecological-systems perspective, in which the universe "appears as a harmonious indivisible whole." This perspective "emphasizes the fundamental interrelatedness and interdependence of all phenomena, and the intrinsically dynamic nature of physical reality."[4]

The organic perspective, as we shall characterize it here, views change as a continuum of dynamic interactions, and not as a single event. When viewed from the organic perspective, transformation is a natural part of evolution — the inner urge to grow. B.M. Hubbard pointed out:

> The balance of nature is continuous, progressive change with a recurrent pattern in the process: the creation of a new whole forms out of the old through synthesis of separate parts. There is no point where the process remains static. The tendency in nature to form ever-greater whole systems which are different from and greater than the sum of their parts is intrinsic — or we would not be here.[5]

This organic perspective is altering the orientation of corporations, public service agencies, educational institutions, and individuals. Change is no longer seen as a compartmentalized, simple process. The analysis, comprehension, and orchestration of organizational transformation is complicated as the various subsystems experience change at different rates, and affect each other in converging patterns of cyclical waves. The individual employees, departments, divisions, and subsidiaries are all involved in a dynamic interaction of different rhythms and tempos of change.

As organizations undergo major transformations necessary for survival and growth, individual lives are also transformed. The success of an organizational change largely depends on the employees' ability to integrate the changes. The individual experiencing transformation in an organizational context will discover that a cycle of transition begins with the unconscious stage.

THE SEVEN STAGE TRANSITION CYCLE

Unconscious Stage

Organization transition begins gradually with an unconscious period. Basically a passive time, the period of organization unconscious builds a readiness for change. During this gestation, the organization develops the capacity to acknowledge that something is wrong. Certain clues in the informal networks — unconnected bits of random information, sporadic symptoms, and tentative new ideas — indicate that an organization is experiencing the unconscious stage. Messengers within the organization could include someone in a powerful position with an inspiration or vision; an old-timer with an intuitive sense that something needs to be changed; or an employee identifying surface symptoms of a failure in the system. Other catalysts might include growing internal dissatisfaction, or changes in the external environment (*i.e.*, new competitors, national economic trends, or international disturbances).

An organization's cultural or owned values can support or hinder its ability to respond to internal or external signals of the need for change. If the corporation bases its values only on stability and security, dissident voices or innovative ideas may seldom be heard. The employee responds to this suppression by withholding valuable information, becoming apathetic, or withdrawing personal responsibility from the success or failure of the organization.

An organization that values new information as critical to continued success will experience less lag between the time individuals or departments become aware of new information and the time it becomes a part of the organization's awareness. This shortened response time increases the organization's ability to manage proactively and to facilitate a transformative change.

Many corporations are benefitting from employee suggestions. As reported in *Leading Edge Journal*, executives at Control Data Corporation in Minneapolis confirmed this:

> Suggestions for changes in policy and structure have been so useful and specific that management is now committed to work on any issue raised by employees. Some 2,000 employees in engineering services are now redefining their own organization. They are creating a climate of self-reliance, therefore changing the destiny of the organization.[6]

Once new information becomes part of the organization consciousness, it becomes apparent that changes are necessary. The organization begins to identify, and finally to confront, the existing situation. Awakening to the need for change, the organization enters the next stage of transformation.

Awakening Stage

Suddenly, the organization awakens to possibilities and problems present in the current situation. The unconnected pieces of information from the unconscious stage are synthesized into a message of needed change. The awakening has occurred as the organization is jolted to confront the existing environment.

The need for transformative change may be identified by several different sources. Often it is a new CEO with innovative plans and a fresh perspective. The articulator could be a "natural" leader[7] with an ability to perceive the truth, and with enough passion and insight to be heard. A pocket or division also may point to a new direction. A failure in the system, a crisis, an articulated new vision, or a natural inclination to grow may also trigger the awakening.

Awakening to needed changes introduces instability into the system, and disrupts the harmony of the previous plateau. Because little information is available, management's anxiety, and that of their subordinates, begins to grow. Organizational members sense an impending change, and wonder what the impact will be. The rate of awakening will vary depending on the receptivity to change. Those who first perceived the needed changes provide an impetus for the rest of the organization to awaken as they move through the stages of reordering and translation to commitment. If the articulators try to move too fast, presuming that others share their new understanding, resistance may build rapidly in the organization.

An example of awakening, from the consulting practice of one of the authors, occurred at a prestigious university when the president and the dean realized that the quality of education in America was declining, and that curricula did not respond to rapid technological advances. The president realized he could use the university's reputation to bring attention to the problems in education. Simultaneously, the dean decided that the school of education needed to move out of its ivory tower and improve the quality of education. Sharing an intention to align education with technology, the president and the dean decided to use the university as a catalyst. Already committed, they moved through the transition cycle to embodiment. Spreading the awakening in ever-widening circles, they brought together the faculty of the school of education to express perceptions, ideas and concerns. Once a shared reality was established, they formed task forces to gather data and analyze the present state of education and technology. Acceptance spread further throughout the institution as task force members sought input from different departments, other universities, computer consultants, and corporations.

The awakening stage has included informal data collection through exploration of potential dilemmas and identification of possible opportunities. With significant numbers awakened to the message of needed change, the organization is ready to enter the stage of *reordering*.

Reordering Stage

Reordering is a process of analyzing the existing situation and challenging underlying patterns. The questioning of reordering produces a creative chaos and turmoil necessary for a full grasp of the issues and implications.

This reordering probing process affects the stability of the organization and the equilibrium of individuals. Evidence of instability exists in undefined roles, increased workloads, and unfocused directions. Organizational members begin to ask questions:

- What is happening or not happening in the environment?
- When is it happening or not happening in the environment?
- Where is it happening or not happening in the environment?
- How much is it happening or not happening in the environment?
- Why is it happening or not happening in the environment?

These basic questions identify the substance, time, location, frequency, and cause of the problem. With this data collected, the organization can decide whether to make a minor change, or embark on a major one. In their 1982 work *In Search of Excellence*, Tom Peters and R.H. Waterman state,

> When we reorganize we usually stop at reorganizing the boxes
> on the chart. The odds are high that nothing much will change.
> We will have chaos, even useful chaos for a while, but eventu-
> ally the old culture will prevail. Old habit patterns persist.[8]

Keeping security and stability as top priorities, the organization has, in this instance, chosen a minor change, affecting individuals and the organization with minimum discomfort.

The organization may choose instead to institute major changes leading to a possible transformation. This choice may direct the organization to a new level of growth and excellence. As the organization chooses a deeper level of transformative change, it must recognize the magnitude of the impact on the individual. Traditional change efforts have been primarily oriented to the modification of organization structure, and not to the internal changes of the employee. As the old organizational culture transforms, the individual employee is asked to undergo a profound change in personal thoughts, perceptions, and values. This internal alteration causes emotional insecurity, as individuals let go of the old and adopt new attitudes, behavior, and consciousness.

Until the employee accepts that what *was* no longer *is*, he or she will be unable to move forward with the organization. The organization can reduce individuals' resistance by providing adequate opportunity for early and comprehensive participation. If the level of participation is high, people's perceptions of upcoming changes shift. The organization strengthens the focus of the transformation by the inclusion of those still in the unconscious and awakening stages.

The orientation of transition now shifts from the present to the future. With the introspective questioning of reordering ended, the organization begins to move toward the new vision. The sense of potential and benefit inherent in the new vision provides a driving force for change. Final clarification of the future vision, and development of strategies for implementation occur next in the *translation* stage.

Translation Stage

Translation is the process of formulating a vision from the integration of information, metaphorical images, personal visions, and feelings collected in the unconscious, awakening, and reordering stages. The vision evolves into a clear image of what the organization wants to achieve, which then organizes and instructs every step toward the desired future. Specific long-range goals and strategies for implementation emerge from the vision, enabling individuals to move forward in a concerted effort.

As John Naisbitt has pointed out,

The extraordinarily successful strategic vision for NASA was 'to put a man on the moon by the end of the decade.' That strategic vision gave magnetic direction to the entire organization. Nobody had to be told or reminded of where the organization was going.[9]

Individuals can discover their personal "fit" when the vision has been successfully translated. Effective packaging of the vision generates excitement, and unifies the organization. Employees who previously resisted change may find themselves joining the team. As a stone dropped in a pond sends ripples to a farthest shore, so an articulated new direction ripples out to affect the health and vitality of the organization. In an organization with a cohesive, clear vision, reflective of the "right" purpose, a resonance field develops. Resonance occurs in organizational life when the individual and organization are in alignment with the vision. A.H. Maiden explained resonance as:

> . . . a rich concept used in many fields. For an electrical engineer, it is the state of adjustment of an electric circuit which permits maximum flow of current when impressed by an electromotive force of particular frequency. In physics, resonance occurs when the vibration of the created force equals that of the natural vibration of the system to which the force is applied, as with a tuning fork. When the vibratory qualities of the various parts and processes of the group are consciously brought into resonance, the actual effect of group work is magnified many [times].[10]

From the excitement and support generated around the vision, the organization develops ways to make it work. The organization must be wary of replacing or altering the ideas of the vision that have evolved through the transition, simply because of perceived difficulties in making it work. An attempt to adopt alternative visions may disillusion some individuals, resulting in a withdrawal of widespread support and participation. A reactive stance of resistance or a "things will not change, it has been this way for years" stance of indifference may develop.

The translation stage establishes a cohesive, focused direction that will provide the foundation for total commitment of the organization. In the next stage, *commitment*, all of the forces in the organization pull together toward the single goal.

Commitment Stage

Commitment is when the organization takes responsibility for implementation of the new vision. Commitment has evolved throughout the transition cycle, as greater numbers of individuals commit to the new direction. A few key players may have made the commitment in the beginning, while others committed during the questioning of reordering, or the public articulation of the vision in translation. Let us refer to the education example, in which the president and the dean simultaneously committed to improving the quality of education. By presenting their intention to the faculty, they rapidly advanced to embodiment. The faculty awakened to the need, experienced their own cycles of reordering and translation, and eventually committed to participation in the project. Once committed, they embodied the intention by developing task forces to study specific areas of concern. Commitment happened in the early part of the transition for the president and dean, and in later stages for the faculty. Still later, the university at large and the public school system made the commitment to participate.

The commitment stage is a pivotal point in the transition cycle. So far, the organization and individuals have only been considering the possibility of transformation. This is the time when the level of ability and readiness to "travel the distance" become key factors in transformative change. An organization's readiness can be assessed on attitudes, behaviors, and actions: Do the prevalent attitudes show willingness to change, high levels of trust, and a sense of agreement? Are exhibited behaviors focusing on the future, teamwork, and establishment of informal new boundaries? Are the stakeholders allocating resources, signing contracts, holding special meetings, and interacting with the community and the news media? Individuals become ready to commit when they can see personal benefits inherent in the proposed plan.

For both the organization and individuals, the commitment stage is a time of being torn between the potential of the new direction and the security of the old. The tension between these two forces can cause an imbalance that creates internal disequilibrium and external strife. Moving forward and yet holding back, the individual experiences attachments to the past and fear of the unknown future. If the organization does not prepare the individual to handle these stresses, the transition may revert to earlier stages, stagnate, or die. Through adequate preparation. the full commitment of individuals strengthens the organization.

Based on an assessment of organization values, attitudes, and behaviors, key leaders can decide whether to proceed with the next stage, *embodiment,* or to return to the previous stages of awakening, reordering, and/or translation for further development.

Embodiment State

In embodiment, the organization has reached the point where its task is to bring the transformed vision into its day-to-day operations. The challenge is to manage the interaction of three elements: 1) consciousness shifts that provide the new paradigm for the organization; 2) structural changes that provide a framework for the transformed organization; and 3) behavioral changes that bring employee actions into alignment with the transformed structure. The alignment of these three elements is achieved through an embodiment cycle of four steps:

- identification
- experimentation
- practice
- internalization.

This cycle requires a start/stop tempo with modification and reorganization of the system. The organization synthesizes old data and beliefs into a new paradigm, in order to affect a shift in consciousness. Alternate structural changes are experimented with until the organization discovers the right fit to the new vision. Employees discard old beliefs and norms as they develop behavior patterns congruent with the new directions.

This is a dynamic process. As Peters and Waterman describe it, "The organization acts, and then learns from what it has done. It experiments. It makes mistakes; it finds unanticipated success."[11] Without permission for this trial and error period, embodiment results in short-term, superficial change. The organization must express unequivocally its commitment to experimentation, with statements like "Let's just try it out for the next two months," and "Let's give it a chance, and then we'll modify as needed."

The embodiment of the desired future happens more easily for some than for others. For some people, it is a tug-of-war between the past and the future. One day, an employee may feel very clear and excited about his or her new role, relocation in the organization, or the new direction. The next day, as the time approaches to abandon security, he or she may experience confusion, sadness, or anxiety. To manage the tension that emerges from either holding on, or letting go and moving on, employees often need emotional support from the organization. If personal support is not provided, individual resistance may block or delay forward progress. In order to successfully undergo embodiment, the individual must have the opportunity and support to develop an inner motivation to change. With the inner motivation to change, the individual can direct his or her own behavioral changes. Self-motivated behavioral changes tend to be long-lasting and to improve the effectiveness of organizational change.

The impact of embodiment is illustrated by a participant in a session facilitated by one of the authors. This woman, in wire transfer for a major bank, had been promoted from systems to operations. She reported:

In one day I went from moving linear pieces of data [numbers] on a copper wire from one place to another, to managing a staff of people and the resources needed to transfer millions of dollars around the world. Previously, if data was delayed, I didn't worry and just got it moving again. Now, if the funds are delayed, I am calculating compensation [late fees] and working to get the data moving again as soon as possible. I was bewildered, and realized that I was not prepared for the psychological impact of the promotion. I had received no training to better understand the complexity of my new job or to handle the stress.

In order to succeed, the woman's consciousness had to shift from a mechanistic viewpoint, to a systems viewpoint that encompassed a variety of factors dynamically influencing each other. It would be some time before she completed the behavioral and consciousness changes necessary for congruence with the simple structural change in position. Eventually, the embodiment is complete, and the organization and individuals reach a state of *integration*, drawing the transition to an end. The behavioral changes are internalized, and consciousness and structural and behavioral alignment deepen in the integration stage.

Integration Stage

As the embodiment of the desired change becomes widespread, the organization reaches a stage of integration. The necessary changes, both structural and behavioral, are instituted and operating. Consciousness has been altered so the organization and individual are functioning from a new paradigm. People feel that the changes are real and are going to stay.

The anticipated future state is now in place in the stage of integration, as the organization reaches a plateau of balanced wholeness. The informal and formal systems align to reach the goals of the organization. A supportive environment of trust, cooperation, and openness develops.

Integration is the stage in a transition where the organization experiences a solid foundation for peak performance. In our experience, an organization's ability to remain solid, yet permeable to new information, determines the degree to which it experiences its "personal power." In a graduate course on organizational behavior, Sabina Spencer, an organization development consultant in Europe, defined organization personal power as the ability to be unique, to be recognized as something that is dynamic, and has integrity. It [the organization] is in touch with its very essence or source of being. It has the ability to be regenerative and examine itself. It integrates its history in a change process, so it no longer holds on, but lets go and moves on. It [the organization] is a positive force that leads and creates.

When the organization experiences personal power, individual energy becomes aligned rather than diffused. In the transition cycle, energy had been diverted to the chaotic process of designing strategy, practicing new behavior, gaining commitment, managing emotions, and transforming consciousness. In integration. the individual experiences increased amounts of physical energy, emotional depth. and mental concentration. The organizational environment is stable enough to support its employees. Innovative solutions and creative ideas result from the stability in the organization, increased availability of natural resources, and refined mental clarity. The shared commitment of integration is to work together as one, and is increasingly evident as management extends the energy to get everyone "on the team." The integration stage is made up of varying degrees of completion. Appropriate adjustments are made to compensate for people who have resisted the transition, and who continue to deny what is needed. For instance, the CEO and top management teams may be in integration, the line manager in translation, and workers on the shop floor in awakening. Affirmation of the change process and commemoration of individual contributions strengthen the shared commitment. Through celebrations and rituals, the community is solidified and the emotional, psychological, and physical ups and downs of the change process are healed.

The organization faces the double-edged sword of stability in integration. Organizations, like individuals, should not prolong stabilization, nor move too quickly into a new change process. Prolonged stabilization can close an open system for lack of stimulus. Too-brief periods of stabilization can cause the organization to become reactive or dysfunctional from the anxiety created by constant change. In integration, a stable foundation has been built to enable the organization and individual to move into the next change cycle in a timely fashion. A strategy for assessment keeps the system responsive to feedback and open to emerging ideas. This passage through the transition cycle is now complete, and the organization once again enters the unconsciousness stage, developing readiness for the next cycle.

SUMMARY

A major challenge for large organizations is to maintain high productivity while experiencing transformative change. Successful institutions are realizing that change is a natural part of the organization's life cycle, and are beginning to prepare for and manage the complexities of organizational transformation.

Progressive managers and consultants understand that successful passage through the transition cycle is contingent upon the readiness and willingness of individuals and the organization to align with the new direction. These organizations are using the stages of *unconsciousness*, *awakening*, *reordering*, *translation*, *commitment*, *embodiment*, and *integration* to build a corporate context for an upcoming period of rapid change. The stages provide a common language to facilitate cross-level communication. Used as a diagnostic tool, they also become a method to anticipate future needs. In the celebration of a completed transition cycle, the seven stages build a foundation for future change.

As we have seen, the process of transformation is essentially a death-and-rebirth process. In our traditional mechanistic bias, we have imagined that transformation comes through fixing something defective, or supplying something that is missing. The transition cycle demonstrates that transformative change is a cyclical process from disintegration to reformation. Organizations and individuals choosing to transform will be stronger in their response to societal shifts and changing values affecting business in today's rapidly changing world.

Notes

1 R. Beckhard and R. Harris, *Organizational Transitions: Managing Complex Change* (Reading, Massachusetts: Addison-Wesley, 1977).

2 "Auto Plant's Operations Revised to Fit New Outlook," *Leading Edge Bulletin*, Vol. III; 8 (1983), pp. 1-2.

3 F. Capra, *The Turning Point* (New York: Simon and Schuster, 1982), p. 53.

4 F. Capra, "The Turning Point: A New Vision of Reality," *The Futurist*, Vol. XVI; 6 (1982), p. 19.

5 B.M. Hubbard, *The Evolutionary Journey* (San Francisco: Evolutionary Press, 1982).

6 "Management Committed to Work on Issues Raised by Workers," *Leading Edge Bulletin*, Vol. III; 11 (1983), p. 1.

7 See Beckhard and Harris.

8 Thomas J. Peters and R.H. Waterman, Jr., *In Search of Excellence: Lessons from America's Best-Run Companies* (New York: Harper & Row, 1982), p. 3.

9 John Naisbitt, *Megatrends* (New York: Harper & Row, 1982).

10 A.H. Maiden, "Resonance," *Gaia* [quarterly publication of the Institute for the Study of Conscious Evolution], Vol. II; 2 (1980), p. 3.

11 Peters and Waterman.

5

Metanoic Organizations*

CHARLES F. KIEFER
PETER M. SENGE

Comments on the Second Edition

When we wrote this article over fifteen years ago, the ideas made great sense to us. They had, after all, arisen from about ten years of prior experience, from consulting and workshops with senior- and middle level managers. But they were viewed as "on the fringe" of management theory and practice — often deemed idealistic. How widely have some of these ideas spread! Vision, alignment, empowering people, systems thinking, and more decentralized organization designs permeate contemporary management thought.

None of this means, however, that the notion of metanoia, a fundamental movement of mind, is either well understood or widely embodied in today's organizations. In some ways, the more basic ideas become familiar to us, the more the deeper meanings that lie behind them may elude our grasp. We all speak the right words, but in so doing may mislead ourselves into thinking that new words mean new understanding and new practices. Everywhere today, people speak of "vision;" but how many think about purposefulness, what it would mean if each and every person worked from a deep sense of "their work?" Likewise, "empowerment" has become a buzzword in recent years; but how many have really thought about the key assumptions that lie behind it — assumptions both about people and the inability to control complex living systems from the top? The same rise in popularity seems now to be happening with "systems thinking;" yet, how many organizations are actually seriously investing in developing new capabilities to understand cause and effect as "distant in time and space?" How many are starting to escape the addiction to "quick fixitis" that afflicts industrial-age institutions, the incessant focus on short-term fixes that end up creating more damage in the long term?

Looking now at this article, it is also possible to see the flaws in the picture we painted fifteen years ago. For example, we surely gave too little attention to the importance of learning processes that can increase the intelligence of local decision makers and align local actions across large organizations.

The absence of such learning processes can prove fatal for inspired innovators seeking to empower and decentralize. At the time, we had little experience with the extraordinary personal, political, and cultural challenges involved in redistributing power in large enterprises. We talked in the article mostly of younger, smaller enterprises and neglected the important questions of bringing about change in large, tradition-bound institutions. These are things we have all been learning a good deal about in recent years.

All in all, we found that re-reading our ruminations of many years ago left us proud of sticking our necks out, and should encourage all of us to be more bold in moving forward. The notion of organization metanoia is as important today as it ever has been. The role of such organizations in creating a sustainable society is crucial as well. Certainly, it is not likely that the next fifteen years will bring fewer dramatic changes than have the past.

— Charles F. Kiefer
Peter Senge

*©1984, Charles Kiefer and Peter M. Senge. This paper is based on "Metanoic Organizations in the Transition to a Sustainable Society," published in Technological Forecasting and Social Change, 22:2, October 1982.

Society faces a host of fundamental problems that are unlikely to be remedied, given present ways of thinking and acting. These range from urban decay and economic vulnerability, to third-world poverty and the arms race. Each reflects the mismatch between the nature of complex social systems and our everyday methods of defining and attempting to solve problems generated by those systems. What is needed are local environments where experiments can be conducted with new, more effective ways of designing social systems. A small number of businesses are now providing just such environments. Nurtured within these organizations, new insights about human nature and the systems in which people operate are already being demonstrated on a local scale. The consequence is a fundamental shift of mind, in which individuals come to see themselves as capable of creating the world they truly want rather than merely reacting to circumstances beyond their control.

BACKGROUND

T wo distinct, long-term dynamics are now merging to create unique forces for social change. One is the life cycle of industrial growth. The other is the economic long wave. The life cycle is a one-time phenomenon, based on depletion of finite natural resources such as land, oil, natural gas, water, and the capacity to dissipate pollution. Abundant resources, often at diminishing real costs, gave rise to a period of unprecedented industrial expansion with little attention to the longer-term consequences of growth.

In the transition to a post-industrial society, the interdependencies between the economic system and the environment become clear, and basic shifts in attitudes and values occur. *The Limits to Growth,*[1] published in 1972, and subsequent studies point to the present as a time of unprecedented stress, where the attitudes, values, and expectations of the industrial-growth era are challenged for the first time. Pitirim Sorokin,[2] founder of the department of sociology at Harvard University, forecast over a half-century ago that industrial society would become increasingly disillusioned with its materialistic goals, decline, and then perhaps re-emerge as an "integral culture" characterized by a balance between material and spiritual values. With twenty years of survey evidence, Daniel Yankelovich[3] today sees just such a shift. He argues that "instrumentalism," which views material possessions as the instruments for generating satisfaction, is gradually being supplanted by a "sacred" outlook that seeks the intrinsic value of human experience in the family and the workplace.

The transition to a post-industrial economy probably spans 30 to 50 years. What makes the 1980s a period of particularly rapid change is the concurrent cresting of the economic long wave, or Kondratieff wave.[4] This is historically a period of economic stagnation, as shown by the major depressions of the 1830s, 1880s and 1890s, and 1930s. But it is also a period of experimentation and innovation. Economic growth since World War II has been built primarily on a series of remarkable innovations — television, jet propulsion, digital computation — that came to light in the 1930s and 1940s; that is, during the last long-wave transition.

The long-wave transition is a period of great stress for private business. Bankruptcies are high, particularly in older, traditional industries. Pressures to cut costs and to maximize flexibility handicap the top-heavy bureaucracies of the former period of relatively stable growth. Economic conditions favor more resilient organizations that can adapt to complex technological and market changes.

The simultaneous transitions of the life cycle of industrial development and the economic long wave are causing fundamental changes in the business environment. The life cycle is creating fundamental shifts in values and attitudes, while the long wave is creating extreme economic stress.

In response to these pressures, a small but significant number of corporations are emerging as prototypes of a new kind of organization. We call them *metanoic* organizations, from a Greek word meaning "a fundamental shift of mind." The term was used by early Christians to describe the reawakening of intuition and vision. Simply put, a metanoic organization operates with a conviction that it can shape its destiny. The climate created within such an organization can have profound effects on people, particularly by nurturing understanding of and responsibility for the larger social systems within which the individual and the organization operate.

Metanoic Organizations

We use the term "metanoic organizations" to describe a unifying principle underlying a broad base of contemporary organizational innovations. This principle is that individuals aligned around an appropriate vision can have extraordinary influence in the world. Antecedents of the metanoic organization can be found in many places: the management theories of Douglas McGregor in the early 60s,[5] the writings of systems theorists like Jay Forrester later in the same decade;[6] and the basic beliefs in freedom and self-determination expressed in the founding of the United States over 200 years ago. In metanoic organizations, these beliefs form a coherent organizational philosophy with five primary dimensions: 1) a deep sense of vision or purposefulness, 2) alignment around that vision, 3) empowering people, 4) structural integrity, and 5) the balance of reason and intuition.

At the heart of the metanoic organization is a deep sense of purposefulness and a vision of the future. While values (such as excellence, service, or creativity) can be abstract, vision must be a clear picture of the future that people are striving to create. In an organization, vision may have several dimensions, some dealing with the product, such as building the world's most powerful computers, and some with the organization, such as freedom and personal responsibility. What matters is not so much what the vision *is*, but what it *does*. By taking a stand for something that truly matters to people, the organization creates an environment where commitment is the norm rather than the exception, and people have an ever-present standard against which to judge their own actions.

The Apollo Moon Project provided a superb demonstration of the power of a clear and compelling vision. By committing themselves to "placing a man on the moon by the end of the 1960s," the leaders of the project took a stand. The clarity and conviction they generated touched people at all levels of the enterprise. One can imagine how much less spectacular the results might have been if they had adopted an alternative mission statement, such as "to be leaders in space exploration." Unfortunately, such "motherhood" mission statements are the norm for most organizations.

A clear and timely vision catalyzes alignment. Alignment is a condition in which people operate as an integrated whole. It is exemplified in that profound level of teamwork that characterizes exceptional sports teams, theater ensembles, and symphony orchestras. When a high degree of alignment develops among members of a team committed to a shared vision, the individuals' sense of relationship and even their concept of self may shift. Abraham Maslow observed that for a highly-aligned business team,

> the task was no longer something separate from the self, something . . . outside the person and different from him, but rather he identified with this task so strongly that you couldn't define his real self without including that task.[7]

Alignment is crucial for two reasons. First, it bounds a group of disparate individuals into a common body wherein each feels that his or her contribution matters. Second, highly aligned teams can produce results most people think impossible. Just as the 1980 U.S. hockey team shocked the world by winning a gold medal against the vastly more talented and experienced Russian and Finnish teams, overall performance can improve dramatically in highly aligned business teams.

The third characteristic of metanoic organizations is a focus on empowering people. While most organizations espouse personal growth and development for their members, their commitment to this goal is limited. In the absence of alignment, empowering the individual can increase disharmony and conflict. The burden of managing more powerful individuals who are going in different directions can be much greater than managing people with only a limited sense of their personal abilities. By contrast, in the metanoic organization, where the best interests of the individual and the organization are highly aligned, empowering the individual becomes a key to empowering the organization.

Even the most highly aligned and empowered individuals will languish if placed within a poorly designed structure. In the metanoic organization, attention is continually focused on whether the organizational design in the broadest sense — roles, accountabilities, key policies, information flows — is consistent with its purpose. Each of the companies described in the following cases has implemented basic innovations in organizational design. Most are highly decentralized; some break totally with traditional, hierarchical structure. All have developed incentive systems that encourage employee initiative, responsibility, and a sense of ownership. All continually evolve policy and structure as required to move toward their vision.

Cutting across all these dimensions of the metanoic organization is a unique balance of reason and intuition. The quest to continually improve the organizational design is tempered by the recognition that there is no "complete" model of the organization. Consequently, intuition must complement rational analysis and planning in order to understand the company's internal dynamics as well as its interactions with its environment. Vision and empowering people are also intimately linked to intuition. A compelling and inspiring vision, by its very nature, transcends rationality — as does the capacity of artful leaders to create environments where people naturally grow.

Last, alignment develops from the intuitive interconnectedness of people that allows each to act spontaneously in the best interests of the whole. Futurist Willis Harman has observed that at the heart of the world's spiritual traditions is the notion of a personal "life plan" that is known only by listening to our creative "inner voice." In an article titled "The Rationale of Good Choosing," he writes:

> Acting in accordance with this 'plan,' I can expect my actions to be in harmony with the ultimate well-being of all those around me.[8]

In another article, he expands on the subject:

> The founding fathers who set up this nation were very clear on this. They specifically recommended the way in which this nation should govern itself, the way in which choices should be made, namely through this kind of collective listening.[9]

Highly aligned groups perform complex tasks in ways that cannot be planned rationally. Former basketball star Bill Russell described this intuitive component of alignment in recounting games that were

> more than physical or even mental . . . and would be magical. . . . It was almost as if we were playing in slow motion. During these

spells I could almost sense how the next play would develop and where the next shot would be taken. . . . My premonitions would be consistently correct, and I always felt then that I not only knew all the Celtics by heart, but also all the opposing players, and that they all knew me.[10]

CASE STUDIES

The metanoic organization represents an ideal toward which many companies appear to be evolving. The companies described below illustrate how the general metanoic principles can be translated into specific changes in corporate design and policy.

Kollmorgen Corporation

Kollmorgen is a diversified manufacturing company headquartered in Stamford, Connecticut. It markets printed circuit boards, periscopes, electro-optical equipment, specialty-purpose electric motors, and related products. Its 1982 sales were $250 million, having doubled every four years for the past ten. Comprising fourteen virtually autonomous divisions, the company embraces a small-is-beautiful philosophy through decentralization. Each president reports to a division board of five or six other division presidents and corporate officers, replicating the relationship between a CEO and a corporate board of directors. Important decisions, such as capital expansion, R&D expenditures, and the hiring and promotion of senior management, remain at the division level. Divisions are kept small (typically less than $50 million in sales, and fewer than five hundred employees) so that each employee can feel a part of a family where his or her contribution matters. When divisions grow past this point they generally split. Although there are about 4,500 employees in Kollmorgen, the corporate staff number only 25.

This organizational design is intended to expose all employees to the incentives and pressures of a free market. All employees share in their division's profits. Not only are the divisions run as free-standing businesses, but product teams within divisions function highly autonomously. They may share equipment and overhead support with other teams, but they typically set their own prices, determine their own sales goals, and manage their own production schedules. Incentive within product teams is great, for most new divisions grow out of successful ones.

Organizational innovation has recently extended to corporate management. A "partners group" of the division presidents and senior corporate officers has been formed to bring freedom and equality into corporate policymaking. Decisions are by consensus, each partner having veto power over any major issue. In this atmosphere, absolute honesty and trust are imperative.

Cray Research, Inc.

Unlike Kollmorgen, Cray Research manufactures several versions of two basic products: the Cray 1 and the Cray 2, two of the world's largest computers. They are used for such tasks as weather forecasting and simulation of nuclear power generation, which require very large data bases and computational capacity. Sales in 1982 were $141 million, with growth in the 50%–100% range over the previous five years. The company currently employs about 1,400 workers, mostly in the Minneapolis-St. Paul area, where it was founded in 1972.

Although a divisional structure like Kollmorgen's would be inappropriate to Cray's limited range of products, Cray embraces the same objectives of freedom, honesty, and responsibility. Product-development and marketing teams are small and independent, often located in separate facilities. As Chairman and CEO John Rollwagen explains, "We have always found that people are most productive in small teams with tight budgets, time deadlines, and the freedom to solve their own problems."[11]

The technical and managerial challenge of building the world's most powerful computers seems to be shared throughout Cray. Rollwagen believes that it can be easier for an organization to achieve "audacious tasks" than more mundane goals: "Such a vision creates an environment that takes people beyond day-to-day problems. It creates enormous excitement. While this seems very risky, it's not really, because people are focused on a single purpose, and they know that there's no backup." He views this focus on a single vision as the key to Cray's management style: "If we lost track of our overriding purpose, all the other things we do would not be enough to guarantee our success."

Analog Devices, Inc.

Analog Devices, Inc. (ADI) is a Norwood, Massachusetts, manufacturer of analog-digital converters and related devices for computerized measurement and control systems. The company has grown at 30% a year for the past five years (1983 sales of about $220 million), thanks in large part to a clear corporate philosophy that values the contribution of each individual. ADI's value statement could have been taken from any of the organizations we have studied:

1. We believe people are honest and trustworthy, and that they want to be treated with dignity and respect.

2. They want to achieve their full potential, and they'll work hard to do so.

3. They want to understand the purpose of their work and the goals of the organization they serve.

4. They want a strong hand in determining what to do and how to do it.

5. They want to be accountable for results and to be recognized and rewarded for their achievements.

This commitment to the individual is again maintained through decentralization and distributed decision-making. Chairman and president Ray Stata works to erode the mentality of hierarchy. The corporation explicitly places its first commitment to employees (followed by customers, then stockholders). Workers are regularly reminded of this. As Stata puts it, "Human judgment is above procedure and on an equal footing with policy at Analog." Stata seeks "to break the procedural syndrome, whereby people seek to impose themselves on others through establishment of rules."

Stata seeks to create an environment where individual power and influence derive from ability and commitment, not position. "We are not trying to eliminate all hierarchy," Stata says, "but to undercut the value system that is linked to the hierarchy. The greatest limitation in traditional organizations is that people further down the hierarchy somehow consider themselves lesser beings than those above them."

Other Innovators

Many other companies are developing along the same lines. Dayton-Hudson is a $5 billion, 90,000-person retailing organization headquartered in Minneapolis. The company is a leader in decentralization among large retailers, as evidenced by a corporate staff that numbers only 250 (a ratio of corporate staff to total employees that is lower than Kollmorgen's), and consensual decision-making, represented by the four principal corporate officers. The company is also a leader in community affairs, being one of the founders of the Minnesota 5% Club, which now includes about 50 corporations that give at least five percent of their pre-tax earnings to local social programs.

Tandem Computer is a young, rapidly growing company (1983 sales of about $300 million) with a vision of producing computers that offer continuous, nonstop service. It illustrates another characteristic of the emerging metanoic organization: a marked de-emphasis of formal organizational structures and management systems. At Tandem, the structure within working groups is fluid. People avoid memoranda and formal procedures whenever possible, so communication is generally immediate and oral.

There are many other organizations that deserve more attention than is possible in a short paper — Steak and Ale, a highly successful restaurant chain that is now a division of Pillsbury; The Hanover Insurance Companies; W.L. Gore & Associates, makers of a variety of products based on synthetic fibers such as Goretex; and the Herman Miller Furniture Company, to name a few.

BASIC ASSUMPTIONS

More and more, organizational specialists are examining "corporate culture" to determine what distinguishes successful corporations. Edgar Schein,[12] well-known organizational theorist at the Massachusetts Institute of Technology, suggested that corporate culture can be considered on at least three distinct levels: artifacts (language, rules and procedures, and organizational structure), values (explicit goals, and principles for their pursuit), and basic assumptions. He emphasized that basic assumptions, however difficult they may be to observe, represent the deepest level of culture and must be examined to understand how an organization affects its members.

People are Good, Honest, and Trustworthy

A central theme in every metanoic organization is that people are basically honest and trustworthy, and that each wants to contribute to the organization. It is assumed that failure to behave accordingly signals the organization's failure to create an atmosphere conducive to such behavior. Kollmorgen's 1979 Annual Report expresses

> an unspoken conviction that man is basically good, that each individual is the basic measure of worth, and that each, by pursuing his own good, will achieve the greatest good for the greatest number.

People are Purposeful

That people are basically good and want to contribute is well-known as the "Theory-Y" view of management,[13] to which the metanoic viewpoint adds a still more spiritual, visionary dimension. Rollwagen of Cray says it is important to "share the spiritual benefits of our success with all people in the organization." Stata of ADI sees alignment of personal and organizational purpose as a prerequisite for productivity. In his words, "I cannot commit a large part of myself without a 'rationalization' — that is, seeing the relationship between what I care deeply about and what the organization stands for." He believes that an organization's vision must reach from concrete business plans to a sense of cosmic purpose aligned with people's deepest values.

These views reflect a deep belief that personal satisfaction lies not in material rewards alone, but in the opportunity to pursue a lofty objective. Metanoic organizations do not reject material rewards or the role of private enterprise in generating wealth. They do reject the "instrumental" view that people work solely for purchasing power, for they find no inherent conflict in the pursuit of a lofty vision and financial gain. Indeed, most argue that the two are complementary. This assumption is nowhere more clearly articulated than in Kollmorgen senior management's mission statement:

> to fulfill its responsibility to Kollmorgen shareholders and employees by creating and supporting an organization of strong and vital business divisions where a spirit of freedom, equality, mutual trust, respect, and even love prevails; and whose members strive together toward an exciting vision of economic, technical and social greatness.

Each Individual Has a Unique Contribution to Make

It is frequently assumed in organizations that only the extraordinary individual matters, and the only power that matters is positional power. Those not in formal positions of power can at best connive to influence those who are. In metanoic organizations, positional power is secondary to what James MacGregor Burns[14] and Warren Bennis[15] called "transformational power," or the capacity to empower oneself and others to realize a common vision. Such power grows from the clarity of the individual's personal purpose and his commitment to the organization's vision, not from position in the hierarchy.

John Rollwagen illustrates the importance of individual commitment by relating that within the Cray 1 computer there is a cylindrical mat (about a foot thick, four feet in diameter, and five feet high) of some 70 miles of hand-woven copper wire. It takes three shifts of four people working three months to wire a Cray computer. In the past two years, many have been completed without a single mistake in over 100,000 connections! Not only is this a source of tremendous pride for the wiring teams, it has had a direct impact on the company as a whole. When the wiring is completed on time and is mistake-free, the computer passes inspection rapidly and is ready for delivery a month early. The result is not only a significant saving in cost, but a direct gain in revenue, since a Cray 1 computer rents for about $300,000 a month. Everyone in Cray benefits because all employees share profits.

Complex Problems Require Local Solutions

Traditionally, in large organizations, be they corporations or government bureaucracies, most people assume that major problems must be solved from on top. By contrast, metanoic organizations show that small institutions can typically be more responsive than large ones, and that local decisions can be more effective than centralized ones. They have developed ways of making the smallest feasible unit an autonomous and effective decision-making body. As Stata explains,

> we try to adopt an organismic approach to management control. We continually emphasize local control for local problems, because it's simply not possible to figure it all out from the top.

> We try to decouple local control from hierarchical control. The management hierarchy needs to provide direction, awareness, and a sense of how the game is played, but it needs to respect the greater ability of small groups to solve their own problems.

Rollwagen adds that "We need to rely on individuals and small groups to identify and correct their mistakes. By the time a mistake gets to top management, it's often too late for effective correction." Decentralized, participatory decision making at Dayton-Hudson is exemplified by the weekly "ad meetings" at Mervyn's, where merchandising managers from the entire company lay out a week's advertising. The open, free-flowing, and often confrontational meetings are a far cry from centralized advertising planning, and so are the results — new ads are produced in three weeks, whereas competitors average sixteen.

A company's commitment to decentralization can be no stronger, however, than its faith in the wisdom and responsibility of the individual worker. Many managers do not trust people to function efficiently and effectively without elaborate rules and procedures. Yet companies like Kollmorgen and others we have studied function perfectly well with no procedure manual whatsoever. The key is obviously a deep level of trust, within what Max DePree, president of the Herman Miller Furniture Company, calls "covenantal relationships" — relationships where each party assumes responsibility for an outcome and for the quality of the ongoing partnership.

The Concept of Leadership

In traditional organizations, including our federal government, the people at the top are seen as the people in control. By contrast, leaders in metanoic organizations are responsible for sustaining vision, catalyzing alignment, and evolving policy and structure. They frequently conceive of themselves as teachers, but they do not control the system. Most don't even think it's possible to control an organization effectively from the top.

In the past, those who lead and those who are led have represented separate, if not antagonistic, classes. Leaders were assumed to possess unique understanding and power. This authoritarian attitude runs deep. As Stata observes, "Much of our traditional organizational thinking is derived from the Catholic Church and the Roman Army, institutions predicated on the notion that the person on top has information and influence not shared by others." To overcome such notions, leaders in metanoic organizations typically involve themselves heavily in teaching employees how the organization operates.

At Tandem, which invests heavily in teaching people how the business operates, Jim Treybig says, "Each person in the company must understand the essence of the business." "We want to run the company in a completely open way," says Swiggett of Kollmorgen, "so that there are no information monopolies — everybody knows everything. We don't want secrets. We don't want 'closed books.' We don't want people feeling special by virtue of the fact they have certain information."

However, efforts to break down the barriers separating different levels in the organization are not always welcome, particularly by those who come from authoritarian backgrounds, be they managers or not. Swiggett says, "Many people have been brought up with the idea that they cannot operate if they haven't got somebody telling them what to do. People are comfortable with authority; they've built their lives on it." Leaders in metanoic organizations recognize that they must continually work to overcome the authoritarian mentality, because it is inimical to the spirit of equality and responsibility they seek.

Me and You *versus* Me or You

Traditionally, there is an underlying assumption of separateness and competition in organizations. The spotlight is on the distinct, often conflicting needs, desires, and aspirations of individuals. People operate according to what Buckminster Fuller called the "me or you" orientation, vying for scarce resources such as money and recognition, because they assume there is not enough to go around.

Metanoic organizations do not avoid competition; in fact, they seem to share a unique zest for it. They are energized by the risks and rewards of a challenging game. What is different is the context. Competition is transformed by the pursuit of a common vision, agreed-upon ground rules for how the game is played, and strong ethics of honesty and integrity. People insist on fair play and clear rules. They want clear winners and losers. When people have, in Swiggett's terms, "an honest game" to play in pursuit of a lofty vision, creativity and innovation are maximized. In such a context, competition becomes a strategy rather than an end in itself. Under these conditions, there may be interim winners and losers, but all benefit in the long run.

Robert Galvin, chairman of Motorola, describes how this "me and you" attitude extends into the organization's relations with its environment:

> Generally in an industrial society, we are simultaneously suppliers and customers, licensors and licensees. We can't do without each other. Each of us is better off that the other survives. We must and do compete vigorously. At times, one of us will be a little better than the other, providing the opportunity to win on that occasion. A next time the other may be the winner. Each competitor is important to the market and to each other, for we need multiple sources. The world requires diversity. The American society, to be dynamic and strong, needs the aggregate of all the ideas and all the efforts.

A Petri Dish for Systems Thinking

The study of complex social systems is a particularly grim business. Case after case reveals disturbing similarities. Cause and effect are not closely related in time and space; ameliorating symptoms often makes matters even worse in the long run; trying harder typically results only in more resources — mainly people and money — used, not more results. In short, fundamental socioeconomic problems cannot be solved from the mindset that generated those problems:

> The world is a complex, interconnected, finite, ecological-social-psychological-economic system. We treat it as if it were not, as if it were divisible, separable, simple, and infinite . . .

> No one wants or works to generate hunger, poverty, pollution, or the elimination of species. Very few people favor arms races or terrorism or alcoholism or inflation. Yet those results are consistently produced by the system-as-a-whole, despite many policies and much effort directed against them.[16]

Despite considerable progress in understanding the nature of complex social systems, system theorists have been conspicuously unsuccessful in developing strategies for implementing systems thinking. Many individual problems have been solved, but few minds have been changed. The process of applied systems thinking remains the province of a small cadre of experts.

Perhaps emerging metanoic organizations offer an element of such a strategy. They present a radical alternative to our accepted methods of managing complex systems. They replace top-down control with decentralized control. They replace rules and regulations with alignment around a common vision. They foster the assumptions that everyone can win and that each individual has a unique part to play. And they demonstrate that leaders who catalyze vision, alignment, and personal responsibility and who can be effective teachers can be far more effective than traditional authority figures.

When biologists want to create a new strain of bacteria, they create local conditions suitable for the bacteria's development. Perhaps metanoic organizations are like the biologist's petri dish — a local environment where a new, more systemic way of looking at the world can take root and eventually spread. It is much too early to be sure, but there are interesting indications.

Systemic Awareness and Responsibility

Systemic thinking starts with a heightened awareness and sense of responsibility for the larger system within which the individual operates. Awareness of a larger system arises naturally from alignment around a common vision. This is exemplified by the individual players in an orchestra, who know that their success is intimately tied to the success of the others.

Metanoic organizations nurture systemic awareness and responsibility in many ways. By continually dividing into small, autonomous business units, they thwart the paralysis of size that stifles conventional organizations that grow beyond the point where each individual can "get his hands around the business as a whole." By eschewing formal rules and procedures, the organization encourages the individual to be responsible for results, not for following rules. Individual responsibility is reinforced by leaders who act as teachers rather than as omnipotent and omniscient controllers of the destiny of the company and its employees.

Responsibility for larger social systems carries over to the corporation's interaction with its environment. The corporate responsibility programs of the metanoic organization tend to address the long-term well-being of the communities and regions within which they operate. Unlike the narrow, self-serving social activities of many companies, aimed at protecting business interests, the metanoic organization sees its self-interest more broadly. For example, beginning with a pledge of a million dollars in 1977, Dayton-Hudson helped found the Whittier Alliance, a nonprofit community-development partnership aimed at revitalizing the depressed Whittier section of Minneapolis. Since its inception, the Alliance has assisted in over 650 home improvements, developed cooperative home ownership, and upgraded streets, sidewalks, and public squares. Dayton-Hudson is now repeating this process in Pontiac, Michigan, with plans for seeding additional community redevelopment organizations in other communities. The company sees such programs as good business, since its long-term profitability is intrinsically linked to the economic and social well-being of the communities in which it operates.

Similarly, Analog Devices helped found the Massachusetts High-Technology Council (MHTC), an association of business leaders that has worked toward property tax reductions and increased corporate support for higher education. Ray Stata has been a leading champion of the "2% solution," a pledge of two percent of corporate R&D expenditures to institutions of higher learning. To Stata, "Such a pledge isn't a charitable contribution; it's an investment in the company's future."

System Principles

Systemic awareness and responsibility form a foundation upon which shared understanding of system principles can develop. Although these principles are rarely noted as such within the organization, they set a unique tone in dealing with the outside world.

One such system principle is *better before worse behavior,* where management interventions improve conditions in the short-term only to lead to further deterioration in the long run. This principle has led to opposing legislation that, although directly beneficial in the short run, may be detrimental in the long run. Swiggett and Rollwagen have been directors of the American Electronics Association (AEA). The AEA opposed the business tax cuts of the Reagan Administration that were felt to be inhibiting to free-market forces. They felt that short-run benefits to member companies of accelerated capital depreciation or investment tax credits did not justify the likely long-term costs to the economy as a whole. By artificially boosting short-term profits in stagnating businesses, the Reagan tax cuts would force society to carry these businesses beyond their productive lifetime.

A second principle is the need for policies designed to *work with the forces in a system rather than against them.* Futurist Buckminster Fuller often accused nonsystem thinkers of trying to "invent the future" rather than understanding the laws governing change as a guide to planning. Swiggett, in a 1982 speech to Kollmorgen's stockholders, criticized the Reagan economic program for its failure to recognize the long-term forces causing economic stagnation. Despite strong support for Reagan's intention to reduce government involvement in private affairs Swiggett stated that "By implying we can make major changes in three or four years, President Reagan is running the risk of building high expectations and being washed out of office on a tide of disappointment." He went on to assert that the economy is in the midst of a long-wave transition to a new mix of dominant technologies and industries, and that policies designed to speed that transition are needed. Swiggett backs up his speeches with action: he and the AEA helped to initiate the 1978 Steiger Amendment reducing capital gains taxes to spur investment in new business.

A third system principle understood by metanoic organizations is *shifting the burden to the "intervenor,"* the tendency of natural control mechanisms to atrophy in the presence of external assistance, becoming dependent on still further intervention. This principle is central to understanding reinforcing spirals of external assistance, whether involving food aid to developing countries, federal assistance to cities, or medical dependencies. The emphasis on autonomous business units in all the companies we have studied grows out of their understanding of the principle of "shifting the burden." Frequently, when product teams at Kollmorgen seek assistance, managers inquire whether the assistance represents a one-time need for help or is likely to lead to increasing dependency. They ask, "Are you shifting the burden?" Sharing and intergroup assistance is commonplace, but only where it strengthens both parties.

Understanding how external assistance can foster dependency makes most metanoic organizations strong believers in free-market mechanisms. They vigorously oppose government assistance that may undermine the self-reliance of individuals and businesses, even when that assistance may be in their own short-run interest. They recognize, however, that for a free-market system to remain viable and responsive to society's changing needs, an uncompromising commitment to honesty and integrity coupled with a strong sense of social responsibility must prevail. None of the companies sees itself as a social missionary, preaching morals to fellow businessmen. Rather, they see themselves simply as demonstrating that freedom, honesty, and responsibility make good business.

THE METANOIC VIEWPOINT

The vast majority of organizations simply do not work as well as people would like. Disillusionment, dissatisfaction, lack of alignment, and inefficient use of human resources are accepted as normal — "Things don't work, and there's nothing I can really do about it. I'm dissatisfied, but I'm stuck in a system too big, too unresponsive, and too complex to influence." This point of view is so pervasive it easily becomes an "absolute truth" and a self-fulfilling prophecy. It not only permeates most organizations and institutions, but is the root cause of our sense of powerlessness in tackling the problem of creating a sustainable society.

The essence of the metanoic shift is the realization within each individual of the extraordinary power of a group committed to a common vision. In metanoic organizations, people do not assume they are powerless. They believe deeply in the power of visioning, the power of the individual to determine his or her own destiny. They know that through responsible participation they can empower each other and ultimately their institutions and society, thereby creating a life that is meaningful and satisfying for everyone.

The dominant belief in society at present is that the individual is at the mercy of huge, hopelessly complex, and unresponsive systems. Yet such beliefs can change, and when they do, everything else changes with them — even one's physical environment and perception of reality. As Willis Harman wrote:

What you believe determines what you perceive as reality.

What you believe determines what you feel you can do about it.

What you believe determines the exhilaration and joy you get out of life.

Some beliefs are wholesome; others are definitely unwholesome. (Along the way most of us pick up a lot of unwholesome beliefs.)

Beliefs can be changed.

A life that is constructed around an inadequate or erroneous set of basic beliefs, will include a lot of problems and pain.

If a society is guided by an inadequate or erroneous set of basic beliefs, it will tend to foster a great deal of human misery.

At the level of society, too, beliefs can be changed.[17]

One such change is the emerging belief *"We can collectively envision and create the society we want."* If metanoic organizations can provide a safe environment for this most basic belief to take root, they may have a profound effect on the future.

It is too early to gauge the long-run effects of metanoic organizations. The number of companies operating in this manner will need to increase before their impact is felt on society. But this seems the least uncertain element. As one Kollmorgen manager put it, "Our way of operating is just so far superior in organizational and human terms to the way most companies work, others will have a hard time competing. In a free society, this is the most potent force for change."

Notes

[1] D.H. Meadows, D.L. Meadows, J. Randers, and H. Behrens III, *The Limits to Growth* (New York: Universe Books, 1972).

[2] P. Sorokin, *The Basic Trends of Our Time* (New Haven: College and University Press, 1964).

[3] Daniel Yankelovich, "New Rules in American Life," *Psychology Today* (April 1981), pp. 35-91.

[4] Understanding of the long wave has been advanced at several research centers in the United States and Europe. Although still controversial in mainstream economics, the theory has developed substantial credibiltiy as one of the few systemic explanations of the worldwide economic stress of the 1970s and early 1980s. See G. Mensch, *Stalemate in Technology* (Cambridge, Massachusetts: Ballinger, 1979); J.W. Forrester, "Innovation in Economic Change," *Futures*, Vol. 13 (1981), pp. 323-331; A.K. Graham and Peter M.

Senge, "A Long Wave Hypothesis of Innovation," *Technological Forecasting and Social Change*, Vol. 17 (1980), pp. 283-311; N.J. Mass and Peter M. Senge, "Reindustrialization: Aiming at the Right Targets," *Technology Review* (August/September 1981), pp. 56-65; C. Freeman, J. Clark, and L. Soete, *Unemployment and Technical Innovations* (Westport, Connecticut: Greenwood Press, 1982).

[5] D.M. McGregor, *The Human Side of Enterprise* (New York: McGraw-Hill, 1960).

[6] J. W. Forrester, "Common Foundations Underlying Engineering and Management," *IEEE Spectrum*, Vol. I (1964), pp. 66-77; J.W. Forrester, "A New Corporate Design," *Industrial Management Review* [currently *Sloan Management Review*], Vol. 7 (1965), pp. 5-17.

[7] Abraham Maslow, *Eupsychian Management* (Homewood, Illinois: Richard D. Irwin, Inc., and the Dorsey Press, 1965), p. 122.

[8] Willis W. Harman, "Rationale of Good Choosing," *Journal of Humanistic Psychology* 21 (1981), p. 10.

[9] Willis W. Harman, "Visions of Tomorrow: The Transformation Ahead," *OD Practitioner* 13:1 (February 1981), p. 7.

[10] B. Russell and T. Branch, *Second Wind: The Memories of an Opinionated Man* (New York: Random House, 1979), pp. 155-156.

[11] All quoted statements are taken from direct communications to the authors unless otherwise noted.

[12] E.H. Schein, "An Organizational Culture," [working paper] (Cambridge, Massachusetts: Sloan School of Management, Massachusetts Institute of Technology, 1981).

[13] D.M. McGregor.

[14] J.M. Burns, *Leadership* (New York: Harper & Row, 1978).

[15] W. Bennis, *Leading Edge Bulletin* (22 February 1982).

[16] D.H. Meadows, "Whole Earth Models and Systems," *CoEvolution Quarterly* (Summer 1982), pp. 98-108.

[17] Willis W. Harman, *Institute of Noetic Sciences Newsletter* 9:2 (1981), p. 22.

II.

LEADERSHIP IN

TRANSFORMING

ORGANIZATIONS

6

Leadership and Strategy for a New Age*

ROGER HARRISON

Comments on the Second Edition

In my professional autobiography, *Consultant's Journey,*** I have described at length the story behind this paper. The ideas about organization culture that it set in motion are set forth in my *Collected Papers.**** During the 15 years since writing *Leadership and Strategy for a New Age,* I have found the central concepts of this paper, alignment and attunement, to be extremely robust. In 1982 there were few organizations that were truly aligned to a clear vision, and where members were willing to merge their individual goals and purposes with those of the whole. Since then, literature on business and management has been full of such examples.

We have seen both the positive and the darker sides of alignment; the former in the camaraderie and spirit that a high-performing team brings to its work, the latter in the exploitation, burnout, and stress that aligned organizations can demand of their members. But whether for good or ill, the notion of human *will* mobilized through vision and charismatic leadership, rather than through roles and rules, is much more pervasive now than then.

Attunement has fared less well. The concept of an organization that exhibits a resonance among its parts, and harmony between the parts and the whole, in which the members *dance* together, has not become an idea in good currency. At the time I wrote the paper, talking about love in organizations seemed professionally risky, and I remember pacing the floor of my family's cabin in the woods, where I had gone to work on this piece, wondering out loud to my spouse, Diana, whether I was about to sacrifice my credibility as a rational, clear-thinking consultant by "coming out of the closet" about the importance of love in organizations.

My timing was probably not bad; the *idea* of human love as a powerful motivating force in organizational life has become discussable. However, the years between have seen love's actual *availability* to organization members shrink due to decreased trust in organizations. The mistrust has various causes. The most fundamental are probably the final (?) triumph of individualism as the dominant ethic of our culture, and the massive increases in addictive behavior in organizations today. Downsizing, increased competition for personal power and political advantage, and the unilateral abrogation by organizations of longstanding, though implicit, agreements with their members have all played their part. In many if not most organizations, empathy, understanding, caring, nurturance, and mutual support are scarce satisfactions in these latter days.

For myself, I have changed little in my mistrust of charisma, visionary leadership, and commitment to realization of the organization's dreams at whatever cost. Cohesive, fanatically committed groups are often as tyrannical and destructive as were the power-hungry authority figures they were supposed to supplant. And I maintain my faith in the healing powers of love and community for our organizations, their members, and for the planet that our unbridled greed is fast rendering toxic to many forms of life (our own, for example). I am heartened that most of the more creative recent innovations in organization development aim at embracing community and the quality of communication and understanding of the whole, which are so essential to attunement. Examples are "dialogue" (Davis Bohm), "future search" (Marvin Weisbord and many others), "appreciative inquiry" (David Cooperrider), and most approaches to the "learning organization" (Peter Senge and many others, including myself).

These approaches can only flourish, of course, in that same climate of reduced fear that is essential to all the other processes of attunement. I wish I could see more clearly how these reductions in fear are to be achieved. For now, I continue my own focus on endeavoring to facilitate healing and deeper understanding for those organizations and individuals with whom I work, and I strongly encourage others to do likewise.

— Roger Harrison

* ©1982 by Roger Harrison

** R. Harrison, *Consultant's Journey: A Dance of Work and Spirit.* (San Francisco: Jossey-Bass, 1995).

*** R. Harrison, *The Collected Papers of Roger Harrison.* (San Francisco: Jossey-Bass, 1995).

It is often said that if something doesn't work, we are likely to continue doing it, but with increased intensity. Harrison observes that this often has been the case in our organizations, as extensive training and development efforts seem to have done little to overcome the new breed of problems facing contemporary organizations. In this chapter, Harrison argues for new ways of approaching these problems through focusing on the powers of intentionality, alignment, and attunement to foster high-level performance. He also suggests that strategic planning needs to be conceived as a search for meaning, a discovery process, rather than the creation of an organization's purpose. Throughout the chapter, Harrison insists that we consider the inherent daimonic nature of humanity as we work with these concepts. He closes with a series of questions leaders can discuss with their groups to test the usefulness of the concepts he presents.

D uring the last few of my twenty-five years as a management consultant, I have been impressed with the seeming intractability of organization problems. I ask myself why it is that so many of our attempted solutions seem either to produce no effect, or else appear to exacerbate the problems they were designed to solve.

For example, why is it that decades of human relations training for supervisors and managers have not produced committed and happy workers? Is it only a coincidence that as information systems make more information available to managers, it becomes more difficult to make decisions? Why have incentive systems so often failed to keep productivity high, and why have more psychologically "sound" attempts to motivate workers had similarly ambiguous outcomes? Is there any connection between the development of sophisticated planning systems and the increasingly unpredictable fluctuations in the environment? How is it that organizations seem so unmanageable just at the point when we have learned so much about the art and science of management?

It seems to me that our relationship with our clients resembles eighteenth-century medical practice. We bleed and physic our patients, and when they become sicker and weaker, we bleed and physic them some more. When they do die, it is not clear whether they were carried off by the disease or the treatment. It would seem that we, too, would do well to heed the

Hippocratic admonition: "First, do no harm." We seem impelled to action even when we may suspect that our interventions may merely be applying more of what caused the problem in the first place. To do nothing in the face of our problems would be painful, even though it might be as efficacious as the actions we take.

Contemplating this sorry state of affairs, I have slowly and reluctantly come to the conclusion that the tools and approaches that got us where we are today are not the ones we can use to advance to another level. I sense that, like the drunk in the story, I have been looking for my lost keys under the street lamp simply because there is more light there. If there are answers, they lie in the dark beyond the circle of illumination given by our current concepts and methods.

WHERE TO LOOK?

Where to look? It is hard to venture out of our little circle of light into the vaster darkness without some guidance or sense of direction. Far easier to go busily over the same ground again, hoping we may have missed our keys in the last circuit.

We may not yet be at the beginning of a New Age, but we do seem to be ending an old one, if that can be measured by the increasing unworkability of current forms and by the failure of old beliefs and values to give peace, certainty and satisfaction. It is a time when many varieties of heresy flourish, amid calls for a return to traditional virtues.

I do not know which heresy to choose. Return to the past has little heart for me, and as I contemplate the plethora of choices, I am little by little drawn toward a constellation of ideas embodying that ancient admonition of gentle Hippocrates. We live in a troubled world, beset with forced changes. Surely the answers will not lie in ever more-drastic intervention and frantic activity, but rather in some organic approach that allows healing forces to emerge.

The idea of "conscious evolution" constitutes one of the many varieties of New Age thinking. So far as I know, few efforts have been made to apply such ideas to organizations in general, or to business in particular. Indeed, at first glance the ideas seem bizarre and otherworldly when seen from the viewpoint of the business world. They are quite definitely outside the circle of illumination that our traditional ideas and concepts cast upon the functioning of organizations. Let us see whether they have anything to offer by way of lighting a path through the dark.

Conscious Evolution

The term "conscious evolution" refers to the idea that after millennia of evolution, we humans are on the verge of becoming aware of the transformative process in which we are involved. As we become aware, we can begin to participate voluntarily in our own evolution and that of the planet. We can influence the quality of life on earth through our thoughts and beliefs.[1]

Thought is seen as the *source* of outer reality. We create reality through thought. Thus, we need not struggle with things-as-they-are. Instead, we may change our mode of perception, and thus the quality of our experience. At any moment, the possibility exists for transformation of our reality into new paradigms. If we don't like current reality, we are invited to think an alternate reality into existence.

There are, of course, laws and principles of manifestation that govern the transformations of reality. For example, the development of organisms takes place through differentiation and integration. In differentiation, the parts take on unique and distinct qualities, becoming different from and more independent of one another. The principle of integration unifies and harmonizes these diverse parts in the interest of the health and transformation of the whole. Each organism lives in creative tension between these opposing principles.

Each organism forms a nucleus, or center, which bears in mind the integrity of the organism and the establishment of "right relationship" between the organism and the universe. This center also turns the attention of the parts towards the evolutionary transformation of the organism. When "critical mass" is reached, the idea of the next transformation is transmitted to all the parts, and an evolutionary leap occurs.

During the process of differentiation, each part develops its own purpose. Between parts and whole, relationships of greater and lesser "alignment" and "attunement" come into being. When a resonant relationship (attunement) occurs among the parts, the organism experiences peace, love, and mutual nurturance among its parts. When a part consciously chooses to serve the evolution of the whole, alignment occurs, enhancing the well-being of all parts of the organism.

These ideas are neither very clear nor particularly precise, and they must be appreciated intuitively if at all. For the most part, New Age thinkers write for others who have crossed over into the modes of thought of the "new paradigm." What is intuitively obvious from the inside is, from without, intellectually unsatisfying and mystical. As is usually the case, truly new ideas are seen by some as giving great illumination and insight — and by others, as creating further obscurity and gloom.

Rather than trying to explain the ideas of conscious evolution, I am going directly to the application of those ideas to business organizations, to test whether the ideas are *useful*. If they promise us viable ways to heal and nurture our organizations and to facilitate their evolution, then perhaps these ideas are worthy of closer study on the part of business leaders. If they do not, there is no point in trying to explicate them further.

A New Age Conception of Leadership

Managers are fond of saying that people's attitudes toward work have changed, and the low productivity in the United States is often so explained, in part. In place of a voluntary commitment to hard work and high quality, we manage with systems of rules, regulations, checks and controls. This is not only costly, but the low trust and depersonalization that are engendered further reduce the motivation to contribute, and the system becomes self-perpetuating. In the effort to make up for the inadequacies of voluntary performance, more and more sophisticated systems are developed, often replacing humans with more reliable machines.

Of late, interest in leadership has been reawakening. The leader — as opposed to the mere manager — is seen as a source of vitality and vision, who can articulate values that organization members can live by. Through his or her articulation of common purpose and exciting future possibilities, the leader lines up the organization members behind him or herself, and the organization marches forward into the future. Indeed, in most arenas of contemporary life, we lament lack of leadership and await its charismatic emergence, which we hope will lift us from our apathy. I believe it is true that most organization members hunger for some purpose higher than mere career success, a nobler vision in which they can enroll.

The two ideas in conscious evolution that are most relevant for our conception of leadership are those of *alignment* and *attunement*.

Alignment

Alignment occurs when organization members act as parts of an integrated whole, each finding the opportunity to express his or her true purpose through the organization's purpose. According to Kiefer and Senge[2], who have explored the concept in depth, the individual expands his or her individual purpose to include the organization's purpose. Kiefer and Senge point out that this concept differs from that in which the individual sacrifices his or her own identity to the organization, a process which is said to achieve only "a degree of alignment." It is not quite clear, however, what kinds of leaders and followers achieve the one result rather than the other.

There lies the difficulty. Most Americans mistrust — and rightly so, I think — the easy giving over of one's will to any collectivity, whether it be the nation-state, one's employer, or even one's nuclear family. Even while we acknowledge the startling superiority of Japanese productivity over our own, most of us are unwilling to find our own fulfillment in the purposes, no matter how noble, of any business organization. And for the most part, our business organizations are indeed lacking the nobility of purpose attributed to the large Japanese firms of whose productivity we have read so much.

Organization alignment behind charismatic leadership must involve the merging of the individual's strength and will with that of the collectivity. In high-performing organizations animated by a noble purpose, this may not feel like much of a sacrifice. But even high-performing organizations have their inhumanities. They burn people out; they take over their private lives; they ostracize or expel those who do not share their purposes; and they are frequently ruthless in their dealings with those outside the magic circle — competitors, suppliers, the public. It seems to me no accident that many of our most exciting tales of high-performing, closely aligned organizations are either literally or metaphorically "war stories." War is the ultimate expression of unbridled will in the pursuit of "noble" ends.

There are close parallels between what conscious evolution has to say about alignment and recent research and theory on high-performing groups and organizations. It seems to me that both tend to ignore the dark side of man's nature, what Rollo May calls the *daimonic*.[3] The daimonic is that aspect of man which seeks to express itself and to have impact on the world no matter what the cost or consequences. It is amoral, and, if unchecked, it tends to take over the whole person. We find the daimonic in all sorts of obsessions, for there is hardly any human faculty that does not have the capacity, in some persons, to overcome and direct the personality. We find the daimonic in the passions of the social reformer, the libertine, the dictator, the actor, the artist, the evangelical preacher, the lover. We find it in the expansive dream of the entrepreneur, in the limitless personal ambition of the dedicated careerist, and in the dedicated money-making of the financial genius. Where it is checked and balanced by other parts of the personality, its energy fuels great achievements and contributions. Where it gets control of the person, it turns against nature and creates the tragedy of an Oedipus, an Othello, or a Julius Caesar.

People in groups seem to find one another's *daimons*. Mob scenes, sports stadiums, family quarrels, and battlefields are favorite haunts of the daimonic. Its power has always been with us, and I find it hard to conceive of any evolutionary leap that would rid us of it. New Age thinkers seldom write about the daimonic, and they tend to imply that it will wither away in the coming global transformation, as the state was supposed to under communism. I have my doubts.

Attunement

However, conscious evolution does add one very powerful concept that is missing or understated in much contemporary writing about leadership and high-performing organizations. It is the concept of *attunement,* meaning a resonance or harmony among the parts of the system, and between the parts and the whole. As the concept of alignment speaks to us of *will,* so that of attunement summons up the mysterious operations of *love* in organizations: the sense of empathy, understanding, caring, nurturance, and mutual support.

Love — what a closet word it is in organizations! Far better to talk openly of those old shibboleths, sex, money, and power, than to speak of love. This is the true male chauvinism in business: the discrimination against women masks the deeper fear of love.

Yet love is far too powerful ever to be truly exorcized. We find it everywhere, if we but look. Love is evoked by beauty and by quality in the products or services we produce. It is present in the comradeship of co-workers, in the relationship of mentor to protégé, in the loyalties between people that transcend personal advantage. Love is found in the high ideals of service and contribution, which are articulated in the published values of many corporations. It speaks through our dedication to workmanship and excellence of performance.

There is a mystery in words. When we call the love we find in our organizations by other names than its own, it loses its power. I suspect we are reluctant to name love because to do so will release that power, and we do not have forms and processes with which to channel it. Love has its daimonic side, too, and we are perhaps not wrong to be wary of it. We do speak, somewhat gingerly, about caring, open communication, consideration, and the like. Not about love.

When we do think about love and organizations, we are apt to see love as a disruptive force, destructive of order and good business judgment. Images come to mind of managers making personnel decisions on the basis of affinity and friendship, or setting prices based on the needs of the customer. Of course, people do sometimes make business decisions by consulting their hearts, but it is seldom admitted, and there are certainly no business school courses on how to do it.

New Age organizations, by contrast, attempt more often than not to invoke the power of love in their decision-making. They have developed forms and processes for effective decision-making: group meditation to enable members to "go inside" and consult their hearts, asking themselves what they are "called" to do, and other similar approaches.

Alignment and attunement are both processes for achieving *integration* and unity of effort among the differentiated parts of a system. The idea of organization alignment is getting a good press of late through the awakening interest in the role of superordinate values, top management leadership, and the characteristics of high-performing systems. I believe we also have much to learn of attunement. Alignment channels high energy and creates excitement and drive. It evokes the daimonic. Attunement is quieter, softer, receptive to the subtle energies that bind us to one another and to nature. It tames and balances the daimonic by opening us to one another's needs and to our own sense of what is fitting and right, what is the "path of the heart" which best expresses our higher selves.

Without attunement and without evoking the power of love in our organizational lives, I think we shall not find peace, but only ceaseless striving. During the decades since World War II, we have unleashed in our organizations and in the world an enormous amount of personal power, through changes in expectations, aspirations, and values. Many of us learned to aim high in our careers and personal lives, and to believe we could realize our dreams through our own efforts and through the abundance that science, technology, and cheap energy brought us. We became net "takers," more concerned about what we could get and achieve for ourselves than what was needed to maintain our organizations and social institutions. In the process of "doing our own thing" we became highly differentiated in our goals, values, tastes, and lifestyles — and as we did so, our differences and conflicts with others increased. In our efforts to get what we believed we deserved, we became increasingly issue-oriented and litigious, careless of the fragile webs of relationship which bind any society together. We did indeed find "personal growth," but we pay an increasingly high price in conflict and stress for what we have achieved. We have created a world in which it is increasingly difficult to *compel* anyone to do anything. How else shall we find order, peace, and harmony if we cannot learn to open our hearts to one another?

The "how" of attunement is beyond the scope of this chapter, and indeed the forms and processes that may work in business organizations are still unclear to me. I think we have something to learn from intentional communities, many of which have been extremely inventive in their search for non-coercive means of making and implementing group decisions. I believe that attunement begins in stillness, in some quasi-meditative process for connecting with our own higher purposes. As is true with any intuitive process, attunement can be facilitated by ritual, by music, and by the visual arts. I can imagine business meetings in which participants begin in an atmosphere of soft lights and meditative music, with a few minutes of silence in which they go inside to seek guidance as to the higher purposes to be achieved in the work of the meeting. When I think of my current clients engaging in such rituals, however, I am aware that there is some distance to be traveled between here and there!

Stewardship

What does the foregoing imply about leadership? The picture of the leader that emerges looks remarkably like that which Michael Maccoby proposes, proceeding from a social-psychological perspective. In his 1981 work *The Leader*,[4] Maccoby looked at the emerging social character of the workforce and then projected the leadership traits that such a character would demand. The picture of the new leader that he draws has much in it of attunement. The new leader is seen as having a caring, respectful, and positive attitude towards people, and a willingness to share power. He or she is more open and non-defensive regarding his/her own faults and vulnerabilities than former leaders, and less likely to use fear, domination, or militant charisma. The picture is one of a personally secure and mature individual who can articulate the values and high principles that give organizational life meaning, but who is more humble and receptive than we normally expect visionary leaders to be. Perhaps this conception of leadership is best expressed as *stewardship:* leadership as a trust that is exercised for the benefit of all; the leader as serving the followers, guided by a vision of the higher purposes of the organization. Thus, the organization is seen as animated by the sense of its own higher purpose. The leader focuses the attention and consciousness of the members on those purposes. But the leader also knows that the parts have legitimate purposes of their own that are not completely expressed by the purposes of the whole, and he or she facilitates the attunement processes, by means of which organization members can come to know, respect, and care for one another's needs and individual purposes. The flow of human energy is not one way, from the members to the organization; the uniqueness of each part is also preserved and nourished by the whole.

In the past, leaders we call "great" have generally been very strong, ruling through fear and respect, and/or very charismatic, releasing and focusing the daimonic for their followers. Our concept of leadership is clearly different. Without being soft or avoiding conflict, our new leader avoids the use of fear and arbitrary authority. He or she is a visionary, but the daimonic thrust implicit in the charismatic style is balanced and tamed by a nurturing receptivity. The leader brings healing and harmonizing influences that we can only call love into the organization.

We are clearly a long way from the point where we could imagine the majority of business organizations in this country as animated primarily by noble purposes and love. There are far too many situations that engender feelings of fear and weakness in organization members, and it is not possible to be truly loving when one is powerless and fearful. How could we ever get from here to there?

Conscious evolution tells us where to start. We are told to create reality with our thoughts. We are informed that the events we experience as the world unfolds are actually manifestations of thought, having no existence independent of our willing and believing them into being. Thus, if we call love by its proper name, look for it in ourselves and others, and affirm its potency in our organizational lives, we shall summon it into being — much as Aladdin summoned up the genie from the lamp. At first glance, not an idea likely to appeal to most hard-headed business people.

Yet the idea of manifesting reality through thought has actually been around on the fringes of business for a long time, and it seems to be gaining currency. Motivational speakers, such as Norman Vincent Peale on "the power of positive thinking," have never been more popular. Most of us (at least in California) have friends who practice the manifestation of money, career success, or love, and many tell remarkable tales indeed of the results of their efforts. (I manifest parking spaces, myself, but I always make a joke of it when I mention it to others.)

We make jokes, too, about the stories we hear of the regimented, inspirational group-singing in Japanese companies like Matsushita and Toyota (or, closer to home, in IBM and Tupperware). We may not respect their methods, but we certainly respect their success. In one way or another, mysterious or mundane, positive thinking in groups works for these organizations. Would they harmonize more sweetly at work if they sang of love? I do not know, and I know of only one way to find out.

Studies of high-performing people — athletes, managers, researchers — consistently turn up findings that suggest the power of thought. Successful people are prone to visualize the results they want in their lives and work, and to affirm to themselves that they can accomplish their goals. They create a clear and conscious *intention* as to the desired outcomes, and allow their actions to be guided by that frequently-affirmed intention. Rather than planning in detail what they are going to do, they start by creating an intensely-alive mental representation of the end state. That representation then works through the individual's intuition as he or she makes the multitude of everyday decisions that bring the goal ever nearer.

In fact, I have never in all my years as a consultant seen anyone change an organization in any fundamental way through rational planning. Plans have their place, of course, but the managers I have seen deeply influence their organizations' characters always operated by intuition, guided by strongly-held intentions. They communicated their intentions verbally to others who could share their vision, and they communicated it daily to others through their real-time actions and decisions. In due course, enough people shared the vision/intention for it to reach "critical mass," and the dream became reality. I guess if we are to have organizations that are animated by both love and will, it will be through the efforts of a few strong people who have a vision of what such an organization could be like, who share that vision with others, and who together *intend* it into reality.

New Age Concepts of Strategic Thinking

We usually think of strategy as the art of predicting the future, and then planning how to change the organization so that it will perform well at the future time. It is a frustrating business for a number of reasons, not least because the organization is always defined as wanting, when compared to the strategic ideal. Add to that the fact that the most dramatic aspects of the future are the ones that are the least predictable from an analysis of the past (e.g., the sudden increase in oil prices in 1973–1974), and it is little wonder that many managers have little taste for strategic planning.

We seem to do more planning in organizations as planning becomes less and less effective, in a desperate attempt to make the future behave. In fact, planning can only help us to deal with conditions and variables that we already know or suspect are important.[5] Planning defines what we know and don't know within a given context. Any future changes in context (changes in variables not known or thought to be important when the planning was carried out) will invalidate our plans to a greater or lesser extent. Planning, for example, can estimate the risk of a downturn in the economy, based on known historical factors, and the probable impact of that downturn on, say, the launch of a new product. Planning cannot tell us anything about either the likelihood or the impact on our marketing plans of unforeseen events such as the sudden rise of a new religion or an epidemic of some new form of plague.

Most of us seem to be aware that unforeseen events are looming over our futures. We know that we do not know. We imagine wars, economic disasters, and cataclysmic natural events, but we do not believe we can predict their likelihood by reference to historical data trends, so we cannot plan for them. If we could assign a probability to these events, we would still find it difficult to plan, because the events we imagine are so sharply discontinuous with our current experience as to paralyze both mind and will. I think it is fair to say that because we cannot plan for the future we fear and imagine, we plan instead for the future we hope for — one in which even the projected negative events possess a comfortable familiarity.

Planning and Planetary Purposes

If we cannot plan for the future, how can we best prepare our organizations and ourselves for it? The suggestions provided by conscious evolution involve attuning our organizations to planetary purposes. This means moving out of the rational and analytical modes of thought typical of the planning process, and into intuitive and intentional mental processes.

A radical leap is required to move from our normal habit of thinking of organizational purposes as defined internally, to thinking of an organization in terms of planetary purpose. Seen from the planetary point of view, the organization exists only as part of a larger reality, supported and nurtured by the larger system on which it depends. Its purposes are not solely determined or decided by itself, but are "given" by its place in the larger system. Organization purpose is not simply decided by its members, but is rather to be *discovered.* The process of discovery is partly internal to the organization, involving an inner search for values and meaning. It also has an external aspect, that of discovering meaning through the transactions of the organization with its environment. Viewed in this way, a primary task of the organization is the discovery of its place and purpose in the larger system. Every event in its history can be viewed as part of a lesson, the meaning of which is to be intuited by the organization's members.

Adopting such a point of view requires a fundamental change in one's orientation to goals, and to the success and failure of one's plans. We can begin, in Kipling's words, to "meet with triumph and disaster, and treat those two impostors just the same." If one's orientation is to learning, then failure carries just as much information as success. In fact, failure may be more valuable, because in our failures are embedded nature's messages about required changes.

Most business organizations today strive to succeed and to win against their competitors, against the government, and sometimes against their suppliers and customers as well. The tougher conditions become, the harder they strive. Since conditions are increasingly tough, there are a lot of people out there striving. Because of these conditions, those people experience a lot of failure, and consequent blame from themselves and others. They are under a lot of stress, as can be seen from the ever-increasing popularity of alcohol, tranquilizing drugs, and "stress management" courses.

When one is striving to achieve goals, one's learning is oriented to *means*; one learns more and more about what to do or not to do to achieve those particular goals. The excitement and stress are likely to blind us to the question of whether the goals themselves are worthy. Stepping back and taking the perspective of planetary evolution forces us to ask the large question: are these goals in line with our higher purpose? Is the fact that they are becoming increasingly difficult to achieve perhaps a signal that they are no longer appropriate to this stage of our evolution? If we find on reflection that there is no longer joy in the struggle, that we are burning ourselves out in the effort, that we are no longer energized by what we do, then that may be a "signal from the universe" that it is time to move on to find a "path with heart."

The Search for Meaning

From the point of view of conscious evolution, then, strategic planning is a search for meaning, rather than a search for advantage. It is an intuitive process in which the goals and activities of the organization are examined against the criteria of the heart. Does this task enliven the doer, giving value and meaning to life? Do we still experience satisfaction in the attainment of this goal? Do we strive joyously, or with desperation? Do we feel that we are net contributors of value in our work in the world?

In approaching strategy from the point of view of purpose, our aim is definitional, rather than positional in a market domain. Our endeavor is to forge a shared view of reality that will serve the organization members as a base for day-to-day decision making, and will direct the leadership thrust of the dominant coalition.[6]

The activity is definitional in that we are attempting in a variety of ways to penetrate the forms of the organization in its internal and external relationships, in order to discover its essence. Our belief is that when the forms (systems and structures) and processes (doings) of the organization flow from its essential qualities (being), the organization will become energized and integrated and will be effective in dealing with its environment.

The questions we ask in order to determine the essential qualities of the organization are simple, though the process of answering them may be difficult. First we may ask who we are, and what are our gifts. What are our distinctive competencies; what have we to contribute that is unique or different? What special knowledge do we have? What do we value? What do we believe in?

We may also ask what we are called to do. What needs do we see in the world that we are moved to meet? What activities have "heart" for us? What do we love doing?

We may examine our "core technology" — those processes we use to transform inputs into outputs. How does the core technology link us to those parts of the environment that supply us with our inputs and receive our outputs? What do these key domains in our environment need from us, and what do we need from them?

We may ask ourselves what other messages we are receiving from the environment, from government, the public, and special interest groups. Do these tell us more about our mission or calling in the world?

Of course, answering the questions can become extraordinarily complex when our organization is made up of many diverse constituent parts, each of which may produce markedly different answers to key questions. In heterogeneous organizations, it may be necessary for each part to go through the strategizing activity on its own. Then some integrating process is needed to attune the parts to one another and harmonize their differences. I am not underestimating the difficulty of this task, but it is one which must be faced by any strategizing activity in complex organizations. It is perhaps more difficult when we adopt the aim of preserving the essential integrity of each part, because then we forego the convenience of using authority simply to override the aims, values, and world views of those who disagree with us.

The result of the strategizing process is a statement of the mission of the organization, along with the values and beliefs about reality that underlie it. The mission statement forms the basis for a projection of the organization into the future. This statement of intention, the "willed future," describes the organization's state of being and its relationship with its environment at a later point in time when its essence will have been realized in its forms and processes, and it will be making its maximum contribution to the common good of the planet.

The statement of the willed future becomes the basic operating document of the organization, to which all plans and decisions are related, and upon which the *intentions* of the organization members are focused. In this way the power of thought to create reality is brought into play. By consulting the willed future at each point of uncertainty, and endeavoring to keep plans and decisions in conformity with its statement of intentions, the organization aligns all its efforts with the strategy.

Evaluating the Approach

How shall we evaluate the usefulness of an approach to strategic planning that says, in effect, "Get your values right, know what you want, go for it with all your heart, and trust in the Lord"? Certainly it has the advantage of simplicity in concept. It is consistent with the growing interest in leadership as a value-transmitting activity. Because of its comprehensiveness, it can have a unifying and stabilizing effect, compared with strategies that are responsive to transitory changes in markets and competitive position.

On the other hand, there are real obstacles, in modern organizations, to the establishment of a common vision of purpose and a unified idea of the willed future. For one thing, most large and complex organizations are heterogeneous and highly differentiated. If it is difficult to keep a coordinated planning activity going between, for example, the production and marketing people, what shall we say of the chances of their agreeing on ultimate values and the meaning of life?

The idea of establishing consensus with one's business associates around values implies a high degree of mutual commitment between the individual and the organization. It is one thing to contract with the organization to give it control over our activities for a certain period each day. It is quite another for us to pledge to one another "our lives, our fortunes, and our sacred honor." Such deeper commitments to purpose are implicit in New Age strategizing. They are quite evidently not for everyone.

Then, too, I wonder why it is that so many nonprofit and grassroots organizations dedicated to the highest principles are badly managed, undisciplined, and prone to personal backbiting and political strife. Why, I ask myself, have I frequently found more kindness and human decency in organizations committed to commercial pursuits than I have in those espousing lofty ideals?

The answer to the paradox lies, I believe, in the operations of the daimonic. In many business organizations the daimonic is repressed beneath layers of structure and impersonal systems, kept in check by authority and regulations, and bought off with financial rewards. It is as though the implicit contract is, "Leave your daimon at home, and we'll give you the wherewithal to indulge it during your off hours."

By contrast, many nonprofit organizations, and particularly the more activist ones, unleash the daimonic in the service of their ideals, but fail to tame and channel it. It is easy for their members to fall into the tragic error of identifying their own egos with the ideals they serve, which results in their sometimes becoming self-righteous, arrogant, and quarrelsome. To me, the message seems clear: It is not sufficient simply to align oneself with high ideals and set off down the road in pursuit of lofty purpose. We need also to remain receptive to those we meet along the way, both companions and strangers. Through the heart-opening process of attunement and through the humility and reason that enable us to accept discipline in the service of order, we can keep the daimonic in check without losing its energy and vitality.

After due consideration, then, I remain basically optimistic about the possibility of introducing New Age thinking into business organizations. In the first place, the personal needs are there. There is a hunger for meaning, commitment, and service that is often not fulfilled in work. There is a reservoir of positive energy waiting to be tapped, if we can give people something to enroll in that is larger than their own careers.

At the same time, there exists in business organizations a willingness to be led, to accept discipline and to respect and follow rational authority. There is an ability to forego immediate ego gratification for the sake of getting a job done. I believe, in fact, that many business organizations are ripe for the transformation. Their members slumber uneasily, knowing there is something missing, that there should be more to working life than this. This energy and vitality wait to be released by a vision of purpose and love. At the same time, they fear the awakening, as we always fear unknown powers. We know that change is coming, for the signs and portents of change are all around us. It is hard to believe, in the midst of increasing disorder, scarcity, and confusion, that the changes will be positive. Thus we cling to the past without really believing in it, and we distract ourselves with business as usual and with our personal careers. Even if the promises of the New Age are real, how shall we awaken ourselves and others to their messages?

THE PROCESSES OF PARADIGMATIC CHANGE

I said at the beginning of this paper that I am drawn toward a gentle stance on intervention and organization change — one which seeks to release the organization's own vitality and healing energies. Are there such organic approaches to transforming organizations in the rather fundamental ways discussed above?

In fact, I do not believe that organizations are changed much, if at all, by consultants. They are occasionally changed by managers. They are mostly changed by events — markets, technology, economic cycles, social and political developments. Managers and consultants can assist an organization to change in more productive and less painful ways, and that assistance may be decisive for the organization's health and continued survival. Few of us are given the opportunity to make history, though we consultants have shown some talent for rewriting it to our own advantage.

If events were going well, and we were all prosperous and expecting to become more so, no amount of intervention and management activity would be sufficient to accomplish significant changes in perceptions and values within business organizations. Crisis provides the stimulus and opportunity for change. The ingredients for transformation exist now in our organizations. We have to concern ourselves with what prevents change, not with how to create it.

Elizabeth Kubler-Ross and others have studied personal reactions to terminal illness and other traumatic losses. They have discovered that there is a predictable sequence through which individuals pass when they suffer major trauma or loss such as impending death, loss of limb or crippling accident, death of a spouse, etc. I believe that we may be going through a similar sequence as we face the death of our world view, the concepts and values that have served us throughout our oil-fueled ride to prosperity and high technology.[7]

The early stages of the sequence are characterized by denial and rage; the later stages by depression and despair. These emotional reactions are followed by acceptance, and a change in self concept and world view that is appropriate to the individual's new circumstances. With acceptance and reorientation, the individual experiences new energy for learning and coping with life as it is.

I do not think it is far-fetched to state that we are suffering just such reactions to traumatic loss, as our dreams fade, our cherished institutions work less and less effectively, and scarcity takes the place of abundance. Since we are not one individual but a multitude, all of the emotional manifestations can be found at once, rather than occurring in an ordered sequence.

Some resort to denial: "Reports of resource depletion and environmental damage are exaggerated. There is not really any scarcity. We have coal and oil resources for hundreds of years." "Concerns about nuclear pollution are overdrawn. Technology will take care of these minor problems, just as it has done before." "We will soon be able to feed the population of the earth and provide ourselves with abundant nuclear power, which will usher in the dawn of a New Age of global prosperity."

Some are angry: "It is the prophets of doom who are responsible for our doubt and uncertainty." "We have betrayed our traditional principles, and we're being drained of vitality by the freeloaders and the welfare cheats." "Our confidence is being undermined by a socialist conspiracy." "We are being exploited by the dominant military-industrial complex." "The youths of our nation are morally weak, dissolute, and unwilling to do an honest day's work."

Some are in despair and apathy: "War is inevitable." "We are headed for economic collapse." "The ecosystem is irreparably damaged." "We are headed for a new Dark Age." "The Day of Judgment is upon us."

Depending upon whether we use denial, anger, or despair, we go on with our lives as if nothing crucial were happening; we strive to overcome or protect ourselves against the forces of change; or we sink into a planless apathy and dread. Since the sequence is by no means irreversible, we may migrate between these positions, depending on how we are affected by events. I have certainly experienced all of them in myself at one time or another.

People who have worked with the dying and the severely traumatized know that explanations, arguments, and pressures are ineffective in moving the sufferer through these stages. Indeed, opposition tends to fix the individual in whatever stage he or she is at the moment, or sometimes to move the person back to an earlier and even less adaptive stage. Effective help consists first of all in offering empathy, understanding, and love. The helper neither forces unacceptable reality on the other, nor does he or she join into any delusions or distortions of reality. The unacceptable truth is offered without pressure. Acceptance of the person is offered too, and it is not contingent on the individual's readiness to deal with reality.

I think that in our organizational lives we are groping for ways to come to terms with the death of our paradigm — that complex of assumptions, values, and perceptual frames that constitutes our world view. In the struggle to hold onto our dreams and beliefs, and in our attempts to deal with their demise, we have great need of one another's understanding and support. We also need new dreams and hopes, but we cannot use them until we have done our grieving for the world we have lost. In this process we all stand in need of help, but instead we tend to set off one another's defensive reactions with our differing interpretations of reality.

Against such an appreciation of our current dilemma, I have asked myself how managers and consultants can aid organizations in achieving a new, positive, energy-releasing world view. As I have struggled with this question, I have come to understand more deeply my intuitive distrust of old-style charismatic leadership in this period. It is evident that if the model I have outlined is correct, charismatic leadership can only appeal to denial or anger, so long as most people have not yet accepted the changes that are in process. That is perhaps a reason why great leaders are so notably lacking in our world; the new paradigm has not yet acquired enough vigor to be led.

If not charismatic leadership, then what? I have come to the idea of conscious evolution too recently to have a program to propose for transforming organizations. What I am clear about is that the changes in consciousness that are required cannot be forced. The seeds of those changes are in all of us; we each need to experience conditions that support the growth of those seeds. One way to create those conditions is through discussion with others — discussion that goes beyond our day-to-day work and deals with our deeper hopes and fears for our work, our organizations, and our connections with others. I believe that in small discussion groups, we can experience that combination of mutual support and gentle confrontation that we need in order to change. We need to be reminded that reality is changing, and we need to be understood and accepted in our struggles to come to terms with that change. I know that the properly managed small group can provide that balance of conditions, nudging people to change through exposure to different views of reality, while creating a climate of mutual support that transcends differences of belief and opinion. (We all know that groups can be destructive, tyrannical, and intolerant, as well, but we have learned a lot in the last three or four decades about how to create conditions for more positive outcomes.)

Concretely, what I would propose to those business leaders who wish to explore the relevance of New Age thinking to their work, is that they meet regularly with a few others they trust and respect to share their concerns and thinking. Explore the issues outlined here. Spend enough time at it that you can share your deeper hopes and fears. Open your hearts to one another a little at a time, as you test the others' willingness to accept you as you are. Here are some questions you might address:

- Can we see the daimonic at work in our organization? How does it express itself? If it is suppressed, what are the effects?
- Where do we see love at work in the organization? What stops us from talking about it? Does it matter?
- What does the idea of stewardship mean to us? What kind of leadership does our business need? What kind would we follow ourselves?
- Can we change reality with thought? What is the role of intention in bringing about the results we achieve? Do we visualize our desired results? What would happen if we visualized as a group?
- Do we use intuition to make decisions? For what kinds of decisions? How can reason and intuition work together?
- What kinds of future events do we ignore in our planning? What would happen if we allowed for them?
- What is our organization's purpose? What is its driving thrust, its distinctive competencies, its values? How do these relate to our own purposes and values?

- Of what large purposive systems is the organization a part? How, if at all, does our organization's purpose become attuned to the larger system's purposes? If the planet had a purpose, how would our organization relate to it? How would we know?

- Does a focus on goal-achievement block learning in our organization? How, and how well, does our organization learn?

- What messages do we receive from different parts of our environment? Are there some parts whose messages we consistently ignore? What would happen if we listened to them?

- With respect to goals, are we for the most part pushed by events, or pulled by our vision of a desirable future outcome? Does it make a difference in the stress we experience in work?

- What is the relationship between our stated strategy and what we do? If our strategy doesn't determine our actions, what does?

- As an organization, can we identify a "willed future"? How does it focus our efforts? If we don't have one, would it make a difference if we did?

- What losses do we fear in the future? How do we deal with that fear? How do we react to people who have different fears? How can we help each other with our fears?

Lastly, if the discussion of these issues in a small group of your peers has been a useful and productive experience, how might you offer such an experience to others in your organization? Is it possible that, given the opportunity to open our hearts and minds to one another, we shall discover that we know our way home?

Notes

[1] For a more complete development of this concept, see B. McWaters, *Conscious Evolution: Personal and Planetary Transformation* (San Francisco: Evolutionary Press, 1982).

[2] See Chapter 5.

[3] See Rollo May, *Love and Will* (New York: Norton, 1969).

[4] Michael Maccoby, *The Leader* (New York: Simon and Schuster, 1981).

[5] See, for example, S.M. Davis, "Transforming Organizations: The Key to Strategy is Context," *Organizational Dynamics* 10:3 (1982).

[6] I am indebted to my colleague, David Nicoll, for this view of the strategizing activity.

[7] Also, I am indebted to Nicoll for the idea of applying this model to the paradigmatic shift.

7

The Flow State:
A New View of
Organizations and Managing

LINDA S. ACKERMAN ANDERSON

Comments on the Second Edition

As I re-read this work, I was struck with the continued relevance of the message. I still feel strongly that organizations would be incredibly more effective, responsive, and healthy if there were more of the flow state mindset, strategy, and systems in place today, and less of the fear state and solid state mentality and practices. Change would be enormously easier if leaders had greater understanding and competency in working the energy dynamics of their organizations.

Over the course of the 13 years since this book was published, my partners and I have worked with organizational leaders to raise their awareness of the issues and benefits of moving in the direction outlined in this chapter. Our work has taken the form of facilitating transformational change, driven by helping leaders to recognize and evolve their mindset, leadership style, guiding principles, behavior, and culture.

What is presented in this chapter is a particular leadership orientation. It represents a preferred set, style, principles, and behavior. In teaching this work in the mid-80s, we found that the flow state orientation was quite compelling to open-minded leaders, consultants, and trainers — but largely as information. We might touch individuals or inspire a team, but the interest of key line executives stopped with their intellect. Whether it was generational differences, cultural conditioning, or their exclusive bottom-line orientation, the work of actually changing leaders' mindsets, behavior, relationships, and change strategies toward the flow state was neither on their agenda nor in their comfort zone. Discovering just how fear- or solid-state oriented they currently were, and acknowledging how it limited them and their organizations, was not acceptable.

As the runway for building readiness to do the actual work of changing mindset, we shifted our focus to raising awareness of the importance of mindset as a concept. Once leaders could acknowledge that 1) they had a mindset, and 2) it in fact influenced their decisions, perceptions, and results, we could begin to introduce new and different principles and strategies that might get them improved outcomes.

We have not publicly named the new strategies "flow state," but we still incorporate what is offered here as a vision of what is possible. To date, we are still dealing with the issue of organizational readiness to do this work, and we have had more success with individuals, teams, and organizational units, but not yet at the organization-wide level, although that level of work is in progress. As rapid cycle time, speed to market, Wall Street expectations, and bottom-line pressures take even greater precedence, the time, resources, and priority for this kind of work goes down, despite the fact that it could have lasting impact on organizational performance over time. Unless, of course, the transformation crisis hits, and leaders are literally forced to look at their business approach, mindset, and decisions in new ways, or go out of business.

This work has gotten a significant boost from the Quality and Process Improvement trends, the Learning Organization, and "partnering" as a long-term strategy, as well as reengineering and the increasing intrigue with the New Sciences and Chaos Theory. It is fascinating to look at the aspects of the 1984 flow state orientation as it is now found in these latest management trends. Where the flow state orientation is still a lot for today's executives to swallow all at once, it seems to be finding its way into leadership development conversations through other means, which is positive and satisfying to all of us working to help organizations recreate themselves for the 21st century.

If I were to pinpoint one area that continues to surface as a glaring need for building change leadership, it is the capacity to think in dynamic, responsive, and choiceful ways — a skill called Process Thinking. Process Thinking is at the heart of the flow state approach, reflected in its orientation to time, complexity, responsiveness to new information, relationships and change. As executives increasingly recognize the need for managing large-scale change in this rapidly changing environment, the door opens wider on the opportunity for teaching the flow state orientation and its principles and practices in real time.

— Linda S. Ackerman Anderson

This chapter describes the need to work with organizational energy as well as the traditional, formal aspects of organizations to significantly enhance the positive impact of management. This shift has implications for how managers approach their work and for their management styles. Ackerman calls this new style of managing "the flow state." She contrasts this with a style she calls "the fear state," and with the more traditional style of managing, which she calls "the solid state." After comparing and contrasting these leadership styles, Ackerman explores the flow state style in depth. She concludes the chapter with a series of inquiries about the desirability of the flow state style, how to implement it, and how to maintain it.

Management literature over the past few years has been crowded with concepts and success strategies taken from the Japanese. With the myriad of demands facing American managers today, it is no wonder that their doors and minds are open to these new ideas. Old practices no longer satisfy today's and tomorrow's challenges. Unfortunately, in many cases the Japanese approaches have added to the frustration of American management as well. Why? Two reasons have surfaced. The oriental methods are successful because the Japanese culture supports them; American culture usually does not.[1] The approaches are foreign to our way of working and our organizational traditions. They are easily rejected because of this strangeness. Second, many companies have used these new practices as techniques, or band-aids. Applied to a problem that has evolved over decades, they can do very little to help. Again, they are readily cast off as failures.

We must ask ourselves what is missing. The Japanese tradition works for them because their management practices are based on a consistent way of thinking — a belief system. This belief system, their management approaches, and the needs of their industrial environment are congruent and supportive of one another. Given the painful symptoms in American organizations, it is evident that our way of thinking, our management practices, and the needs we have are somehow not compatible in the same fashion. We are not functioning in a way that inspires our full potential. We must begin to unravel the issues by challenging our fundamental assumptions about how we have been managing organizations. To do this, we must also confront the image and the role that managers have played as well.

This chapter will describe a particular way of viewing organizations, and will explore the implications of this view for American managers. I will begin by briefly discussing two contrasting views of what management is about: managing organization form vs. managing organizational energy. This will be followed by a description of a new way of looking at managing that is worth consideration for effective leadership: managing in the *flow state*. To emphasize this perspective, I will contrast it with two other approaches that are prevalent today in our organizations. These alternative views are presented not as truth or new solutions; they are constructs that help explain a different way of managing that may assist us in our current struggles.

OUR TRADITIONAL VIEW OF ORGANIZATIONS

Traditional models of organizations provide us with an effective description of the component parts of organizational systems. There are numerous examples of these models and, overall, they vary only slightly. One illustration (Figure 1) was offered by D.A. Nadler and M.L. Tushman.[2] They presented the organization as made of tangible parts, such as structure, processes, people, tasks, and resources. The model also describes some less tangible aspects, like history and "informal" components such as values, politics, and leadership.

Models like this offer us a way to capture what is at work in the organization — the form or the substance. They enable managers to see the "big picture" of what to look for when assessing or designing their organizations. They also help reveal the complexity of how organizations work, given the many variables or parts that contribute to the total system.

There is another important dynamic offered by most organization models. In Figure 1, the arrows between the boxes indicate that a relationship, or an interdependency, exists among the parts. In the example given, Nadler and Tushman said that the parts must be congruent, or "fit together," for the organization to work effectively. As a statement in itself, getting the parts to fit together makes common sense. The most effective organizations do have parts that work smoothly together. This becomes a fundamental assumption in our management thinking.

In theory then, good managers define what parts are necessary, based on organizational needs; ensure that each part is uniquely essential to the overall strategy; and then see that they work well with one another. When carried a bit further, this type of thinking can lead to the tendency to "fix" the parts so that they fit, in order to maintain or regain the status quo. This is consistent with the belief that good managers are skillful problem solvers. Come up with

Figure 1. Organizational Model.
This model identifies the component parts of an organization and conveys that, for the organization
to work most effectively, the parts must fit together congruently.
Nadler and Tushman (1980)

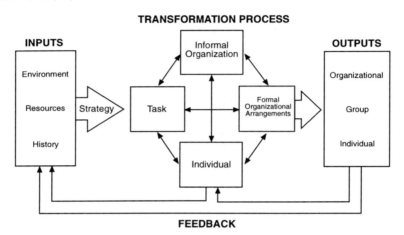

a solution and consider yourself successful. Achieve your goal and complete
your task. Design ways to maintain control over work, schedules, and people's
needs. Plan by the numbers. Keep those parts fitting at all costs!

Here is where the theory begins to break down. Reality reveals that life
in the organization is somehow more dynamic, more complex, more out of
control than the models describe. John Naisbitt[3] said, "The world that once
seemed so certain, solid, has changed radically. Now, conflict, confusion, and
great uncertainty is the norm for sure." This supports the possibility that on any
given day, the parts of the organization may look more like those in Figure 2.

With the attitude that good managers must solve problems, meet their
numerical goals, and figure out how to control things, it is no wonder that
serious frustration occurs. Somehow, trying to keep the parts congruent
becomes an organizational comedy or, worse, tragedy. We become entrained
in a pattern of "start with a problem; stop with a solution. Prevent problems
by staying in control." If not this common-sense approach, then what?

It is important to keep this belief within our reach because it is valuable:
Good line management is about producing tangible results. We must expand
the approach, however, and shift our view of the organization in a subtle but
very important way. I propose that management begin to focus its attention on
the arrows in the model rather than just the boxes. If we work more on the
relationships and the pushes and pulls between the parts, there will be less

Figure 2. The Organizational Reality.
This illustrates that organizations are in the state of flux at all times, their component parts often working against each other.
Ackerman (1983)

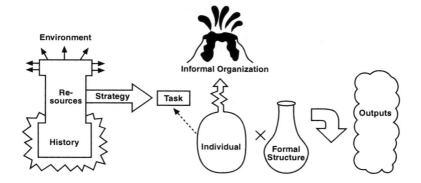

attention needed for what form the parts take, or how to control them. This shifts our attention to daily, or even momentary, experience of what is happening in the organization — what is assisting the fit, what is blocking the flow, what is needed in the long range for things to unfold the way management would like. The key to viewing organizations in this way is to see them as dynamic energy: moving, changing, shifting, pushing, pulling.

Energy? What a peculiar word to use in conjunction with management and organizations. Given that we don't have a familiar language to discuss this phenomenon yet, bear with me as I demonstrate how to view an organization as energy.

ORGANIZATIONS AS ENERGY

Webster defines energy as "the capacity for action, or performing work." Applied to the organization, this is a primary reason why we organize in the first place: to accomplish something of value. The act of accomplishing, or performing work, is the very nature of energy: movement.

The closest theoretical base we have for explaining energy is offered to us by quantum physicists, who have developed a language to describe the behavior of the particles that compose atoms, which in turn make up form or mass. In very simplified terms, physicists hypothesize that there really is no such thing as form, only energy particles that are perpetually moving in unique ways. From this analog, we can extrapolate some notions that support the idea that organizations are also perpetual motion, or energy.

If this is so, what do we do with the logical organizational models that describe their form so well? (As in physics: How do we deal with the "reality" that objects still appear to be solid mass?) We use these apparent realities as stepping stones to understanding the nature of what it is we are to manage. The *form* is the noun — *organization.* Webster defines form as "shape, structure; the orderly method of arrangement; the established method of doing something." It is important to hear in this definition the finality or control implied by the terms "structure," "orderly," and "established." These feel tangible, like good line management. This is consistent with the very assumption we are questioning: the need to make things fit, to regain the status quo, to manage the form.

The energy model we seek is contained in the verb *to organize,* or in the process of organizing. The movement is in the "act of," which is a constant phenomenon in life, as things are always changing. There is in fact perpetual motion in the organization. Managers are continually faced with new data and new challenges. Decisions always need to be made.

There are inevitable forces emerging that alter the way things seem to be going. New goals are constantly being set or redefined. There is very little that does *not* change at some time in the organization. Dealing with the process of managing, rather than the result, may be perceived of as "soft," like staff work. In order to achieve a balance, we must first acknowledge and legitimize an emphasis on the process, which is what energy is all about.

An attempt to capture the organization as energy is made in the model in Figure 3. It names the aspects of energy in the organization, but does not depict the behavior of energy *per se.* At the core of the organization is its *purpose,* or reason for being. The purpose gives meaning and direction to the energy and the form of the organization. When fully appreciated throughout the membership of the system, it becomes the life-blood, or central linking force, of everything and everyone. Ideally, the core purpose of the organization is the one energy force that touches every person in common and ties them all together. It is the single mechanism that guides the way in which the parts and structures are shaped and aligned.[4] Everything seeks to contribute to the pursuit of the purpose.

The outer rings of the model in Figure 3 describe other aspects of energy in the organization. The second ring identifies the *sources* of energy — where it comes from. The third ring describes typical *channels* through which energy flows in the organization. The outer level identifies another characteristic of energy, the *fields* that are created when energy is having a widespread effect in all, or large portions, of the organization. The sources, channels, and fields are described further below.

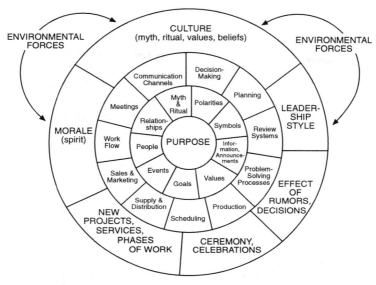

Figure 3. The Organization as Energy.

The context for managing energy is found in the purpose of the organization, which is the central linking force in the model. The next ring of aspects are SOURCES of energy. The third, CHANNELS of energy, and the fourth ring, energy FIELDS. The organization is also influenced by ENVIRONMENTAL energy forces.

© Linda S. Ackerman, 1983.

The rings of the chart describe the energy inside the organizational boundaries. However, since boundaries are also form, energy flows through and around them as it does with all forms. The world outside the organizational boundaries is also filled with energies that directly affect the functioning of the organization. These energies are *environmental forces,* most of which are quite familiar to us. They include:

- social values and culture
- the economy
- government regulations and politics
- the marketplace and customers
- competitors
- suppliers
- technology
- the labor force and unions

It becomes quite interesting to view the demands of the external environment as energy forces entering into and influencing the behavior and effectiveness of the organization. Part of what today's managers are experiencing is the turbulence that occurs whenever two or more dynamic forces meet, such as in union-management negotiations. The roller coaster ride we are on is the outcome of energy forces that are misunderstood, ignored, or let loose without guidance, care, or leadership. This model reveals again the need for a new perspective on how organizations are working and how best to manage them. Let's look more closely at the sources, channels, and fields of energy in the organization.

Sources

In order to manage the energy, we need to know where it comes from — its sources. A primary source of energy is the variable competing forces that exist in the organization. These forces are *polarities*. They create energy from the tension that exists between the pushes and pulls of two or more real and opposing sides. Tension in this case need not be perceived as negative, but rather as a description of the force set up between the poles. The pull can be felt as the desire or need for movement in one direction or another. Neither side is "better" or "right" in a polarity. There is a fundamental and natural reciprocity between them, which is why they continue to exist. At any given time, one side will be more attractive or powerful than the other. At another time, as circumstances shift, the opposing side will draw the attention. J.D. Ingalls[5] described a term used by Carl Jung, "enantiodromia," which is the tendency of all things to turn into their opposites over time.

Ingalls went on to describe a series of polarities that underlie human energy, such as control vs. creativity, and ambiguity vs. certainty.[6] Another significant example is the one we are addressing in this chapter: managing form vs. managing energy. As mentioned earlier, the emphasis on energy does not replace form; it plays off it and surrounds it. This chapter makes the case for moving our management attention toward energy and away from form, where it has been for most of the Industrial Age. Ultimately, we are after a balance of the two.

As you read on, feel the energy created in you by this polarity. The attraction or rejection you feel is an experience of the push-pull dynamic, of which we must become more conscious.

There are many other examples of polarities in the organization. A sample list includes:

- long-term *vs.* short-term needs
- risk-taking *vs.* safety (conservatism)
- freedom *vs.* control (constraint)
- change *vs.* stability
- individual autonomy *vs.* collective effort
- centralization *vs.* decentralization
- quantity *vs.* quality
- differentiation of tasks *vs.* integration of tasks
- spend *vs.* save
- creativity *vs.* routine, standard methods
- line *vs.* staff

Polarities are only one source of energy, however. The building and evolving of human, as well as functional, relationships generates energy as well. Bosses and subordinates, peers, job-related ties and social relationships each create and use energy in the organization. Observe the effect when a relationship between two people is particularly strained. Everyone uses up energy worrying and strategizing about it. When relationships between people or departments are going smoothly, everything seems to flow. The health of relationships can greatly add to or drain an organization's life forces. When relationships are trusting, supportive, and encouraging, they contribute positively. When they are competitive, provocative, or fearful, they waste energy. When a great deal of activity and feeling occur in the organization, it is always around some source of energy.

Additional sources of energy include:

- individuals who are key figures in the organization
- important events
- announcements
- values
- myths or stories
- ritual acts or ceremonies
- symbols such as logos or mementos
- rewards

- goals
- information and language

Again, each of these can add to or detract from the organization, depending on their positive or negative effects. These effects can change over time as well. Tracking whether these sources are being helpful or hindering becomes part of management's responsibility in this view of the organization. Ingalls describes a matrix between action and consciousness.[7] For this perspective to be useful we must become conscious of the energy, to understand how it can guide our actions. And we must be able to translate our conscious aims into action to feel any result of this approach. Let's go farther into the model to raise this awareness.

Channels of Energy

What happens to energy in the organization? Where does it go? Depending on the circumstances, it can scatter wildly, build or die naturally, or it can be *channeled* through the forms existing in the system. This is where effective management practices come into play. For instance, energy flows through the communication networks in the organization. It moves during all decision-making, planning, review, and problem-solving processes. All meetings have the potential to move energy or to block it, depending on their outcomes. Work flow, scheduling, supply, and distribution systems each channel energy when working effectively. Sales, marketing, and production lines move energy as they carry out their roles in the organization. As any thing happens, whether by plan or not, energy does what it does naturally — it is flowing.

There are many ways in which energy gets blocked as well. Delays can stop the flow, as can confusion, inefficiency, bureaucracy, battles, inhibitions, and breakdowns. Over time, tradition can become a hindrance to energy flow. Rules, policies, and cumbersome procedures can get in the way, even if they were initially created to assist the process. People's attitudes and beliefs can act as obstacles to the energy flow, as can negative emotional states, fear, and distrust. The "grapevine" is an interesting phenomenon; it can set off deep stirring and resistance in the organization because of the potential for rumors to carry negative energy. One key to managing effectively is to keep the channels clear and to ensure that the flow of energy, in the form of information and behavior, is as clean and as accurate as possible.

Energy Fields

In situations where a feeling or mood is widespread, an energy field is created, almost like a blanket of mist that envelopes the organization. All who are within the energy field experience the same mood — the effect of the field. Those outside it do not experience the same impact, unless they enter the field somehow. Organizational morale is an example of an energy field. Low morale is a rather contagious emotional state. High spirit, on the other hand, is also an energy field and is equally contagious. Energy fields can occur spontaneously, within minutes, or grow over a long period of time. The "rumor mill," when spreading a loaded message into the depths of an organization, can create a field like wildfire. Some energy fields disappear or change radically very quickly; others take a very long time, or never disappear at all.

The following are examples of what generates energy fields, in order of increasing magnitude:

- *Specific events:* changes in leadership, acquisitions of new business or products, divestitures, start-ups, ceremonies, celebrations
- *Information:* announcements, policies, rumors, key decisions
- *Leadership style and philosophy:* authoritarian, inspirational, humanistic, maverick, entrepreneurial, participative
- *Culture:* values, norms, myths, rituals, feelings, beliefs, rewards, tradition.

Lasting and profound energy fields like culture are great challenges to managers in times of change. The patterns they create become hypnotic and habitual; the density of the field tends to blind people's ability to see anything but the field. In order to change anything, we must first face up to where we are and then begin to create new options that are more appropriate to our desired outcomes. Understanding how energy and energy fields work gives us a technology with which to assist the change process.

There are times when it is necessary to alter an organization's fields, channels, and key sources of energy. This leads us to look at the implications of this model of the organization for people who are in a position to influence how change takes place. How do we manage the energy of an organization to achieve a desired result? What sorts of skills, beliefs, and styles are needed to be an effective manager and leader of change?

A CONTINUUM OF MANAGEMENT STYLES

There are three management styles that can help or hinder energy flow in varying degrees. The ideal manager for the model is a true agent of change, one who smoothly facilitates the release and channeling of energy. I call this style *managing in the flow state.* The manager on the opposite end of the continuum is one who works against the system, one who constrains or blocks the natural flow. The belief system and the emotional state of this manager lead me to call this *managing in the fear state.* Somewhere between these two poles lies the manager who is effective at working the traditional model — the organization of form. This style works the system from the point of view of results, decisions, and structures. I call this *managing in the solid state,* in honor of the form. The following table displays these styles on a continuum and describes the orientation of each style. At any point in time, a manager can alter her or his style. A manager feeling intensely threatened is likely to move toward the fear state. One feeling particularly potent and effective is likely to move toward the flow state. Let's look closely at each of the styles.

THE CONTINUUM OF MANAGEMENT STYLES

Factor	Fear State Management	Solid State Management	Flow State Management
WORKING STRATEGY	works against the system	works with the structures of the system, tries to insure that they "fit"	works with the energy flow in the system; works for harmony; alters structures to free up energy
ATTITUDE TOWARD COMPETITION	win/lose mentality; destructive competition	win/win when possible; competition within reason is useful	winning and losing are not important; doing what is necessary is
ORIENTATION LEVEL	self oriented	department, function oriented	total system oriented
RELATIONSHIP TO OBSTACLES	strategically creates obstacles, barriers	rearranges obstacles; moves around the numbers and structures	removes, dissolves obstacles; changes the structure to respond to the energy needs

TIME	slave to time, frenetic	tries to manage time; still crisis oriented	respects imposed time-tables and uses sense of "right timing" for events
REWARDS, IMAGE	preoccupied with payoffs, rewards, image	concerned with rewards; respects and responds to external influencers; image is important	motivated from within; sees rewards as tools; image is an illusion
CONTROL OF INFORMATION AND RESPONSIBILITY	overcontrolling; withholding of information and responsibility	controls through formal systems, policies, rules; shares information as necessary; delegates when appropriate	lets the flow of energy guide behavior; uses information to unblock the flow and indirectly guide events; encourages others to take on responsibility
RESULTS	gives lip service to results which serve own needs	results and outcome oriented, management by objectives	oriented to process; results are only temporary realities
MENTAL STATE	distracted, scattered anxious, confused, depressed, sick	pulled in many directions; concerned; seeks information for understanding; works regardless of mental state	clearly focused; attentive without concern; comes from clarity and foresight; alive, active, healthy
KNOWLEDGE OF LIMITS, FEEDBACK	uncertain of own limits; closed to feedback on performance	accepts responsibility without knowledge of own limits; aims to please; accepts feedback when given	clear about own limits and those of others; seeks feedback from self and others
SENSE OF TRADITION	buried by tradition	respects, preserves tradition	respects purpose of tradition; alters it when necessary
RESPONSE TO POLARITIES	cannot see polarities; sees only one way	sees polarities; fights for right answers; resists shifts	allows polarities to emerge, shift as necessary; embraces both sides as legitimate; dialectical thinking

Factor	Fear State Management	Solid State Management	Flow State Management
MEANING OF WORK AND PURPOSE	work has little meaning; totally ignorant of the organization's purpose	meaning is in results, numbers, profit; organization's purpose is perceived of as a number	meaning is in the pursuit of the organization's purpose, its viability, the process of making a contribution to the larger social environment as well as people's lives; purpose is used to connect everyone together
BELIEFS ABOUT RESOURCES, REWARDS	believes in complete scarcity of resources, rewards; must fight for them	resources and rewards are finite and must be distributed in logical, standardized ways	believes in abundance of resources and rewards; knows how to create them from existing or new sources
MISTAKES AND LEARNING	mistakes are suicidal; hide them	mistakes are inevitable, and to be avoided; move on quickly if they occur	mistakes provide the most valuable source of learning and are welcome if they occur; it is important to understand them
FOCUS ON OTHERS	focus on controlling others	focus on using others to carry out tasks	focus on empowering others
POSITION, POWER, AUTHORITY	attachment to own position; power hungry; holds on to authority irrespective of position	looks after own position; seeks power opportunities; exercises authority over others consistent with position	nonattachment to self, power, authority; can move in and out of these conditions with ease
BRAIN AND BEHAVIORAL ORIENTATION	mental processes and behavior erratic	left-brain, analytically oriented; traditional male behavior	right and left brain balanced for synergy; androgynous in behavioral orientation

Managing in the Flow State

There is little question, given the pressures felt by today's executives and the arguments laid out above, that an expanded perspective is required for our leaders. J.B. Quinn[8] referred to this new image as "the guiding executive" — one who sees change as ongoing, and who understands how to work with the many variables that must unfold for things to proceed in the organization. It is from this notion of "going with the flow" that the new style emerges.

The concept of flow can be traced back to the Eastern philosophy of the Tao, which urges harmony with the natural order of things. The Tao is the path, or the way the universe is meant to unfold. It states that there is a natural sequence to life; that change, like a flowing river, is perpetual; and that we can best facilitate the flow by unblocking it and removing obstacles from its way. Applied to management thinking, to be in a flow state implies seeing the large picture: understanding objectively the most appropriate changes or shifts that must occur and assisting these changes with the least amount of cost or disruption to the people and output of the organization. Being in the flow state means working in harmony with others and looking after the good of the whole, not just the favored parts of the system.

The experience of the flow has been well documented in the research of Mihalyi Csikszentmihalyi,[9] who stated that the flow is "the holistic sensation that people feel with total involvement." The person in that state "experiences a unified flowing from one moment to the next, in which he is in control of his actions, and in which there is little distinction between self and environment, between stimulus and response, or between past, present, and future." The manager in this state, then, is totally immersed in his or her work, completely attuned with the needs of the moment, and has no conscious expectation of reward.

Building upon this, R.G.H. Siu[10] described the ability in this state "to act from an instantaneous apprehension of the totality." Grasping the totality requires a broad perspective on what is going on all around the manager. To act from the apprehension of the totality means having a sensitivity to, or intuition about, what is needed. Intuition, or having a "feeling", comes from *within* the manager, most often accessed when he or she is in a relaxed, poised state.[11] Managing in the flow state is trusting the connection between one's intuitive inner knowing and the reasoning power gained from seeing the big picture of what's happening in the organization. It is balancing the factual data in each situation with the allowing and following of one's hunches on how to act. As mentioned in the table, this balance also can be seen in managers who effectively use the functions of both brain hemi-spheres: the left being analytical and structured, the right being intuitive and creative. It is the synergy between the two that enables the flow to occur.

Values That Support the Flow State

There are certain values espoused by flow state managers. They see themselves as being in service to the larger purpose of the company. They strive for the fulfillment of that purpose as well as for the potential of the individuals who con-tribute to it. They have a deep sense of patience with, and trust in, people's inten-tions to work for the good of common goals without sacrificing their personal identity. Work to them is meaningful, and they feel enriched from their effort and time spent on behalf of the organization. They believe there is an abundance of opportunities in which to demonstrate competence and effectiveness.

Flow state managers encourage the best efforts from everyone and value a work environment that supports learning, exploration, and creativity. In their efforts to ensure harmony among the parts of the organization, they also pro-mote opportunities for group synergy and group recognition. They understand that their values must be shared in order to have a positive impact.

Many of the values of the flow state manager are illustrated by the life of Mohandas K. Gandhi, a popular model of a visionary leader. Gandhi was deeply guided by his inner purpose, his beliefs in equality, justice, peace, and patience. Having no resources or form with which to manage his cause, he became a master at managing energy. He used himself and other public fig-ures as models and sources, created a widespread energy field on behalf of his vision, opened new channels for action in the British government and in the Hindu and Muslim states, and trusted that the flow of events for and against his vision would work out in his favor. This dramatic illustration also brings to mind the potential risks and personal sacrifice that may be required — tai-lored, of course, to the realities of organizational life.

Before going further with the flow state manager, let's look at the other styles on the continuum for contrast.

The Fear State

You may think, "This is all well and good in theory, but in most real organiza-tions people strive to advance their own causes; they compete for scarce resources; and they are rewarded solely for how they control results." This is true in many cases, but we must look at the cost of such realities. In and of themselves, each of these acts may be a positive condition if it serves the col-lective purpose of the organization, instead of the individual alone.

It is the individual, self-centered focus, rather than the collective one, that drains the potential performance of the system. The self-centered focus comes from an attitude of fear and defensiveness. Fear can be observed in managers who have a win/lose attitude, who play political games, and who control and grasp self-servingly at events and information in the organization. Fear can be seen in managers who over-control meetings and assignments, overprotect themselves, and engage in destructive competition.

People who act out of fear are threatened by the forces around them. They assume there are not enough resources or rewards to go around. The assumption of scarcity makes them act in selfish ways. Life becomes a game of win/lose, and these people believe they have no choice but to go for winning, thereby forcing others to lose. They come from a position of distrust, and they typically hear and see everything in the organization with the question in their minds, "How will this hurt me?"

It is nearly impossible to have a clear sense of how to proceed appropriately when one is worried, anxious, or driven in this way. The physiological reactions to fear shut down our ability to breathe, respond freely, and be open to new input. Typically, the fear state creates negative situations that leave costly residues of bad feelings, physical pain, and wasted energy. The organization becomes a battlefield. This state drives people to withhold and protect information and power, to become entangled in political quagmires that cripple the most reasonable of people, and to demonstrate blind allegiance to tradition, for fear of losing ground.

This description is purposely extreme to emphasize the point of how costly the fear state can be when allowed to escalate. Under normal conditions, the state can be observed in individuals who lose their tempers frequently, become workaholics, have difficulty delegating responsibility, are reluctant to let go of a lost debate or unpopular decision, or frequently blame others for bad conditions. These signs, unfortunately, breed greater strain and fear in others. The fear state is highly contagious, and unfortunately very prevalent in contemporary organizations.

The Solid State Manager

The *solid state* managerial style is more familiar because it reflects the mainstream of Western business school teachings. These people are ideally very skillful at managing the traditional structures in the organization: charts, policies, schedules, numbers, and "head counts." There are a variety of familiar management styles that fall into this category: the authoritarian, the task-master, the organizer, and the administrator. Some of the more people-oriented managers are also within this range on the continuum. The common factor among them is that they manage the components — the *form* of the organization — and don't see or emphasize the relationships, dynamics, and processes that exist as well. They are largely left-brain oriented, influenced solely by external forces in the organization such as goals, deadlines, and policies, rather than by their own intuitions about trends, patterns, and energy flow. They respond instead to rewards and punishments, visibility, political expectations, and traditions. They plan according to available, quantifiable facts and are truly the "good soldiers" of management. The table lists more specific characteristics of solid state management.

Where they are situated on the continuum does not detract from the success of these managers in what they attempt to do. Within their views of the world, the best of them are truly successful. However, these managers are faced with the dilemma laid out in the beginning of this chapter. Their best strategies somehow do not work. We no longer live in a time of stability and certainty. The only thing that we are sure of is that pressures, polarities, and ambiguity make up our reality. The door opens again on the need for a new vision of management. Let's now return in more depth to the flow state.

HOW THE FLOW STATE WORKS

I've discussed the flow state manager's values and perspectives on organizational life. There are additional attitudes held by this individual, which become the foundation for his or her way of thinking and deeply influence decisions and behaviors. I'll describe several here, along with brief examples.

1. Abundance of Opportunity. To begin with, the flow state manager feels that the organization offers an abundance of opportunity to those who seek it. The "one big chance" mentality is an illusion; there is no scarcity of options and potentials. Believing in abundance releases energy and excitement. If now is not the time, another chance will emerge — or, better, an opportunity as yet unforeseen will surface. This attitude creates a sense of drama and enticing novelty. Life is filled with curiosity and the seeking of new events. By staying fresh and aware, one actively participates in the opportunities of the day.

2. Learning Is Essential. To sustain this kind of openness, the flow state manager values calculated risks and continual learning. People must have the freedom to explore and make mistakes. Without testing limits, it is difficult to know whether or not one is on or off course, moving too fast or too slow. True faith in the process means believing that the process will indicate how to self-correct, or how to reorganize in order to keep moving, much like water seeking new open channels to keep flowing. Each event, positive or negative, provides more information about where one has been and where one needs to go next.

3. Structures Are Necessary and Changeable. This does not imply that the flow state manager advocates a "free-for-all." She or he recognizes that certain structures are necessary and useful. For instance, people's jobs must be clear and distinct from one another; job descriptions aid this. There must be some semblance of order as well as reasonable boundaries between functions. Each department must understand its unique task. For the flow state manager, however, job clarity and boundaries are like walls — while they are useful for defining what is inside them, they inevitably close some things out as well. People need boundaries to help define their identity and role; the flow state manager uses them to serve this purpose, and they are seen as changeable at any time to facilitate new events or to alter people's jobs. This is true for all structures in the organization; they are vehicles to facilitate the flow — easily created, easily removed. This has major implications for how one organizes, plans, and uses policies and rules. Nothing can be perceived as carved in stone.

4. Using Common Purpose as a Bond Between People. Given the uncertainty in organizations, most people require some form of security or stability to perform effectively. This security comes from two major sources: shared acceptance of the purpose and future goals of the organization, and the sense of togetherness or community that is created by collective effort. The flow state manager encourages people to feel connected and attuned with each other at some level. By participating in the organization together, they commit to a common purpose. At all levels of the organization, the sense of community can be built to enhance people's motivation to work together effectively, especially during periods of uncertainty or change.

An example of this was seen in 1982 at Braniff Airlines. The employees shared the burden of the financial state of the company because collectively they believed in the overall purpose. Although the airline went bankrupt, the spirit demonstrated by the common bond inspired many other organizations.

5. Attend to All Stakeholders. Because the tides can shift at any time, it is important to heed and value all stakeholders, or constituents, of the organization. Siu[12] warns that taking constituents lightly can come back to haunt an executive. Paying some form of recognition and attention to all interested parties is wise. To do this, the flow state manager may ask for input or feedback, may test out a new idea, may praise a point of view, or may reward some contribution as a way of revitalizing the relationship with each of the stakeholder groups. Again, the principle at play here is to keep all doors open and all parties actively involved.

6. There Is Meaning in All Events. Events and circumstances in the organization may change radically, disrupting people and plans. A shift in leadership or direction, for instance, may cause pressure or conflict. The flow state manager respects all events and the wishes of influential people, whether he or she agrees with them or not, because each change in the organization serves some purpose in the long run. Being learning-oriented and patient, the manager seeks and spreads the meaning or value to be gained from every event.

An example of this was seen in a petroleum company whose chairman left the organization after a nine-year effort to diversify the business. His reign had been largely successful, but the organization's board of directors finally concluded that the company needed to revert to its initial roots and reorient to petroleum-related specialties. Although his departure was abrupt and awkward, the executive gracefully articulated this strategy and supported the change publicly. His wisdom and dignity assisted the company's rapid implementation of the change.

7. Seeing the Big Picture That Surrounds Polarities. The preceding example also demonstrates the flow state manager's openness to conflicts, differences, and polarities. In martial arts training, one is taught to "embrace the enemy," for only then can one see the larger picture and know how to proceed. It is empowering to be able to experience a situation through the eyes of your adversaries, since their view is as legitimate to them as yours is to you. Conflicts are often dealt with as either/or, right/wrong situations, and seeing the situation from both sides is essential, as was explained earlier in the discussion of polarities. The solid state manager can usually see two sides of the issue or conflict and select one or the other based upon an analysis of advantages or disadvantages. Often, a compromise can be reached.

The flow state manager has the ability to see both sides from above the big picture — and to seek a synthesis of the two poles. This is *dialectical* thinking. This view allows a more complete and objective perspective from which to make decisions. It enables the manager to rise above the conflict without ascribing rightness or wrongness to either position. Instead, decisions can be based on appropriateness to the circumstances at hand, since at any time one force may have the stronger influence. Not falling prey to "rightness" or "wrongness" protects the manager's future options should the situation turn around. The key here is to be able to observe what happens to the weaker force, knowing that, over time, it will gather strength and emerge again. In the flow, all forces are cyclical in nature.

A formal decision-making system built upon this principle was offered by R. Ackoff.[13] He described a method for deciding upon major capital investments by setting up a task force to thoroughly investigate why a major decision should be made (the advocacy position). A second task force is created to formally study why the same decision should *not* be made. The deciding body can then maintain a clear grasp of the large picture and still have both sides thoroughly and legitimately reviewed.

8. *Non-Attachment to Self, Action, and Power.* The flow state manager knows that there always will be a circumstance larger than what presents itself at any moment. One always must be ready to respond according to the emerging need. One must be prepared to act or to stop an action, to give up a position of power or to step into one, to take on leadership or to demonstrate loyal followership. This requires letting go of one's ego and attachments to favored positions. Ego becomes blindness. Attachments become constraints very quickly. There is tremendous freedom, and often exhilaration, felt from this awareness and approach. Flow state managers are self-responsible and self-directed, capable of choosing the most appropriate actions in any given moment.

9. *Focus on Empowering Others.* This "freedom from self" allows a valuable focus on what others need. The flow state manager seeks new opportunities for others to make a contribution. The guiding principle here is to facilitate higher levels of performance, to empower others to act on their best intuition and skills. One accepts that every individual is unique, and that the greatest gift one can give is to free up people's internal energy and then provide the stage for their acts of excellence to play out. Through delegation, giving away responsibility and authority, and demonstrating trust, a manager can unlock a tremendous amount of motivation and excitement. Becoming an advocate for what others want to do, especially subordinates, is a key strategy for unblocking human energy in the organization.

FLOW STATE STRATEGIES

In accordance with flow state principles, anything that helps facilitate the unfolding of events in the organization is considered a valuable approach. There are a few strategies in particular to consider closely.

Managing Ambiguity

Given the high degree of ambiguity in organizational life, managers need to be able to cope with uncertainty. Most people, however, want information, clear choices, advantages and disadvantages spelled out, and reinforcement from others before they are willing to act. Flow state managers are aware of these natural tendencies and work to generate as much clarity and understanding as possible. Quinn[14] wrote of managers who strive to amplify people's understanding of different alternatives and their seeking of clear criteria for making decisions. This takes time and care, which is not always available. According to Pascale,[15] a basic management skill in an uncertain environment is knowing the distinction between having enough data to *decide* and having enough data to *proceed*. It takes courage to proceed, and the flow state manager knows that further action will reveal more data than taking no action. Situations become clearer over time as trends emerge from taking careful steps or sending out "trial balloons." Others also will grow more comfortable with new directions if given an appropriate adjustment period and an opportunity to sample a new approach.

Five key strategies in managing in highly ambiguous times, then, are:

- Pursue as much clarity and understanding as possible.
- Shape criteria to test the decision.
- Create lead or slack time for more information to surface and to facilitate people's comfort levels.
- Take slow or partial steps that do not risk the entire ball game; test ideas and watch for emerging trends or tendencies.
- Encourage people to air their concerns and frustrations with the unknown, and reinforce the climate for learning.

Sense of Timing

In certain times, knowing *when* to act is a fine-tuned skill that assists the unfolding of events in the organization. People often react to an event by saying, "The timing is all wrong," or "Perfect timing!" The flow state manager has two abilities concerning time: knowing how to order events on a linear timetable and knowing the best timing for action. The Greek words *kronos,* or clock time, and *Kyros,* or right timing, illustrate this point effectively. *Kronos* provides the logical, organized sequencing of events so necessary to planning and implementing complex changes. *Kyros* deals with the process of sensing the energy, readiness, and momentum in the organization for implementing critical changes. *Kyros* requires knowing when to act, when the moment is right, and when not to act. To be effective at this, the flow state manager senses the political climate, people's need for direction, and their openness to change.

Building Readiness: The Use of Critical Mass

The notion of building readiness is a key component of the flow state perspective. How does the manager get changes to occur? Nuclear physics offers us a term that is a useful way of viewing how the tides shift in organizations: critical mass. Critical mass is the point at which the momentum necessary for action to occur is reached; it then continues to spread, and action follows. Up until this point, one is building awareness, understanding, and support for a particular desired outcome. Critical mass can be viewed as the necessary number of "ready" people. More than this, it symbolizes a building of momentum or an energy field, where the effort proceeds on its own without constant support. The analogy of a snowball rolling downhill is useful here. The size and weight of a snowball, appropriate to the angle of the decline, reaches the right proportions so that it proceeds to overcome all resistance and rolls of its own accord, picking up speed as it picks up size.

In organizational terms, a flow state manager identifies people throughout the organization who are best suited to advocate a desired change. She or he invites their support and describes the collective effort that is required for the change to occur. They then use their skills, reputation, influence, and resources to attract others to the effort as well. When the people who advocate the move, with their combined energy and intention, outweigh those who resist or have not committed themselves, a critical mass is reached and the effort proceeds.

It is important to emphasize that this is a strategically *proactive* move for the flow state manager. It illustrates that this approach is not just to be responsive and accepting, but is highly active as well. The intention to act with this form of influence grows out of a manager's personal accountability to an intuitive sense of what is needed and congruent with the "big picture." Maintaining this requires keeping the self finely tuned.

Nurturing the Inner Flow State

Organizations that function effectively are healthy. Their purpose is clear; their members work together in pursuit of the purpose; the structures in the organization remain adaptable and responsive; the energy flows smoothly. This picture of health is a collective mirror image of the health of members of the organization. There is an inner flow state in every person that directly affects their personal level of performance. This flow is a reflection of the individual's ability to be in synchronization with the flow of the larger organization.

The flow state manager is keenly aware of his or her inner state. He or she lives by a model of balancing and caring for four core aspects of the person: the mind, the body, the heart (emotions), and the spirit. As in the organization, these components are interlinked. Peak performance is the outcome of the health of all four working in support of one another.[16]

It is valuable to reflect on the fact that the mind-body-heart-spirit model is applicable at the organizational level as well. The flow state manager looks after the mental functioning (seen in decision making, planning, and problem-solving, for example), the physical ability (reflected in operations, structure, and use of resources), the emotions (such as morale, creativity, and culture), and the spirit (felt in meaningful work, alignment of the parts, and sharing a common purpose). The balance of these core aspects directly indicates the health of the organization and the degree to which the energy can flow naturally.

THE FLOW STATE MANAGER'S MIND IN ACTION

I've described the flow state manager's values, abilities, and strategies for working effectively in the organization. Given this picture, how might this person approach a situation in real life? How would these principles guide his or her thinking and actions? It is valuable to translate the characteristics described above into actual questions that might be posed in any given situation in the organization. The questions offered here illustrate various beliefs and mental functions of this managing style. The list is not inclusive or sequential. Consider these questions as doors to opening up your own thinking channels for a management situation presently facing you.

- Fit With Purpose: How does this situation fit the larger purpose of the organization?

- Opportunity/Risk: What is the opportunity here? What is at risk? What is needed to have this situation turn out positively for everyone involved?

- History: What circumstances and events have led up to this point in time? How does this historical perspective influence the way we might proceed or the outcome desired? What polarities have been at play? What is the existing energy field?

- Support/Obstacles: What do we have going in our favor (people, resources, excitement, timing, etc.)? What real or potential obstacles stand in our way?

- Direct Control: What is within our direct control that can easily be created or removed to assist this effort? What channels can be opened up? What structures are needed?

- Indirect Influence: What actions would require indirect influence, longer lead time, or special consideration? How might that happen?

- Critical Mass: Who is essential to the critical mass (for political reasons, expertise, stakeholders, to build support and trust, etc.)? How can these people be reached and involved to help open channels and build a positive energy field?

- Assumptions: What assumptions are we making about our desired outcomes or the need/opportunity facing us? Are these consistent with other people's views?

- Motivation: What is my interest in this? What is in this for others? How can I be an advocate for them? Empower them?

- Timing: What is the best timing for events to occur? What is an appropriate sequence?

- Degree of Activity: How proactive should we be, or is it best for us to let things unfold for now?

- Visibility and Pacing: How visible shall we be with our efforts? Shall the total effort move ahead at once, or should we proceed a step at a time or in phases?

- Contingencies: What other pressures might emerge (e.g., resistance, removal of resource support, political factors, change of leadership, etc.)? How will we build in contingencies?

- Learning: What can we learn from this experience? What is meaningful about it?

- Intuitive Sense: As I look at the big picture, what hunches or feelings do I have for how to proceed?

The information derived from these questions shapes a strategy for action. From each action, new learnings and data emerge and help shape ensuing strategies. Flow state managers scan these questions, plus any others that arise, on an on-going basis, keeping this underlying principle in mind: *What is the best way to proceed to serve the highest purpose for all involved?* At times, even with all the possible steps that might be taken, they choose to do nothing actively but watch and support.

IMPLICATIONS OF MANAGING IN THE FLOW STATE AND THE ORGANIZATION OF ENERGY

The concepts offered here describe an ideal state of being. As mentioned earlier, this is a construct of reality created to help explain an expanded view of managing. We must ask ourselves, "Is it really possible, or practical, in today's organization?" Upon reflection, several realistic questions and needs come to mind and prompt further exploration.

How would our organizations be different if we held this frame of reference? We must ponder the implications of the flow state on our existing organizations and managers. To do this, certain things are needed. They include:

- Need for a new terminology to discuss energy and flow operationally. Need for awareness of the shift from talking about nouns (form and results) to verbs and gerunds (process). Describing reality in terms of action enables us to better see and feel the energy flow.

- Need for new organizational forms and systems that are more readily responsive to the energy flow rather than obstacles to it. New forms must be self-organizing, self-correcting, and adaptable. For instance, the traditional bureaucratic decision-making procedures and record-keeping systems do not fit these criteria.

- Need for greater focus on the purpose of the organization and what is done with it once created. The purpose of the organization must ensure that the system remains viable, given the demands of the larger environment. In addition, the purpose can excite and mobilize the members of the organization to work in greater alignment with one another when it is kept in the forefront.

- Need to assess the existing sources, channels, and energy fields to better understand what helps the organization to adapt to greater complexity and what hinders it. Pervasive cultural factors, (such as the message "Don't rock the boat") may be seen as major blocks to the greater self responsibility, creativity, and adaptability which are necessary for change to occur.

- Need to assess people's beliefs about the future, the organization's viability, management style and responsibility, and change. This information can raise awareness about the need for new perspectives and actions. What beliefs would support desired changes?

- Need to look at the model of energy as an organization moves through its natural life cycle. Different management strategies would be appropriate to an organization that is growing rapidly vs. one that is declining.

Assuming that it is desirable, how would we implement changes in organizational forms and management style? The things needed for implementation might include the following:

- Need information upon which to build a case (an energy field) on behalf of this view. The above questions suggest several types of information that can be gathered to raise management awareness. Also, we must study whether existing energy channels can be opened up or new ones created in the organization to demonstrate the effect of energy flowing freely. Experiencing this is essential.

- Each manager can ponder the way she or he sees organizations (as form, as energy) and where she or he sits on the continuum of management styles.

- Need to identify the key sources of energy (people, events, etc.) in the organization and how to best use them to serve the larger purpose. Develop a strategy for building a critical mass of supporters within the targeted system. It is necessary to identify whom to initially invite in, how to use them, and how to spread the awareness (events, communications, symbols).

- Need to carefully study the impact on existing structures and managers. What would specifically need to be changed? Who would assist the effort? What forms of resistance might be encountered? What sacrifices must be made, compared to what gains? What would the cost be in dollars, time, resources, and emotion? From this information, organize an approach that sequences and paces changes appropriately. Caution must be taken not to push the existing system beyond its limits to absorb and respond to changes.[16] Plans must model the flow!

- With the explosion of technology, need to explore how computers can be introduced as a way of enhancing information and energy flow.

- Need to study whether managing in the flow state can be learned. We know it must be experienced, not just talked about.

- Need to find out if the flow state can be taught. Learning experiences, language, and feedback mechanisms must be developed which reflect the state itself.

CONCLUSION

What would life be like if everyone in the organization were in the flow state? Is it possible to maintain it? I do not presume to have the answers. Thorough discussion, and probably some free-form fantasy, will help with this question. I personally can see people caring about each other, working collaboratively across functions. I can see lively debates for certain decisions to be made, and then clean resolution and responsible follow-up, no matter what the outcome. There would be high spirit, constructive tension, a lot more trust and patience, a more satisfying quality of life, pride in excellent performance, and a deep attunement with the purpose of the organization.

In reality, we work toward the flow state as a process, not an end result. It is a state of being, not a place to achieve. Managing in the flow state is an attitude, not an absolute. If certain aspects are appealing to you, then work toward making them happen, and don't worry about the concept in its entirety.

A great deal of personal commitment and integrity is necessary to maintain the flow state frame of mind. As a way of viewing the world, this is a place to come from, the inspiration for behavior. Do what aids the unfolding of events, and that is the flow state. This is about using any action, observation, or appreciation for how to make things occur with greater ease. The value felt will match the situation at hand; the possibilities are limitless.

With the crush of demands, increasing complexity, and need for change, it is no wonder that anything that makes life in the organization smoother will be welcome. Executives cannot fight or ignore the challenges they face today, nor can they hope to solve fundamental problems by superficial changes. Some shift in our perspective is essential before we can experience relief. That shift is internal, in our attitudes and beliefs. Fear *can* be transformed. Form and energy *can* work in harmony. No matter what we actually do, things will continue to unfold. Managers can assist the unfolding, if only by not blocking the way.

As Lao Tse said, we can consider ourselves successful if, when the leader is finished with his work, the people say, "It happened naturally."

Notes

[1] See E.H. Schein, "Does Japanese Management Style Have a Message for American Managers?" *Sloan Management Review* 23(1):55 (Fall 1981).

[2] D.A. Nadler and M.L. Tushman, "A Model for Organizational Diagnosis," *Organizational Dynamics* (Autumn 1980), p. 47.

[3] John Naisbitt, *Trend Letter* 2:4 (1983), p. 1.

[4] Peter Vaill, "The Purpose of High Performing Systems," *Organizational Dynamics* (Autumn 1982), pp. 23-39.

[5] J.D. Ingalls, *Human Energy* (Reading, Massachusetts: Addison-Wesley, 1976).

[6] Ibid., p. 1; p. 15.

[7] Ibid., p. 6.

[8] J.B. Quinn, "Managing Strategic Change," *Sloan Management Review* 23(1):55 (Fall 1981).

[9] M. Csikszentmihalyi, *Beyond Boredom and Anxiety* (San Francisco: Jossey-Bass, 1975).

[10] R.G.H. Siu, *The Master Manager* (Chichester, United Kingdom: John Wiley and Sons, 1980).

[11] See M. Gelb, *Body Learning* (New York: Delilah Books, 1981).

[12] Siu.

[13] Russell Ackoff, "Organizational Decision Making and Planning," Seminar Proceedings, Sun Company, Inc. (Radnor, Pennsylvania, 1979).

[14] Quinn.

[15] Richard T. Pascale, "Zen and the Art of Management," *Harvard Business Review* (March/April 1978), 156.

[16] A more detailed description of these components can be found in Chapter 11, Chandra Stephens and Saul Eisen, "Myth, Transformation and the Change Agent."

[17] S. Beer, *Platform for Change* (Chichester, United Kingdom: John Wiley and Sons, 1975).

8

Spirituality in the Workplace

RICHARD McKNIGHT

> *Most people have work that is too small for their spirits.*
> — *Studs Turkel*

> *This is the true joy in life; the being used for a purpose*
> *recognized by yourself as a mighty one.*
> — *George Bernard Shaw*

Comments on the Second Edition

This selection has touched the lives of many people, and I remain proud of it. It has been the inspiration for at least one best-selling book (Dick Richards' *Artful Work),* and it has been the impetus for a score of total strangers to thank me effusively when they've identified me with this piece.

Re-reading the piece fifteen years after writing it, however, I am struck by three things: how darkly I portrayed the effects of corporate life on individuals; the fervor with which I implore the reader to right the wrongs identified; and the extent to which the problems I pointed out so many years ago are still evident.

Corporations are, in the main, probably worse places to be now than they were then, and for the same reason. Most are built on a psychologically injurious system of dependency and external rewards that enfeeble their inhabitants. While there are exceptions, the American business organization I portrayed when I wrote this selection in 1982 differs very little from many of the organizations I consult with today. The rare exceptions are those organizations that have found ways to forge new and more ennobling relationships with their employees.

The famed whitewater formed by the confluence of the information age, global competition, and deregulation had yet to churn when I wrote this piece, and I feel sure that if I had anticipated the resulting downsizings, merger mania, violated psychological contracts, and the like, my tone would have been even more strident than it was. Since then, however, I have come to the view that both employee and corporation will ultimately benefit from these changes.

In this selection, I never come out and describe the ideal corporation as a protective mother, but as I re-read the piece, this implication makes me very uncomfortable. Today I would describe a very different ideal. I reject as cloying and sentimental the model I admired in the early 1980s, and I now favor one that's more like what I imagine an effective movie-making organization to be: temporary alliances of highly competent, autonomous professionals. In other words, a culture in which everyone is free to leave, but only a few — those with the purpose, polish, track record, and ego strength — can join. A culture in which performance and contribution are king, and loyalty and dependence are unheard of.

This may sound like heresy to those who have been so touched by this article. Is loyalty a bad thing? Isn't there more to life than achievement and contribution? Ultimately, this chapter speaks to the idea that organizational life can — and should — bring out the best in people. I still believe this. I am more convinced than ever that groups of individuals, acting in concert toward ends they believe in, can do great things. But I no longer rail against corporations when they don't treat people right. I save my breath, realize that what goes around eventually comes around, and advise my job-holding friends (the list is shrinking) to bring job security to work with them rather than try to find it in monthly paychecks and promotions.

— Richard McKnight

McKnight defines spirituality as the animating life force that inspires one toward purposes that are beyond one's self, and that gives one's life meaning and direction. In this chapter he gives examples of problems that arise when this force is ignored in organizations. He then illustrates what is possible in organizations where human spirit is encouraged, and closes the chapter with suggestions for enhancing spirituality in the workplace.

After ten years as a consultant in American business organizations, I have come to the conclusion that most employees perceive work as a never-ending struggle that requires them to constantly prove their worth, to live in perpetual fear of losing their jobs, and to remain on constant watch lest others impede their efforts or take recognition for their accomplishments. Further, judging from the nervous laughter I hear from employees when I discuss it, most people suffer from what I call the "Sunday night syndrome" — the tendency to count down the remaining leisure hours on Sunday evening prior to bedtime. The way most people feel about work is characterized by the person who says, "Hmm. It's 7 o'clock. My bedtime is 11 o'clock. Therefore, I have four hours of freedom left before I'm back into the grind."

For those who have sought to build a management career in a business organization, work also often represents a never-ending series of political moves and territorialism, as well as "packaging" and "selling" oneself so that one might become and remain acceptable to those whose favor might pay off in promotions.

This is the kind of "cold war" most employees feel they engage in relative to their jobs. They steel themselves against the worst in their jobs, go along with the aspects that are tolerable, and give in totally on other aspects so that they may retain employment and extract the monetary and status rewards that "compensate" them for their pain and sacrifice. In short, most people do not like their jobs very much.

When people do not like their jobs much — when an inordinate amount of energy goes into bickering with co-workers, feeling exhausted and overworked, and into molding and shaping the character to be acceptable at promotion time, productivity suffers, stress-related symptoms of emotional and physical distress emerge, and character development is stifled.

If it is true that most organizations are characterized by such dehumanizing policies and practices, and if it is true that most employees feel used and burned out, resulting in lowered productivity, why do such work climates persist? Obviously they don't exist in *all* companies, as Peters and Waterman[1] found. But where they do, such work climates exist because of the cultural hypnosis we have about the essential nature of a business organization.

For most workers, managers, and executives I have worked with in the past 10 years, business organizations are seen as cold, impersonal machines that take raw materials, capital, and people in one end, perform some transformation, process, or service, and produce — or should produce — money out the other end. According to this model, the primary objective of a business is monetary: shareholder equity, return on investment, and other financial measures. People are seen as resources, and whole departments are set up to "manage" them and make their performance more predictable and profitable. In the prevailing model, the ideal business posture is characterized by words such as "competitive," "aggressive," and "winner." "Our business is only about making money," one executive said to me, "and the only way we can do that in our industry is by keeping everybody uncertain and mean — inside the company and outside of it."

I do not endorse this model of a business organization. I have nothing against competition or making a profit. Like one of the executives quoted in Peters and Waterman's *In Search of Excellence*,[2] I believe profit is like health: the more of it the better. But it is not, by itself, a sufficient reason for a business to exist.

In my view, the prevailing model of *business-as-machine* results in practices that are harmful to employees, to society, and ultimately, to the bottom line. Before I go into detail about more socially responsible models of business, however, I would like to relate an anecdote that I think will reveal how the prevailing model of business is injurious. The anecdote has to do with a chance encounter with a man named Mike, who had been a participant in a stress-management seminar 18 months earlier. Mike is a middle-level executive in his company.

When I saw Mike this time, we were going through the line in his company's cafeteria. I did a double-take: He had lost a great deal of weight. "I almost didn't recognize you. You've slimmed down, Mike!" I said.

"Yeah, I lost thirty pounds," he replied. "They came off quickly following my coronary by-pass operation."

Joining Mike for lunch, I was fascinated by his story. When he was a participant in the stress-management seminar, Mike claimed to have no tension at work — the only stress in his life was at home, he said. His job was great, he insisted, but he revealed a tendency towards violent anger at home. And he had a striking way of "relieving" it: "Oh, some days I come home from the office and feel some tension, and I usually yell at one of the kids or my wife. Occasionally, if things are *real* bad, I'll go into a downstairs closet and punch out holes in the sheetrock. Scares hell out my family, but I always calm down."

In the seminar, Mike maintained that the nature of work was "dog-eat-dog." He worked in an all-male environment featuring a lot of competition, and he claimed to enjoy the challenges. "I'm a survivor," he said. In a part of the seminar on the relationship of work to stress and health, Mike disputed the claim that one's feelings about one's job have a dramatic impact on one's health. He especially disliked my claim — backed up by research data collected in his company — that when one feels that one must routinely compete with others in the course of one's work, symptoms of physical illness are likely to develop.

As Mike listened to my presentation, he said audibly two or three times, "I don't believe it." I asked him what he didn't believe. "I don't believe what I think you're trying to get at. I think you are trying to suggest that people can feel differently about their jobs than they do normally. What you are trying to say is that people in business should matter to each other, they should feel like their work contributes to some social good, that they don't have to go home tired each day." "Well," I said, "that's over-stated, but you're getting my point, all right."

Mike vigorously maintained that being in business means you have to be tough; the weak have no place in business and should get out for their own good and for the good of the company. "Okay," he said, "if a person really hates his job, he might get sick. But it isn't the company's fault. The company isn't in the business of trying to make people happy at work. The purpose of the company is to make money."

Eighteen months and one coronary by-pass later, 30 pounds lighter, Mike's philosophy had changed. That day in the cafeteria, Mike said, "You know, when I was in the hospital, I began to reevaluate my life. My family life had some troubles, so I set some goals about that. But the part of my life that gave me the most trouble was my job. I almost died in the hospital. I was off work for three months. And in all that time, during all that trauma, do you know how many of my coworkers reached out to me? Only two — my boss and my secretary."

Given all this, did Mike still believe that business has to be dog-eat-dog and impersonal? Yes. He maintained that it would be nice if work could draw out the best in people, but he still believed it was impossible. "That's just the way business is," he said. When I asked him how he now deals with the tension this creates in him — desiring a supportive work environment, but thinking it to be impossible — he said, "Oh, I now put my best energy into other things, like my family and my hobbies. Compared to before, I'm just putting in my time here now."

There are many people like Mike reporting to work every day, people who are cynical and tired, who have given up, and who are content to make it to quitting time. Daniel Yankelovich[3] reported in 1982 that a majority of American workers admitted to working less hard at their jobs than they had 10 years earlier, even though more aspects of their jobs were currently under their personal control. Most people felt that while they still believed it to be morally important for them to work hard, they didn't foresee any social or personal benefit deriving from their effort; someone else just becomes richer.

Most managers and executives haven't given up trying to be acceptable and admired by their organizations. On the contrary, as Michael Maccoby[4] found, employees at this level put enormous energy into shaping and molding their character, perceptions, and expectations so that they will more closely fit that which they perceive to be valued by their company. Since most business organizations are set to function as money-generating machines, the result is an executive population with highly refined skills, as Maccoby said, of the head but not of the heart. In other words, these men and women, with the encouragement and reward of their companies, gradually strip themselves of their own ability to feel, to empathize, to take a stand on values they hold dear.

When our institutions require us to shape and strangle our natures, or when we cannot understand and become enthusiastic about their objectives, a part of us dies inside. I call that part our spirit. The business organization that is able to tap into its employees' spiritual centers, to liberate their spirits and give them something to rejoice about, is the company that is most fit for human habitation, and, other things being equal, the most profitable as well. The failure of our current business model to enlist employees in some kind of unselfish, nonquantitative cause is at the root of most productivity problems in the United States.

Reading how the Japanese create a sense of family among their employees, how their employees feel a sense of commitment to the enterprise, and how their employees seem to be enriched rather than "used up" by their work experience, I conclude that something other than quality circles and lifetime employment is behind it. I am impressed by Pascale and Athos's 1981 account[5] of such organizations, especially when I read about the spiritual values, such as their concern for collaboration and harmony, underlying their efforts.

We don't usually think of the term "spiritual" when we discuss corporate life. To most of us, business organizations are anything but spiritual. Most likely, we think of them in terms of money and the pursuit of power. Yet when we ignore spiritual values at work, we inhibit the best in people.

When I use the term "spirituality" in this chapter, I refer to an animating life force, an energy that inspires one toward certain ends or purposes that go beyond self. We can never observe this force directly; it only can be inferred from behavior and social customs. It can inspire superhuman efforts to accomplish something, such as those demonstrated by outstanding athletes, star salespeople, creative laboratory researchers, or first-rate supervisors.

A model that presents the business organization as a cold, impersonal machine denies *humanness*. People have needs in three areas: body, mind, and spirit. Yet most companies, if they acknowledge that people have needs at all, act as if there were only two requirements for producing good work: money and job security. Enlightened business people are beginning to understand that there is much more to performance. As documented by Peters and Waterman, employees perform most energetically, creatively, and enthusiastically when they believe they are contributing to a purpose that is larger than themselves: in other words, when they have a *cause*. The role of purpose in our lives is central to any discussion of spirituality in the workplace.

THE PURPOSE OF PURPOSE

In her survey of 60,000 Americans, Gail Sheehy[6] sought to discover the characteristics associated with well-being and general life satisfaction. Sheehy found 10 hallmarks of well-being that distinguished people who were well-satisfied with their lives. The most important factor found to be characteristic of happy, contented people was, "My life has meaning and direction." Specifically, these people's lives are devoted to something outside themselves. According to Sheehy, this characteristic correlates most closely with optimum fulfillment in life.

Happy people find meaning and purpose through involvement with something beyond selfish concerns, like doing something for others and pursuing various social objectives. Most people in her study, when asked if they were devoted to some purpose or cause outside of and larger than themselves, said "No." By contrast, the most-satisfied people in her study, those who said "Yes," were also freest of emotional and physical symptoms of distress, and had the best outlooks.

Sheehy found that one's purpose need not be so lofty that pursuing it will result in sainthood. Most of the purposes held by her satisfied respondents were earthly, but all of their "causes" went beyond their own self-serving concerns, and enhanced their world. Many were active in community work; others, in their church; and one, a small entrepreneur, was committed to creating a business organization that enhanced the lives of his employees.

Having a clear sense of transcendent purpose — one that goes beyond oneself — has a number of positive consequences. It provides us with a source of enthusiasm and energy, and a goal to strive for. We envision something that we might achieve by expenditure of effort, and we are clear as to how others will benefit from our efforts. Purpose is a catalyst for our conduct. A life purpose gives meaning to our lives and gives us comfort when we are faced with misfortune. Victor Frankl's account[7] of life in Nazi concentration camps is a magnificent testimony that those who have clear, transcendent purposes fare far better under extreme hardship than those who do not. Perhaps the most important aspect of a transcendent purpose is simply that it makes us feel good. As Sheehy suggested, having a transcendent purpose results in being in love with the world.

Much of my work with executives involves helping them become clearer about the presence or absence of purpose in their lives. Through guided fantasies, relaxation, and drawing, I help them gain clarity as to what they stand for, and/or what they *want* to stand for. I ask them to fashion their purpose into a one-sentence statement. Nearly all of these statements reflect humanistic values and have a beautiful, poetic quality about them. Here is a sampling:

- "I am loving and caring with everyone in my family, so that I can flourish and they may grow."
- "I am bringing peace and contentment to myself and others by accepting imperfection in myself and others."
- "I am wrapping others in love and happiness and opening myself to the world."

These executives are reminded of what, usually, they already know but don't often act upon. A life centered around a clear purpose is totally integrated. What goes on inside — feelings, attitudes, plans, hopes — is reflected in our behavior. Our principles, values — and ultimately, our behavior — stem from and are consistent with our purpose. Indeed, our lives are *on purpose*: we have intention and direction.

Are *all* purposes actually life-enhancing? Our history is full of monsters whose purposes were clear. From Sheehy's study, it would appear that decades of speculations by humanistic psychologists and religious thinkers are right: the kinds of purposes that make one fall in love with life, and want to contribute to others' falling in love with life, are the purposes that contribute to one's psychological and physical well-being, and to a more generalized social well-being.

The pursuit of two purposes at once is a source of conflict, and unresolved conflicts result in stress symptoms. When we try to pursue two objectives, such as accumulating wealth and serving our God or country or family, we experience distress. Psychoanalysts have been writing about this for nearly a century, and one religious leader, Jesus, addressed it 2,000 years ago. According to him, one cannot serve two masters.

We also experience distress when our institutions do not share our purpose. Such is the case, I believe, with a growing number of employees who can't find much to identify with in their companies. Their performance tapers off and they develop physical and emotional symptoms of distress. People are becoming more aware of the psychological and physical costs of putting forth great efforts in service of the American Dream. They are discovering that it may be to the company's advantage for them to relocate every 18 months, but it certainly isn't to their own or their family's advantage. They resent being used up and spit out. It is conventional business wisdom that the purpose of business is to increase shareholder equity, but of the employees I've observed, fewer and fewer are willing to devote their lives to the shareholders.

Since becoming interested in the importance and benefits of transcendent purpose in life, I have made a practice of interviewing people I meet who seem contented. This tests my hypothesis that contentment is associated with an intention to transcend one's own concerns, to become connected to some higher good. I was impressed, for example, with an elegant 74-year-old man I met one day. "I wouldn't dream of retiring," he told me. "I'd miss the people who come into my business every day. I love people. And besides, they seem to need someone like me to bring smiles into their day. I am in the fur business. Most of my customers are wealthy. But, you know, having money doesn't bring happiness like so many people think. I tell people I'm in the fur business, but I'm really in the joy business. I keep going because I believe people need help in feeling a little more joy in their lives." He had more energy and enthusiasm than any of the several people he brought smiles to that day (including me!).

THE PURPOSE OF WORK

As I listened to a corporate president speak to a group of managers about his career not long ago, I felt an overwhelming sadness when he made the statement, "If it weren't for the money and prestige I'd lose, I'd go back to my old sales management job tomorrow. I loved that job." This executive, widely known for the stress he causes for others in his organization and his own coronary-prone behavior, went on to describe how frustrating it is to get anything done in a large organization. He deals with these frustrations, he said, by working on antique cars on weekends. When Sunday ends, he puts away his tools, heaves a big sigh, and prepares to trudge back to the office. "You have to realize," he said, "that working isn't fun very often."

This is a vivid description of a person who is alienated from deep meaning in his work. He is hardly alone. Most people who have chosen corporate life have known these feelings. Judging by the dramatic rise in the number of stress-related problems among Americans, *most* of us feel alienated. But most of us press on, blind to what really ails us.

Those familiar with managers and executives in American business know that among this group the work ethic is not dead, or even dying. Toward what end do so many strive? Maccoby[8] saw it as the advancement of their own career. They will make enormous sacrifices for it, will bend over backwards to avoid "making waves" in favor of it, and will treat themselves as an object by "packaging" and "marketing" themselves to advance it. Fromm[9] claimed that this "careerism" qualified as a religion, if one accepts religion as "a frame of orientation and an object of devotion." The consequence of such an orientation to work, according to Maccoby, is that we begin to view life and work as a game; to become motivated primarily by competition, winning, and achievements; and to begin valuing shallow emotional attachments, both at home and at work. (Deeper relationships at home and work, it is reasoned, impede judgment.)

For a growing number of employees, such a work ethic is becoming less compelling. Yankelovich[10] observed that people all over the country are reconsidering the relative merits of conventional objects of success, such as a promotion, and are beginning to place higher value on less financially rewarding but more personally satisfying achievements such as closeness to self, family, community, and nature.

Almost everyone has come across numerous accounts of successful executives leaving high-paying jobs at their career peak, to run restaurants in Vermont or a charter service in the Bahamas. Are they kooks? Are they sufferers of terminal mid-life crisis? I think not. I agree with Ferguson that in many cases, "The mid-life crisis may be due in part to the cumulative effect of denial, the sudden thrust into consciousness of pain that can no longer be sedated."[11] Most employees are in pain from one of two sources: either they are devoted only to non-transcendent, materialistic purposes such as career advancement, or they have a transcendent purpose that doesn't mesh with the purpose of the company they work for. Those in the former category are usually unaware of their distress — although a heart attack can sometimes do wonders for awareness. Those in the latter category are acutely aware of the split between their purpose and that of the company. If they are lucky, they can find jobs in other companies where there is more affinity — but companies with goals that transcend profit are still rare.

A 1980 *Business Week* article on corporate culture[12] noted that employees cannot be fooled. They know and understand the real priorities of the corporation, regardless of what is said in the annual report. At Pepsico, for example, the first and foremost object of devotion is beating hell out of Coca-Cola. One Pepsico executive said that careers ride on tenths of market-share points. If one is continually threatened with termination by a drop in market share, it is hard to remember that one's purpose in life is to contribute, for example, to the advancement of peace.

Increasingly, Americans are concerned about all aspects of health. They are concerned with their fitness, their emotions, and the "healthiness" of associating with certain work associates, friends, and even relatives. Many people have divorced because their relationship with their spouse was not "healthy." Millions of people are buying books on stress, and reading about the consequences of working in an environment that does not bring out their personal best. Some young people, like many who responded to Ferguson's *Aquarian Conspiracy* questionnaires,[13] seem to reject the idea of a career altogether. A young truck driver, asked what he intended to do with his liberal arts education, answered: "I will practice living. I will develop my intellect, which may incidentally contribute to the elevation of the aesthetic and cultural levels of society. I will try to develop the noble and creative elements within me. I will contribute very little to the 'grossness' of the national product".[14]

As Ferguson analyzed the questionnaires of Aquarian conspirators — people dedicated to a vision of a world of wholeness and harmony — she found among them a strong desire to make a life, not just a living. They were seeking a *vocation,* not just a job or career. For them, work had — or, they believed, could have — the quality of a "calling," in which what is given comes from some very deep inner reservoir of intention, not merely the desire for money or status. For the person with a vocation, work becomes a positive contributing factor to mental health. Some people use their sense of purpose like a beacon; it guides them to ever-increasing congruence of head, heart, and hands. For them, greed and ambition are clearly not enough. As Yankelovich noted, such people are beginning to pursue an "ethic of commitment," in which they seek to give more than they take from society.[15]

Evidence is available that business people have such desires. For example, I was fascinated by a 1983 television interview with Stanley Weiss, president of American Mineral, Inc., and founder of Business Executives for National Security, an organization composed of high-level corporate executives who oppose the nuclear weapons buildup. Only half-jokingly, Weiss said, "Being dead is not good for business." Another such group, the American Committee on East-West Accord, is devoted to a nuclear arms freeze and to improving relations with the Soviet Union. Robert Schmidt, vice chairman of Control Data Corporation and a member of this group, said the nuclear arms race is "the biggest single threat I can think of."[16] Such executives hardly conform to the "organization man" stereotype, in which profits are all-important.

THE SPIRITUAL ORGANIZATION

In *In Search of Excellence,*[17] Peters and Waterman demonstrate that a spiritually-oriented business organization is not only conceivable, but also desirable in financial and human terms. They give marvelous examples of successful companies in the United States that promote transcendent values. The authors studied 75 companies that were judged "excellent" according to various financial and other measures. One of the eight characteristics of these companies is of particular relevance to our discussion here. These great companies bring out the best in employees by helping them find transcendent meaning in their work.

In these companies, the primary role of top executives is to articulate meaning and vision for employees and to create an environment of clear intent. The values expressed almost always go far beyond financial objectives. In research that preceded *In Search of Excellence,* the authors found that companies whose only articulated goals were financial did not do nearly as well financially as companies that had more fundamental values. The founders of some of America's oldest and most venerable companies (*e.g.*, Thomas J. Watson, Sr. of IBM, and J. Howard Pew of Sun Oil) were often visionary and spiritual men. These companies retain their founders' visions nearly as strongly today as when they were personally at the helm. In such companies, executives go far beyond the normal bounds of business life, to care for employees and for the larger culture surrounding the business. Pew, for example, refused to lay off employees during the Depression. Watson, in the days preceding World War II, had the word "PEACE" hung beneath his famous "THINK" signs wherever they appeared in his plants and offices. These leaders, paternal and moralistic though they sometimes were, tried to provide a spiritually uplifting climate. This paid off for them in terms of employee morale and loyalty, as well as in profitability.

If successful companies state goals beyond profit, what are they? For IBM, the overarching goal is customer service. For Delta Airlines it's service, plus creating a "family feeling" within the company. At Caterpillar Tractor, there is a commitment to "48-hour parts service anywhere in the world." At a very successful real estate firm in San Francisco, the goal is "to create and play games together, transcending economic limitations in a satisfying environment." J. C. Penney Co. is still operating on "The Penny Idea," which entails, among other principles, "to expect for the service we render a fair remuneration, and not all the profit the traffic will bear." Pascale and Athos described this kind of goal-setting in depth, and referred to such goals as superordinate.[18]

Superordinate goals characterize many Japanese companies. They have identified goal types that include emphasis on the company as an entity (emphasizing that the company will be one which people are proud to be associated with); the company's relationship with customers, employees, and internal operations; the company's relationship to society and the state; and the company's relationship to the culture, including its religion. In the latter case, the company commits itself to advancing cultural values such as honesty and fairness.

Spirituality goes far beyond what is typically thought of as "religion." Where religion refers to a set of beliefs, creeds, and rites, spirituality is the more general need for which religious practices are a vehicle. A spiritually-oriented business organization would seek to create a climate that meets as many facets of this need as possible.

My interviews with contented people have revealed the following facets of spirituality:

- enthusiasm about life
- a clear sense of purpose, which is integrated into their daily activities
- acceptance of self and others (with all our faults, we are still noble)
- lives lived gracefully (let things take the time they take; take time to enjoy others; are perpetual students of life)
- orientation towards giving and away from taking
- optimism
- peacefulness
- routinely demonstrated courage (e.g., are willing to state the unpopular opinion or disclose their true feelings).

Contented, purposeful people are enthusiastic about life. Robert Johnson[19] noted that in the original Greek, the word *enthusiasm* means "to be filled with God." He observed that when a person is "filled with God," he or she tends to be highly creative. We need enthusiastic employees in our organizations, whatever the nature of their personal God.

Excellent companies understand the value of employee enthusiasm, and emphasize its importance in company policies and practices. For example, at Hewlett-Packard enthusiasm is one of the three requirements stated as essential to corporate objectives. Highly contented people have a clear sense of purpose that is integrated into their daily activities. So, too, does the spiritually-oriented organization. A lofty-sounding statement of purpose in the annual report means nothing if company policies, procedures, and structures do not support it. Peters and Waterman found that top executives of excellent companies function to ensure that no corporate decision affecting internal or external practices runs afoul of the company's purpose. If the Dayton-Hudson Company, for example, which states its purpose as "serving the business, social, and cultural needs of our communities"[20] were to begin retailing inferior goods at inflated prices to migrant workers, employees would quickly recognize dissonance between policy and actions. It takes very few infractions of company purpose for internal integrity to be lost.

Alignment is a unifying concept that describes the meshing of purpose with organizational practice. This perspective reminds us that organizations, like individuals, are made up of parts designed to serve some whole. The major aims of aligning an organization are 1) to harmonize the relationships among its various parts (person, team, department) so that each understands and contributes to the purpose of the whole); and 2) to clarify the organization's relationship to the larger purposes of human evolution and environmental health — the spiritual uplifting of the larger culture. Alignment results in lessened competition among component parts of the system, and in greater support for continued existence from the surrounding culture.[21]

Whereas alignment specifies the need for conceptual harmony between organizational units and organizational purpose, the picture is incomplete if we do not consider the emotional tone of the organization. Attunement has to do with the desire of all system units and members to work harmoniously together: the tendency to see the needs and concerns of the whole as the needs and concerns of the individual, and vice versa. Organizations that are attuned are characterized by love; members display empathy, caring, understanding, tolerance, mutual support, and forgiveness. Whereas alignment tends to evoke excitement and drive, attunement is a softer, moderating force. It tends to balance the drive and excitement by helping us keep in mind each others' needs and our own sense of what is right in terms of our own transcendent purpose.[22]

Most of us are so jaded by our past experiences in non-loving organizations that we can't even imagine what such an organization might be like. Yet most of us have experienced working as a member of a temporary project team, or part of a community or religious group, that brought out our best. We probably experienced sadness when we left the group. Such sadness is evidence that attunement probably characterized the group. We don't feel ground down and used up by such experiences; we feel enhanced.

Love is a powerful concept. To the uninitiated, the mere description of a business characterized by love provokes strong reactions. On many occasions I have asked groups of managers and executives to imagine a business organization that has virtually no selfishness; that cares about them as individuals; that is a refuge of sanity and peacefulness from a chaotic and hostile world — always with the same result. The majority think it's impossible to achieve. Many seem so fearful and suspicious of love in general that they claim they would prefer to work for an organization where the norms are more competitive. Sometimes, as a protection against the pain of dashed hopes, we prefer the undesirable "known" to the more desirable unknown.

By inference from Peters and Waterman's work, the importance of attunement and alignment is intuitively apparent to the leaders of many excellent companies. As well as being emotionally satisfying, these concepts have decidedly practical consequences. As Roger Harrison points out in Chapter 6, we have created a world in which it is increasingly difficult to compel anyone to do anything. Outstanding business leaders understand that you really can't *get* people to do things; you can only encourage them to *want* to do things. And this encouragement is not through fear, but through meaning, love, and hope.

Increasingly, I find that business executives long for a work experience that reinforces their connectedness to a larger whole, and cultivates within them a set of aspirations that transcend narrow personal concerns. Following a lengthy management-development experience, one manager wrote:

"When I first heard your ideas about what a business organization could be like, it sounded to me that you were describing a change from a cold and indifferent profit-production plant to a warm family or group of friends. I was profoundly skeptical. I'm not sure, as you suggest, that my organization can ever be really concerned about me, that it can ever get to the point where what we produce and how we produce it adds to the life of all. But I want you to know that I listened intently to that sublime idea, and I'm going to do *my* part — for my own mental health, if not just for the organization."

AIDING AND ABETTING SPIRITUALITY IN THE BUSINESS ORGANIZATION

The fundamental requirement for business organizations to be more concerned with our spiritual nature is a radical change in the concept of business purpose. If we ask a business person what the purpose of business is, we probably will be told without hesitation: "To make a profit." If we press the subject, we also may hear something about "providing jobs" or "keeping the economy going," but we will hear very little about people: their need for meaning, or uplifting contributions to human life. We have created businesses that have become cavalier with respect to such products — resulting in a widely shared view that, within the narrow letter of the law, anything goes as long as profit results. If we are to increase productivity in our country, we must change this paradigm. We must acknowledge that among the primary business products of any company are its internal culture and its impact on the communities in which it operates.

The most promising long-term strategy for changing this perception is to change the business school curriculum. Educational institutions are the articulators and transmitters of culture. If our business schools continue to produce thousands of MBAs with a "profit only" perspective about business, organizational change agents who want to foster more humane businesses will have a never-ending job.

What can a company do internally to increase its attention to spirituality? The best answer is implicit in the Zen dictum, "Find the parade and get in front of it." There is considerable evidence that a growing segment of the American workforce already desires greater significance in its work. Most of us are tired of working for companies that grind us down and offer money and status in return for our stressful, alienated lives. This feeling extends, I believe, to the very top of organizations. I have had numerous conversations with top-level executives who privately mourn having spent so much of their lives serving organizations that won't miss them when they retire, and don't seem to fully value them now. As one oil company executive said sadly, "There will be no flags flying at half-mast at any service stations when I retire." This executive, however — like so many others who have been culturally "hypnotized" — still maintained that an uplifting business climate is sheer idealism.

Yet it is this strong desire for closeness, for collaboration, for being part of something larger, that represents the open door for change agents. What we can imagine, we can create. If we take our pain seriously, we can begin to imagine alternatives. That is what creativity is all about: acknowledging our present discomfort with what is, and beginning to consider new ideas that might change our circumstances and feelings. In a climate of cynicism, alienation, and fear, the person who is able to articulate a vision of hope and connectedness is the one who, if persistent and respectful of the audience, can generate enormous energy to achieve it. This is the most-needed role of organizational change agents today, whether the change agent is a manager, executive, or consultant.

Top executives are in the best position to do this. Organization development specialists and other change agents can help executives gain perspective on people's growing need for spiritual meaning in their work, and on people's basic desire to cooperate in achieving objectives they appreciate as worthwhile, but executives are the ones who actually change business policies, norms, and practices.

Personal conviction, combined with moderation and interpersonal skill, almost always gets attention. If you are a change agent and have access to top executives, make your approach as personal as possible. Ask them what their personal experience at work is like. Ask these top executives what others in their organization feel about working there. Ask if he or she doesn't think that an organization filled with people who regard themselves as family, who are in love with their work and what the organization stands for, will put forth a magnificent effort toward company objectives. Finally, begin a discussion about what has to change in order for this to become a reality.

Top executives who seek to promote spirituality, and the coordinated and creative effort it inspires, must be totally consistent in their approach. Every company policy, procedure, and pronouncement must line up with the superordinate goal, even if this means denying opportunities to make additional profit. Pre-employment orientation programs would give job applicants a chance to learn about the values the company stands for before they decide to take a job offered to them. In this way, they would be able to decide whether or not this was a culture they could support; if so, their investment would be enlisted before they even started work. The company's reward system would be tied directly to the transcendent goals. Employees who contribute to the achievement of these goals in an unusually effective way would be rewarded — not only in financial ways, but perhaps in released time to give service to their communities, or to advise an executive on company culture for a few days.

In a company with transcendent goals, organization and management development specialists can help managers and executives create organizational forms that promote the superordinate objectives. Learning how to learn about employee motivation, about how to create exciting organizational visions that support company values, and about how to help workers find their unique niche in the organization, is the kind of management development that pays off.

Change agents do not usually have client companies whose top executives request help in making the company more spiritually oriented. Usually, we take the company for what it is now, and do what we can to make it a more uplifting place to work. I would like to share a few ideas about how this might be done through management development programs, since this is a well accepted medium of organizational influence.

Remember the Zen dictum, "Find the parade and get in front of it." Most managers and executives want to feel that they are significant, and that their efforts contribute to something enduring and worthwhile. Like most of us, they want to be saintly, if not actually saints. Management development programs can help them express this side of themselves through values-clarification exercises, reflecting on past desirable working situations, constructing portraits of ideal leaders, and helping them understand their personal purpose in life and whether or not it matches their current home and workplace behavior. This should be done in an environment of love, cooperation, and support among participants.

Done creatively, all of this will make managers aware that they are human beings with needs and feelings and that others are, too. Maccoby called this "the development of the heart."[23] A key is to create a learning environment in which mutual caring and nurturance are the norms. Managers must experience the emotional truth and desirability of organizations with heart.

The program should give them an assignment to perform — or better yet, have a senior executive give them one — that represents a difficult, long-standing human problem, such as how to rekindle employee loyalty following a period of massive layoffs. Then, by giving program participants mountains of feedback, teach them how to perform this task in such a way that everyone contributes evenly to the work of creating a project organization that fosters the human spirit.

Finally, the program must cultivate the skills necessary to set transcendent goals and teach the participants how to gauge the extent to which their organizations are now achieving them, the degree to which current organizational forms and practices aid or inhibit their achievement, and so on. Teach participants how to be consultants to each other in this process, too, so that a new network begins to form among managers who value cooperation, who know it can work, and who can foster it.

In our attempts to increase attention to spirituality in the workplace, we must keep in mind that nothing very worthwhile was ever accomplished by zealots and moralists. What I am trying to advocate here is gently helping individuals to discover their own uniqueness, and to find ways of attaching it to some endeavor above and beyond themselves. Let's develop and lead organizations that enhance life, taking the role of nurturing servants, gently guiding our organizations toward ever-closer approximations of everyone's secret ideal: a workplace in which we feel valued and loved, and in which we believe ourselves to be aligned with some great purpose.

Notes

[1] Thomas J. Peters and R.H. Waterman, Jr., *In Search of Excellence: Lessons from America's Best-Run Companies* (New York: Harper & Row, 1982).

[2] Ibid.

[3] Daniel Yankelovich, "The Work Ethic is Underemployed," *Psychology Today* 16:5 (1982), pp. 5-8.

[4] Michael Maccoby, *The Gamesman* (New York: Bantam Books, 1976).

[5] R.T. Pascale and A.G. Athos, *The Art of Japanese Management* (New York: Simon and Schuster, 1981).

[6] Gail Sheehy, *Pathfinders* (New York: Bantam Books, 1981).

[7] V.E. Frankl, *Man's Search for Meaning* (New York: Beacon Press, 1959).

[8] Maccoby.

[9] Erich Fromm, *To Have or To Be?* (New York: Bantam Books, 1976).

[10] Daniel Yankelovich, "Toward an Ethic of Commitment," *Industry Week* 209:6 (1981), pp. 62-66.

[11] Marilyn Ferguson, *The Aquarian Conspiracy* (Los Angeles: J.P. Tarcher, 1980).

[12] "Corporate Culture: The Hard-to-Change Values That Spell Success or Failure," *Business Week* (27 October 1980), pp. 148-160.

[13] See Ferguson.

[14] Ibid., p. 332.

[15] Yankelovich, "Toward an Ethic of Commitment."

[16] See F. Graves, "Are These Men Soviet Dupes?" *Common Cause* 9:1 (1983).

[17] Peters and Waterman.

[18] Pascale and Athos.

[19] R.A. Johnson, *He: Understanding Masculine Psychology* (New York: Harper & Row, 1977).

[20] W.G. Ouchi, *Theory Z: How American Business Can Meet the Japanese Challenge* (New York: Avon Books, 1981).

[21] "Project Update: Organization Alignment," *Gaia* 2:4 (1981), p. 7.

[22] Chapters 5 and 6 have elaborated on these concepts.

[23] Maccoby.

III.

WORKING WITH

TRANSFORMATIONAL DYNAMICS:

IMPLICATIONS FOR FACILITATORS

9

Consulting to Organizational Transformations

DAVID NICOLL

Comments on the Second Edition

Several years after I wrote this article, I happened on a poem by C.P. Cavafy that said much to me about seeing an organization's transformation as if it were a journey. The poem, entitled *Ithaca*,* begins:

> *When you start on your journey to Ithaca,*
> *then pray that the road is long,*
> *full of adventure, full of knowledge.*

My personal journey into organizational transformation has been a long one, an odyssey, in fact — one that has yet to find its own Ithaca. There have been a few Phoenician markets and Egyptian cities along the way, most notably my work with Apple Computer, Northern Telecom, and a small brick manufacturer named National Refractories, where, with my clients, I was able to form solid, productive partnerships. But for the most part, my transformational journeys have been difficult, filled with challenges that all too often have "raised up" my own Lestrygonian demons.

In part, my bedevilment has come about because too few ideas and concepts found here proved to be a good compass for transformational consulting. For example, in the article I describe a seven-step paradigm reframing process, and suggest that this "map" will help us intervene in an organization's paradigm reframing process. This has not turned out to be true. Experience has shown me that this map isn't fine-grained enough to point out useful leverage spots along the road.

Despite this glaring deficiency, however, the model is a good representation of the paradigm reframing processes that I've seen moving through my clients' systems. In particular, the Fertilization, Crisis, Incubation, and Diffusion stages are startlingly accurate portraits of the process that are catalyzed by paradigm reframing. But — and this is a huge "but" — knowing these steps, being able to identify them as they ooze their way through an organization, has not been of much help. In fact, it's been very difficult to help my clients see what I see. And even more difficult to get them to use this model as an aide in finding paradigmatic activity inside their own organizations. Too often, when using this model, I've felt like an English archaelogist with a Sumerian map, trying to point out travel highlights to a tour group full of Vietnamese.

On the margins, there are several discrete pieces of this article that have been valuable. As I said above, my description of the Fertilization Stage turns out to be an especially fine exposition on what happens inside an organization when new paradigmatic concepts first hit. Likewise, the idea that an external crisis is necessary to initialize an internal reframing process has proved to be accurate. And while I underplayed the nature of the last two stages, The Politics of Acceptance and Legitimization, by at least a factor of 10, nonetheless my observations on these two stages stand as solid descriptors of what must go on in an organization before a new paradigm becomes the dominant type of glasses through which everybody sees.

Finally, on the practical side, I do think I made one seriously helpful suggestion in this article, in the section entitled "Stopping Unproductive Work," where I propose that a useful thing to do when an organization is wrapped up in a major paradigmatic transformation is nothing. Absolutely nothing. I've come to believe that in organizations, paradigm shifts move like "the rhythms of an ocean's winds and tides" — and as a consequence, are useable but not controllable. Right now we know far too little about these shifts to intervene with surety and confidence. Consequently, while consulting I frequently see the transformation my clients are going through and know that the best thing to do is to help them ease up and enjoy the ride. What else can you do when their transformational ride is inevitably going to be like one of the roller coaster rides at Magic Mountain: scary from start to finish, and propelled by unstoppable momentum?

— David Nicoll

*R. Dalven, *The Complete Poems of Cavafy*. (Harcourt, Brace & Jovanovich, 1976).

Because of significant changes taking place in our culture, the paradigm reframing process is currently active in most of our organizations, moving people to either defend or transform their organization's world view. The purpose of this chapter is to offer ideas about how we can consult to such transformations. It does this by 1) describing the paradigm reframing process by which organizations transform themselves; 2) describing hypotheses concerning this process that can help us to identify it; 3) offering suggestions for consulting to organizations experiencing such transformations; and 4) suggesting new arenas for thinking and working in this field.

I n most organizations, we attend to visible, dramatic activities. Managers, employees, and consultants alike focus on policy conflicts, operational decision making, and the manufacturing of product lines. This is an appropriate focus, for organizations' survival depends upon the success of these activities. However, our bias in favor of these things, as well as our preoccupation with the rational and the well formed, leads us to overlook a more formative set of processes — herein called paradigm reframing — through which these dramatic activities become potent organizational concerns.

Paradigm reframing is the process that creates and supports an organization's dominant world view and, when necessary, carries a new paradigm into the organization for consideration and acceptance. This process is barely visible, and largely tacit; despite this, it underlies all policy debates, infuses decision-making, and interpenetrates operational procedures, producing for us the points of view that govern the visible and dramatic.

The most typical form of organizational transformation is the renewal that happens either in response to an organization's movement along its maturation curve, or in response to significant shifts in an organization's strategic environment. The change of an organization from a proprietary operation to a professionally managed business is an example of this kind of transformation, as is the reworking of an organization from a sales-oriented to a service-oriented firm. Both of these are "first order" shifts, taking place within our currently accepted definitions of organizational purpose, form, and function.

A "second order" transformation also exists. This kind of change encompasses transformations of purpose, form, and function that occur in response to and because of a paradigm shift in the wider culture. Here, the organization transforms itself because the culture that surrounds it is altering its presuppositional views of the world; the organization, in order to cope and remain legitimate, has to react and respond to these fundamental shifts in its definition of reality and truth. Our world currently is well into such a paradigm shift.

This chapter deals with this "second order" kind of organizational transformation. Because of significant changes taking place in the wider culture, the paradigm reframing process is currently active in most of our organizations, moving people to either defend or transform their organizations' existing world view. We need to know more about this process. The purpose of this chapter is to offer ideas and suggestions on how we can consult to such transformations.

THE PARADIGM REFRAMING PROCESS

Paradigm reframing is an organizational process. Like decision making or problem solving, it happens inside organizations. But unlike these other processes, it finds its impetus in the outside world. It takes place when one or more parties in an organization move to bring others to believe a new definition of reality. Metaphorically speaking, paradigm reframing functions as an organization "lathe," shaping and limiting peoples' perceptions of things, much as the rules of geometry shape and delineate peoples' architectural pursuits.

Paradigm reframing is a process that needs to be described in detail and understood in depth. To do this is not easy; as a process, paradigm reframing hides in closed offices, brief hallway meetings, and after-hours poker games. More important, it shrouds itself in presuppositions and assumptions, taking on — like the mime at a carnival show — many guises and disguises. Consequently, our first task is to sharpen our eyes and tune our ears so that we can identify the process when it occurs. Perhaps the best way to do this is to describe the stages of the paradigm reframing process.

As J.D. Thompson noted in *Organizations in Action,*[1] an organization is a composite of structural, technological, and conceptual activity. The conceptual dimension is the "system" in which the paradigm reframing process operates. The currencies of this system are ideas, both explanatory and visionary. This subtle, *sub rosa* use, growth, and change is both the task and the product of the reframing process. Working within this conceptual system, the reframing process moves through at least seven stages:

1. Fertilization
2. Crisis
3. Incubation

4. Diffusion

5. The Struggle for Legitimacy

6. The Politics of Acceptance

7. Legitimization

As with all stage models, this one is an artifact of (my) imagination. It is a useful artifact, however, because it provides guideposts for finding the reframing process.

Stage 1: Fertilization

The necessary precursor to paradigm reframing within an organization is the birth of a new paradigm outside it. Just any idea won't start the reframing process; it requires new ideas framed as presuppositions, assumptions, and beliefs that explain, rationalize, and define reality.[2] All organizations need perspectives that explain cause-and-effect situations, and visionary models that help people understand events, suggest modes of action, and give meaning to behavior. These kinds of cultural ideas, concepts, and symbols are the type demanded by the reframing process.

New ideas of this sort are necessarily part of a wider paradigm shift, and consequently enter an organization from the outside. They usually are picked up and brought in by individuals or very small groups living and working on the periphery of the system. It is on the edge of systems that consultants, researchers, and marketers take part in one or more of the following idea-producing activities:[3]

Cross fertilization involves the movement of ideas from one organization to another, or from the wider culture into the organization. Borrowing and adapting are activities that consultants, engineers, and researchers frequently use to generate new ideas for their organizations.

Invasion occurs when a new and particularly powerful way of looking at things sweeps an industry or a profession. For managers, "management by objectives" and "One-Minute Management" are stellar examples.

New technology historically has spurred the creation of new systems of thought. New machines, demanding new modes of organization, typically open new ways of thinking about the world. Classic examples are the automobile and the computer.

Pragmatic calculations are valuable sources of new ideas — particularly when current ideas don't work. For the manager in trouble, self-interest and predictable future benefits are a fertile source of ideas.

Play is behavior that is not serious but is nonetheless intensely and utterly absorbing. As such, it is important in creating new ideas, and in generating loose and relaxed thinking and associations. It is a particularly important vehicle by which new paradigms are brought into organizations.

Several years ago, while working with an environmental management group, I happened to find the organization's "hermit." Several people had told me of him, so I went looking. Literally on the back lot, in a trailer, I found Larry happily muttering over a piece of computer software, a simulation of the county's environmental situation. Needless to say, his perspective was strikingly different from those on "mahogany row." He was iconoclastic and somewhat acerbic in his approach, valuing "communal pricing" over decision making. I never did quite understand him, but our conversations suggested several rules that pertain to his kind of peripheral activity:

1. Organizations cannot easily incorporate new paradigmatic ideas into their daily activity without disrupting things, so they buffer themselves against truly novel concepts.

2. Organizations only tolerate these marginal areas and the people and ideas they harbor if they come in playful or innocuous forms.

3. When a new concept from the periphery becomes a "cause" for these "weirdos," or suggests itself unexpectedly from all sides, it will be held back from conscious attention, relegated to a kind of intellectual never-never land, or repressed. All too frequently, new perspectives are consciously and vigorously disconnected from action.

Stage 2: Crisis

The paradigm reframing process is not active all the time, everywhere, in an organization. As explained earlier, it is dependent upon changes in the paradigm of the wider culture. If the society's world view is in transition, then the reframing process will be active. If a culture's world view is stable, most organizations will be paradigmatically stable as well. Moreover, the reframing process needs a catalyst — usually a crisis — to begin.

Paradigm reframing begins when a disruptive event threatens the organization. If the event can't be handled, it sets up a demand for a new paradigm that will help explain the "glitch," diagnose the problems, and remedy them. In this context, "crisis" is any happening managers perceive as fundamentally incompatible with their prevailing notions of reality. An unexpected rhythm-and-blues solo from the lead trumpet during the New

York Philharmonic's playing of a Beethoven sonata certainly would be a fit example — especially if the conductor had cause to think it might happen regularly.

Stage 3: Incubation

Disruption does not immediately overturn an organization's established paradigm. A substantial time lag generally occurs between perception of a crisis, and reorganization of the organization's prevailing paradigm. This is because such a fundamental change is part of — and needs the support of — changes in the wider culture, especially in the organization's industry and its associated professions. This lag may be months or years, but gradually efforts to ignore a paradigmatic crisis will give way to a recognition of its existence, its disruptive nature, and the fallacies contained in customary ways of looking at the world. During this period, managers may become worried, confused, even hostile. Production modes will be tampered with again and again, while employees strike, form worker collectives, or ask for seats on the board of directors. Such acts signal widespread readiness for new paradigms of thought and action, and attention accordingly turns to the free, marginal areas within the organization. New ideas are now either permitted or pushed forward, beginning their move toward awareness, acceptance and "good currency."[4]

Stage 4: Diffusion

For a new idea to emerge as an "idea in good currency," it must claim widespread acceptance. Large numbers of people — or a few powerful people — must embrace it zealously. This aids its diffusion across the organization. At this point in our history, for example, certain ideas — the electric car, the environmentally controlled city, or the programmed transportation system — are beginning to diffuse broadly throughout our society. These ideas are better known than used; their familiarity exceeds their actual use. So too in organizations, where, for example, the concept of zero-based budgeting is much more widely known than used.

In this diffusion, an organization's communications systems play a central role. These systems impose public relations requirements on the reframing process, transforming the creative processes of *fertilization* into media events. In the *diffusion* stage, ideas and concepts that move in from the periphery are massaged until they become palpable and coherent. Only then can they be discussed and debated. No new paradigmatic concept or idea has ever been sold without being packaged (for example, as a proposal to the CEO), or hitting the "briefing trail," however fleetingly. "Catchiness" —

another public relations requirement — also shapes the acceptance of new ideas. The ability to express a concept in a phrase — "Medicare," "the war on poverty," or "guaranteed annual wage," for example — is critical to acceptance. Through such requirements, organizational communication networks both diffuse and transform new ideas.

All this was amply demonstrated to me at a medical center where I was consulting. A chief of service was deeply committed to pursuing holistic and preventive medicine in his department. He knew, however, that these concepts and their associated terms were an anathema to most of his colleagues. Consequently, we labored to find the appropriate terminology for what he was trying to do. He finally settled on "Healthwise" as the label for his efforts, and used this in his efforts to explain his ideas to his colleagues.

Critical in diffusion are the "idea brokers" — consultants, administrative assistants, and analysts — whose brokerage channels are the informal networks connecting segments of an organization. In these channels, new perspectives are adapted and translated as they pass from one subsystem to another. Idea brokers are as important to the diffusion of new ideas as an organization's decision-making systems.

In general, reframing activity is neither straightforward nor homogeneous at this stage. New paradigms diffuse through an organization like plankton, separate bits of a complete world view flowing with the tides and currents over broad areas of the system. They spread unevenly, depending on the susceptibility of subunits to a particular idea, and the varying permeability of these units to new ideas. This difference in permeability defines subcultural boundaries and exerts its own control over the ideas being diffused.

Stage 5: The Struggle for Legitimacy

A new presupposition becomes an "idea in good currency" when 1) it emerges as a perspective significant enough to explain events; 2) it influences policy determinations; 3) it begins to be used as a rationale for allocating influence or money; or 4) organizations begin to grow around it.

Once, in a problem-solving session, a medical director explained his interest in autogenic training as a treatment modality for cancer. "I'd like to experiment with this idea," he said. "It would only take a few thousand dollars for the training and the equipment, and I'm finally convinced it will save us quite a bit more. It's a mode whose time has come." Currency of this sort does not come with simple visibility; it comes with perceived utility and support from the broader culture.

The utility of an idea, however, is not necessarily manifest when it is broadly publicized and recognized. To gain the power to determine policy, explain events, or attract funding, paradigmatic ideas must compete with an organization's established presuppositions, concepts, and symbols. In particular, they must vie for legitimacy with older ways of "seeing," and the established work methodologies that reflect the organization's old views of causality, truth, and reality. To the extent that a new paradigm enters the public arena, it is threatening to the accepted conceptual system. It consequently stirs up conflict and then, like any young tough, it has to fight its way into the gang. Naturally, it finds itself in repeated battles as changing circumstances offer new opportunities to gain acceptance.

A new idea may enter the arena several times as an organization transforms. Even though it may die in one particular form, it can continue to influence the ideas that follow. In my career, "active listening" has had this kind of history, changing from "paraphrasing and perception checking" to "unconditional regard" and then to "assertive communication," all the while maintaining its empathic focus.

Stage 6: The Politics of Acceptance

It may already be obvious that some ideas acquire legitimacy long before gaining broad acceptance; other ideas may gain power and influence with one group long before they gain them from another. In my experience, the differences in the relative potency of concepts like "equity," "minorities," and "racism" demonstrate this, and suggest that what an organization seizes on as a potential idea in good currency depends largely on where in the organization we look, and on where professions and industries are in their general transformations.

Ultimately, the distinction between diffusion and legitimacy becomes blurred, for these stages are interrelated. Ideas spread as they become the center of controversy, gaining pockets of acceptance as they stimulate conflict. Diffusion and legitimacy feed on one another, as diffusion leads to conflict and conflict nourishes legitimacy. However, at some point in this ebb and flow, paradigmatic ideas with the potential for acceptance become political, eliciting champions and defenders. When this happens, the paradigm reframing process sharply changes character and enters the "political acceptance" stage.

The acquisition of a champion or defender usually happens when ideas become 1) overwhelmingly useful for understanding otherwise inexplicable bits of reality, 2) particularly helpful in generating action programs, and/or 3) likely vehicles through which people and/or agencies can gain or enhance their power. In organizations I've studied, ideas with this kind of power are staunchly held to and pushed with vigor. By defending or championing ideas, individuals establish significance for themselves, and spheres of influence for their departments. This phenomenon is commonplace in organizations — so commonplace that we call it "politics." In this context, it's fair to assume that championing good-currency ideas and performing the tasks of leadership are inextricably enmeshed with an organization's transformation.

Stage 7: Legitimization

To form a paradigm that shapes organizational performance, ideas ultimately need legitimization. They must become habitual and implicit in the thought processes and work routines of administrators, commissions, boards, and the like. The significance of this habitualness was brought home to me when a client, a patient-education unit, was struggling to set up a preventive health program. They couldn't get it just right at first, spending endless hours trying to find the right mix of services, staff, and budgets. Finally, in desperation, someone suggested that they take the term "patient" out of their designs, their writing, and their conversations. "Let's come at it a different way," was the suggestion. They did, settling on the term "client" as their new focus, and as they worked to incorporate this new term into their efforts, the structure, flow, and concept of their new program began to gel. Over a period of months, the right services, staff, and budget mix emerged.

This kind of habitualness does not come automatically; like riding a bicycle, it comes from repetitive trials. Ideas must be used again and again before they are perceived by their users as consistently producing the desired results. Only then is an idea on its way toward being firmly entrenched in an organization's cosmology. Only then will it become part of the organization's paradigm, tacitly shaping decisions, policies, and programs.

In summary, paradigm reframing is a process that begins at the periphery of an organization's consciousness. In hidden corners and dark closets, new ideas and points of view are generated, discussed, and massaged. Occasionally, a disruptive event (or, more likely, a sequence of disruptive events) damages or invalidates the prevailing definition of reality. This establishes a demand for ideas that explain new circumstances, or direct effective action; it also moves into the mainstream ideas that are already present in the organization's peripheral areas. The incubation and diffusion of these "new ideas" is mediated by people in special roles, and channeled through the organization by interpersonal networks and by the organization's communications media, all of which exert their own influence on the ideas themselves. These new ideas gain widespread acceptance through the efforts of those who push or ride them through the organization. The clashes created by the interplay of different perspectives, interests, and commitments announce the reframing process. As these new ideas approach centers of policy debate and political conflict, they become more powerful. Toward the end, the paradigm reframing process becomes more political, and the movement of new ideas goes hand-in-hand with bids for leadership. New ideas are taken up by people already powerful in the organization, giving these new concepts and symbols enough legitimacy to influence and determine policy issues. Ultimately, new ideas become an integral part of the conceptual apparatus of key actors, and the issues, concerns, and problems they highlight for these people appear obvious, important, and right. The organization and its actors have a legitimized definition of corporate reality.

BASIC HYPOTHESES CONCERNING PARADIGMS

Here I want to offer a set of propositions about paradigm reframing that highlight its more important characteristics. These propositions are designed to help us isolate our experiences with the process, and thereby understand its gestalt. Once understood, these hypotheses can be used as basic tests for identifying paradigm reframing as it occurs, and for expanding our knowledge of it.

There currently are eight basic hypotheses:

1. In any single organization there generally is room for only one paradigm, and only a few ideas in good currency. Most organizations can accommodate only one "world view."

2. The paradigm reframing process elicits for an organization two specific results: a) a socially accepted and legitimized paradigm, and b) associated "ideas in good currency." A paradigm is that set of precepts which defines the fundamental concerns of the organization. "Ideas in good currency" are concepts and beliefs (like "illness," "patient," "cure," and "doctors") powerful in the definition and formation of corporate policy and, naturally, an inherent part of a legitimized paradigm.

3. New ideas in good currency, ones that reflect and support new paradigms, move through the paradigm reframing process as sets of compatible, mutually- reinforcing ideas. They form an interlocking conceptual system, variations on a single theme, such as "decentralized health services," that is now in good currency in many medical systems.

4. Paradigm reframing generates and maintains implicit precepts about the fundamental cause-and-effect propositions governing an organization. In a hospital, for example, key concepts like "surgery," "pain," and "physician" exist, framing and evoking unquestionable actions.

5. Paradigm reframing establishes boundaries that define for people the scope of an issue, and identify modes of action to which an organization can and will devote its time, attention, and resources. General Motors doesn't treat paranoid schizophrenics; Bellevue Hospital doesn't build sedans.

6. Paradigm reframing is an exercise in emotional and affective judgment. Its function is to generate an unquestioned view of reality for the organization. Consequently, when active, the process is colored by ethical and moral tones. Activity here is highly charged. It also is abstract and characterized by philosophical debate.

7. The paradigm reframing process helps an organization alter existing concepts and visions that no longer accurately reflect the "real" world. The concept "illness," for example, no longer accurately interprets for doctors all the situations in which their medical practice places them — as, for example, when they are confronted with patients interested in autogenesis or homeopathy. In most medical care settings, the paradigm reframing process is at work building a new, more appropriate paradigm.

8. In organizations in transformation, paradigm reframing tends to emerge in relation to three salient concerns: a) the formation of enduring institutional perspectives and arrangements; b) the identification of a system's problems or issues; and c) the formation and legitimization of acceptable modes of action. Thus, given a paradigm shift in the wider culture that has an impact on an organization's industry and its professions, the reorganizations, plant and project start-ups, facilities designs, systems audits, budget cuts, and other similar tasks tend to be vehicles for the reframing process.

CONSULTING TO ORGANIZATIONAL TRANSFORMATIONS

Assume that the tools described above are available for our use. We can see the reframing process; we are able to identify its stages and recognize actors as they play in the process; we can perceive the products of the reframing process and know their influence as they emerge around us. What now? Our increased awareness offers several powerful choices:

1. Stopping unproductive work
2. Utilizing the process for beneficial ends
3. Supporting creative work on the periphery
4. Separating problem solving and paradigm reframing
5. Designing reframing events

Stopping Unproductive Work

Stopping unproductive work is a fruitful alternative. Awareness of reframing activities helps like aspirin with a headache — you feel so good when the hammering in your brain stops.

In 1982, I was off-site with an electronics firm. They were working on a reorganization that had been under review for several months and, while the sessions had been intense, we were, from my perspective, going nowhere. Suddenly, the manager for new product development stood, swept up to the board, and grabbed the pen. He wrote several figures, drew a couple of diagrams, and — after ending it all with a large exclamation point — said, "It's all so obvious; why can't you understand?" At that moment, my mind flooded with images from *Ivanhoe,* and I saw that standing before my eyes was a "knight" flush in the throes of a Diffusion battle.

Quietly, realizing that I'd been on the wrong track, I stopped consulting to their "problem solving" and nudged the meeting toward a break. During this pause I grabbed the manager and asked him, "What is it you're advocating?" After we talked, it became clear to both of us that he was asking for a leap of faith from his people. He had presuppositions about how electronics worked, and was assuming that this was reality for everybody else. We agreed that he would simply ask for this leap of faith, and we returned to the session, which went well.

Utilizing the Process for Beneficial Ends

Paradigms exist below an organization's level of consciousness, and therefore are neither examined nor understood. Most of the time they are not even recognized. They consequently impact everything. By introducing affective, moral judgments in cloudy ways and at particularly inopportune times, they add inertial weight to organizational change efforts. By implicitly injecting world views into discussions, paradigms make it difficult to build and validate appropriate models on an as-needed basis. And, by tempting managers to align with incipient trends and fads before they are legitimized, new organizational paradigms confuse and politicize things.

These dysfunctionalities keep a system from reaching its full potential, because in their cumulative effect, they lock organizations either into definitions of reality that have lost their timeliness or into unending, confusing conflicts.

Recognizing this, we have a choice about whether or not to attend to the problem directly. Of course, foolproof interventions are out of the question. However, it often seems useful to focus the system's attention explicitly on the paradigm reframing process. The dysfunctionalities described above spring from the implicitness of the reframing process. Therefore, amelioration requires recognition of the existence of the process and an acknowledgment that it is potent in the activities of organizational members. The patient-education and electronics firm examples cited earlier demonstrate the power of awareness. In the first example, awareness provoked a simple shift of terminology from one paradigmatic symbol ("patient") that was inappropriate, to another ("client") that provided a better fit, and this helped the staff find appropriate structures and concepts to finish their work. In the second example, the reframing process was contaminating the electronic group's problem-solving efforts. Awareness of this fact helped them drop back and design a process that accommodated a look at fundamental differences (in this case, related to the cause-and-effect logic embedded in the theories of electricity). When they settled these differences, they went ahead to finish their work.

Supporting Creative Work on the Periphery

Any effort to help an organization deal with its own transformation must address the key actors in the reframing process. The actors who occupy roles peripheral to the production process are the ones who need the most support. In this context, encouraging marginality, vanguard roles, and the brokers of ideas seems like a useful tack to pursue. "Benign neglect" probably is the best thing that can be offered to them. Much as one leaves a pot of tea in the sun to brew, organizations could encourage the "steeping" of ideas by building in cross-fertilization, reviews of new technology, and free-form play. Like a chicken farmer who provides a brooder, organizations could promote free areas that cultivate paradigms appropriate to their technologies and domains. A farmer doesn't hatch the eggs himself, but he certainly provides a place for the chickens to roost.

Separating Problem Solving and Paradigm Reframing

Separating reframing from problem solving and decision making is mandatory if there is interest in managing the conflict associated with organizational transformations. In most organizations, reframing penetrates and infuses problem solving and decision making in confusing ways. It makes rational review impossible, and it promotes subtle conflicts over turf. With important issues, or at crucial times, managers and consultants would be well-advised to sequence reframing and problem-solving activities, at least noting any paradigmatic issues before problem solving is attempted. In this way managers would be sensitive to paradigmatic conflicts in their work, recognizing that fights over reality definitions preclude effective problem solving. They also could get on with everyday business which, even during a transformation, doesn't stop.

Designing Reframing Events

Part of the reason why the paradigm reframing process is so confusing and conflictive is that, as I've said before, it is implicit. Organizational members have no models or guides for appropriate action. They have no conceptual or contextual frameworks for effective action in the reframing process, and they are unable to sort out for themselves, others, and the organization what a new paradigm requires. Therefore, they fall back on what they do know, which is "office politics."

Consequently, it seems that a good intervention — particularly during Fertilization, Diffusion, and the Struggle for Legitimacy, where events that bring people together seem to occur naturally — would be the conscious creation of "reframing events." These events would be special occasions convened for the purpose of exploring various aspects of a new paradigm, the similarities and differences between the old and the new paradigm, or the impact of a new presupposition on the structure and process of one or more aspects of the business.

Two kinds of events in particular seem relevant: assessing operational presuppositions, and scanning the environment.

Assessing Operational Presuppositions. Knowledge of reframing allows us, when we need or choose, to look for and test an organization's ideas in good currency. The ideas in good currency held by a police department in a decaying part of Los Angeles included concepts like "criminal" and "justice" but did not include others like "culturally disadvantaged" or "minority rights." Since the cosmology of their community embraced the latter two concepts, this police department often found itself in trouble. Several weeks of intense work helped improve police officers' communication skills, but did little to help them realize that their paradigmatic views of cause and effect were out of step with the community in which they worked. Their lives would have been much easier if they had had the willingness and the ability to step back and examine the base presuppositions they held about what caused crime. Not that they would have had to change their views; they could have easily supplemented them. But they couldn't stop and look, and they went on fighting among themselves and with their community over "right," "wrong," "the facts," "truth," and "causation."

Scanning the Environment. Relevance and timeliness are key factors in the functioning of base presuppositions. The essential question is, "Do our paradigmatic assumptions give us an accurate view of reality?" This being the case, an organization might consciously search its environment for signs of new paradigmatic concepts. If these concepts seem to hold promise, the organization could test their power to produce useful results.

In this vein, a hospital I know of found itself the owner of a store-front clinic in a midwestern city. Not knowing what to do with it, nor how it fit into their operation, they went on an explicit search for similar clinics, looking at organizational structure, budget formats, staffing patterns, etc. Unlike the police department just mentioned, they also spent considerable time asking interesting questions about paradigmatic issues. Their base question concerned assumptions made about patients, patient care, and service delivery. The answers they got from this survey encouraged them to turn this clinic into a "service center" that dispensed health care, preventive medicine, and hospital information services, something neither they nor anyone else in the region had ever done before.

NEW ARENAS FOR WORK

We are only on the threshold of work in the transformational arena. We need to explore new ideas and to develop new methodologies and interventions. There are three fundamental issues our age is bringing us that demand new methodologies:

1. We need improved capabilities for dealing with interactive, "nested" sets of problems. For years we have been concerned with an individual problem and its solution; but issues and problems rarely come alone. Even when single problems do exist, single solutions to them do not. Beyond this, my hunch is that many transformational problems will come as dilemmas and paradoxes. The issue is how to encourage action in the face of a transformational problem, dilemma, or paradox. Finally, the concept of a "problem pattern" needs to be dealt with, for my experience finds predictable sequences of problems occurring over and over again

in organizations undergoing transformation. We need models for promoting organization choice in such situations.

2. We need improved capabilities for simultaneously maintaining and adapting organizations. No transformation will happen instantaneously. Day-to-day business always will be present. Consequently, we need ways of doing business as usual and organizational transformation at the same time. We need to teach ourselves how to design systems that consciously learn.

3. Our old paradigm lent itself, indeed supported, the concept of ownership. Our new paradigm probably doesn't. The revolution of participatory democracy is still alive, and it is being supplemented by our emerging interest in appropriate human scale, cybernetics, and total systems. Together, these and many other concepts are giving renewed prominence to the concept of individual purpose and contribution, which in turn is changing our concept of the ownership of organizations. We need to explore the relevance of this issue, for we seem to be flirting with a presupposition that organizations belong to the public domain, like the beaches, the air, our water, and other fundamental things. As we move toward internalizing these concepts, the people who run corporations will have to begin to see their organizations as a part of the public domain, not subject entirely to private direction and the concept of ownership that seemingly underlies it. To ground this new perception in appropriate behavior is going to be a large task, for which preparation is needed.

CONCLUSION

It is appropriate to suggest that consulting to any organization's transformation will be analogous to trying to harness the tides and currents of this planet's oceans; both move as subtle yet incredibly powerful forces that, as of now, are beyond us. In observing both processes, it is prudent to conclude that these forces cannot be directly controlled or managed in any concrete fashion. However, knowing that these forces exist helps us to use them to accomplish previously undreamt-of things. Like the early sailor learning the rhythms of an ocean's winds and tides, our task is to discover enough to ride unpredictable forces respectfully, toward a distant yet desirable shore.

Notes

[1] J.D. Thompson, *Organizations in Action*. (New York: McGraw-Hill, 1967).

[2] For a fuller definition of a paradigm, and a description of the new one emerging in our culture, see Chapter 1, "Grace Beyond the Rules: A New Paradigm for Lives on a Human Scale."

[3] The ideas reflected in this section are adapted from an unpublished monograph by Dr. G.K. Jayaram titled "Creation of New Settings: A Dynamic Model."

[4] Credit is due Donald Schon for his concept of "ideas in good currency," for his explanation of the process by which they emerge, and for his description of the actors who play roles in the process. See Donald A. Schon, *Beyond the Stable State*. (New York: W.W. Norton & Co., 1971). These concepts, original with Schon, catalyzed my work on paradigm reframing and helped direct the observations and interventions that inform much of this paper.

10

A New Paradigm for Developing Organizations*

CHARLES KIEFER
PETER STROH

Comments on the Second Edition

Over the past fifteen years, we and many others around the world have had the good fortune to have applied the ideas introduced in this article with great success. As a result, we and they are even more convinced that "It is possible to create organizations that have the inspiration and ability to produce outstanding performance while enabling members to realize their highest aspirations."

During the same period, we have come to appreciate much more deeply the complement of Current Reality as a key driver in the creative process. Developing a clear picture of current reality increases personal mastery by establishing creative tension between vision and reality. Reality is still not a problem to be solved, but is the ground from which action emerges. Developing a shared picture of current reality also deepens alignment by enabling a group to experience what they want in relation to where they are. Finally, systems thinking, alluded to in the article only briefly, has proven to be a powerful tool for enabling groups to see current reality clearly and, as a result, to motivate and focus collaborative development.

So, for us, the ideas and methods have not only stood the test of time, they have continued to evolve. If you are reading this article for the first time, we hope you will find it reinforcing. If you are revisiting it, hopefully it will stimulate some deeper reflection on your own experience.

— Charles F. Kiefer
Peter Stroh

In this selection, Kiefer and Stroh discuss their work with innovative managers committed to the highest in both organizational performance and human satisfaction. Understanding their organizations requires a new framework that emphasizes fundamental yet frequently neglected variables of personal and organizational effectiveness. These variables include purpose, vision, alignment, personal power, structure, and intuition. The authors suggest a new paradigm for developing organizations, in which these variables assume primary importance, and some of the more traditional forms become secondary. This paradigm in turn suggests the development of new processes, and the authors describe new programs in leadership and team development they have conducted. The outstanding results provide a foundation on which to build additional new ways of thinking and acting.

Over the past five years, our work with innovative managers has led us to believe that it is possible to achieve the highest in both organizational performance and human satisfaction. The companies that have attained these levels have fundamentally altered our understanding of how a group of people can work together to produce astonishing results. We find employees energetically operating as part of a larger whole. Instead of exchanging their personal identity for an organizational identity, they have expanded their personal identity. Their personal identities are inextricably linked to a higher purpose to which they have committed their organizational selves. The organizations themselves seem to transcend preoccupation with their own survival, and instead exist to attain a unique vision of a better world.

Understanding these organizations requires a new framework that emphasizes fundamental yet frequently neglected variables of personal and organizational effectiveness. These variables include purpose, vision, alignment, personal power, structure, and intuition. They suggest a new paradigm for developing organizations, where these variables assume primary importance, and more traditional factors become secondary. This paradigm in turn suggests the development of new processes. New programs in leadership and team development are already being applied to both these and other organizations. The outstanding results provide a foundation on which to build additional new ways of thinking and acting.

CHARACTERISTICS OF AN ORGANIZATION CAPABLE OF INSPIRED PERFORMANCE

Organizations capable of inspired performance appear to have several key elements:

1. A deep sense of purpose often expressed as a vision of what the organization stands for or strives to create;

2. Alignment of individuals around this purpose;

3. An emphasis on both personal performance and an environment that empowers the individual;

4. Effective structures that take the systemic aspects of organizations into account; and

5. A capacity to integrate reason and intuition.[1]

The viewpoint that individuals and organizations can create the future and determine their destiny unifies these five elements. We call this viewpoint "metanoic," from the Greek word metanoia, meaning "a fundamental shift of mind." Most people look at the condition of their personal and organizational lives from a particular viewpoint. In its extreme form, this point of view is that "Things don't work, and there's nothing I can really do about it. I'm dissatisfied and stuck in a system too big, too unresponsive, or too complex to influence or control." By contrast, people in metanoic organizations recognize that, in some deep way, they are the organization. They know that they are responsible for both the quality of their personal lives and the organization; they believe that they can collectively create what they want, and shape their destiny.

A NEW PARADIGM FOR DEVELOPING ORGANIZATIONS

The characteristics of metanoic organizations suggest a new paradigm that places primary emphasis on the elements underlying these organizations, and secondary emphasis on more traditional variables. As shown in the following table, the two emphases are not mutually exclusive, but variables in column one have greater leverage than those in column two.

Personal and Organizational Effectiveness Variables Receiving Primary and Secondary Emphasis in the New Paradigm.

Primary emphasis	Secondary emphasis
Purpose	Goals
Vision	Solutions to problems
Alignment	Agreement
Personal responsibility and power	Influence of external forces
Results	Process
System structure	Individual behavior
Integration of intuition and reason	Rational analysis

Purpose/Goals

A deep, often noble sense of purpose is perhaps the most salient characteristic of metanoic organizations. Clearly, an organization's purpose or mission is the basis for any sound strategic planning.[2] But perhaps more important, a noble organization purpose provides both the opportunity for shared meaning among employees, and work that is personally meaningful.

The purpose of Kollmorgen Corporation's senior management is "to fulfill its responsibilities to Kollmorgen shareholders and employees by creating and supporting an organization of strong and vital business divisions where a spirit of freedom, equality, mutual trust, respect, and even love prevails; and whose members strive together toward an exciting vision of economic, technical, and social greatness." This strong and inspiring mission is reinforced by a philosophy that holds that "freedom and respect for the individual are the greatest motivators of man, especially when innovation and creativity are the intended results."

Managing according to this philosophy, the corporation has generally increased sales more than 20 percent per year for the past ten years (sales are now about $300 million), with turnover and absenteeism averaging less than two percent in most divisions. Additional examples are provided by Pascale and Athos in *The Art of Japanese Management*,[3] where they observe that "great companies make meaning" for their people. A similar study of excellent American companies by Tom Peters and R. Waterman[4] stressed the importance of an overriding purpose or superordinate goal to enable people to identify with their organization's culture.

The capacity of a highly valued organizational purpose to create meaning is matched by our growing individual need to have work that is personally meaningful. In a comprehensive study of changing American values, Daniel Yankelovich[5] described this as a grass-roots shift from an "instrumental" to a "sacred" world view. More and more people are seeking work that has intrinsic value beyond the creation of financial security. A clear sense of personal and organizational purpose can provide this deeper reason for existence and action.

For all its importance to strategic planning, organizational culture, and personal motivation, we frequently ignore purpose in favor of a more operational measure of direction: goals. Goals established without purpose, however, tend to allow hidden conflict about organizational direction and rationale to go unresolved. Equally important, goals can be achieved without the concurrent, deep fulfillment that comes from realizing a highly valued purpose. (See Figure 1.) Placing primary importance on purpose naturally clarifies basic direction. Goals are significant both for the traditional reasons, and because they establish benchmarks toward realization of the purpose.

Vision/Solutions to Problems

Because the full depth and meaning of a purpose cannot be wholly conveyed by the words of charters and mission statements, metanoic organizations use the vision of a desired future to represent and communicate their purpose. The vision embodies people's highest values and aspirations: for self-actualization, excellence, service, and community. It inspires people to reach for what *could be*, and to rise above their fears and preoccupations with current reality.[6]

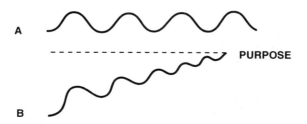

Figure 1. Purpose and goals.
Achieving goals without purpose (A) frequently produces elation (crests) followed by depression (troughs) until the next goal is identified and reached. The achievement of goals within the context of realizing a higher purpose (B) is less subject to emotional fluctuation. As each goal is reached, so too is fulfillment from realization of the purpose.

Kollmorgen holds the vision of a "diamond in the sky." The overall excellence symbolized by the diamond is further enhanced by the brilliance of its facets, each of which represents a company employee. Dayton-Hudson Corporation, a highly successful retailer, envisions itself as the "purchasing agent for its customers" and instills this sense of service throughout the organization. Cray Research, the manufacturer of the "world's most powerful computer," believes that its singular focus on this unique challenge motivates people beyond day-to-day problems, and is the key factor in its success.

By contrast, much organizational development (OD) practice, as exemplified by the action-research model, tends to focus attention on what is wrong with the present by treating current conditions as problems to be solved. This problem-solving approach has several limitations. Most important, getting rid of what you don't want is qualitatively different from creating what you do want. Second, solutions tend to be formulated in terms of what people think is possible, which results in performance that is limited by what people already know how to do.

A vision has the capacity to motivate people far more effectively than a precisely defined solution, because it is not bound by preconceived limitations. As an example, Fred Jervis, founder of the Center for Constructive Change, relates the case of two luxury hotels, serving the same market, that wanted to improve their repeat business, which was five percent.[7] He asked the managers of one hotel to choose a goal that seemed realistic for the problem at hand. They indicated that a seven-percent return rate would be a realistic increase, and subsequently achieved that rate. He asked the managers of the other hotel to set an ideal return rate goal; they envisioned a 55-percent return rate, and subsequently achieved 42 percent!

The leadership styles of former presidents John F. Kennedy and Jimmy Carter also illustrate the difference between the relative powers of vision and problem solving. Kennedy inspired many with his vision of a prosperous nation in a peaceful world. While his presidency is frequently criticized for its failure to solve many important problems, the vision he stood for is still remembered with respect. In contrast, Carter's engineering-like approach to political problem solving was perceived by the electorate as unclear and wavering.

The process of creating visions enables people to clarify and realize what they really want, independent of what presently seems possible. It encourages them to develop their visions of ideal reality, and then builds a bridge between the current and desired states.[8] Building the bridge may require problem solving, but the resultant solutions are likely to be less limiting, more effective, and more satisfying.

Alignment/Agreement

Metanoic organizations develop clarity of purpose and vision to catalyze *alignment* — the special condition wherein people operate freely and fully as part of a larger whole. Alignment is created when people see their organization's purpose as an extension of their personal purposes. People who are aligned identify with the organization and consciously assume responsibility for its success. They naturally support each other out of a recognition that "We are a part of the same whole."

To illustrate, consider a group of people within an unaligned organization (Figure 2-A). While people are generally moving in the same direction, which we could view as the purpose of the organization, they are somewhat unaligned, or pulling in different directions. By contrast, people in an aligned organization (Figure 2-B) pull in the same direction.

Alignment is not the same as people agreeing on where they are going. For example, a strategic planning session may produce agreement on organizational goals and individual objectives, generating a lot of immediate enthusiasm and commitment. Several months later, however — even though individuals are keeping their agreements — collective goals are not accomplished, people are dissatisfied, and there is a pervasive feeling that the organization is not working. In most organizations, people have fundamental *agreement* on organizational goals, and yet we still find these organizations lacking *alignment*. Alignment deals with the more inspirational aspect of organizational purpose and vision,

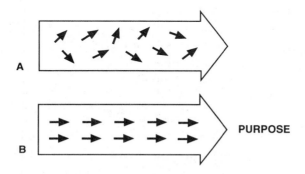

Figure 2. Alignment.
While people (small arrows) in an unaligned organization (A) are generally headed in the direction of the organization, they are pulling in individual directions. In the aligned organization (B), they all pull in the same direction, giving the organization momentum toward its purpose

while agreement deals with the mechanics of goals and objectives. People who agree are saying no more than "We share the same good ideas."

People in aligned organizations are more likely to keep their agreements with each other because of their deeply felt personal commitment to a common purpose. They also are more capable of both disagreeing about ideas, and resolving these disagreements because their commitment enables them to transcend their differences. In contrast, people in unaligned organizations tend to break agreements more easily because of an identification with self-interest.

The shift from agreement to alignment can produce tremendous results in an organization. For example, a project team in a company that builds automatic test equipment had worked unsuccessfully for two years to introduce an important new product. The new product development represented a significant challenge in that, for the first time in company history, it required engineers to design both hardware and software components. The challenge had frustrated the efforts of three vice presidents and three engineering managers; the most recent engineering manager had left to form a competing company, and taken the "best half" of the project team with him. While the remaining team members were still agreeing to accomplish specific tasks, their attitude was "I'll get my part done, but I don't think others will do theirs."

Steps we took here to develop alignment included facilitating people to take personal responsibility for the current situation, to define or redefine the project purpose, milestones, and ground rules, and to make three choices. These choices were to be true to their personal purposes, to support the project as redefined, and to complete the job with the existing team. When the people became aligned, their commitment expanded to "I'll get my part done, and I'll make sure that we all get the whole project done." The result was a 50-percent decrease in expected product development time, followed by stable volume production, and a record-breaking $7 million in new market orders six months after prototype announcement.

Alignment development is a primary strategy because it is an important precondition for building effective agreement. Once people are aligned, it is easier for them to make and keep the agreements necessary to achieve their purpose.

Personal Responsibility and the Power/Influence of External Forces

Metanoic organizations and others recognize that personal power, the ability to create what you want, is a critical factor in personal satisfaction and organizational effectiveness.[9] Consequently, in such organizations there is a conscious, heavy reliance on people to make meaningful contributions to operational results. Employees are placed in situations where the success of the organization depends on their performance. The commitment to people is also held somewhat differently than in most organizations. The focus is on employees' actual and perceived ability to influence company performance, rather than on individual comfort.

People in metanoic organizations believe that they can create their lives the way they want them. This belief is in their best interests because it encourages them to exert influence over both the problems and the solutions in their lives, and to establish new opportunities. Feeling responsible for their own destiny enables them to assume control of external forces, rather than to feel powerless before them. Mistakes, instead of being treated as failures, are seen as opportunities for learning. Any "outside" forces, including the boss, the organization, and the environment, are potential partners rather than obstacles to the creative process.

The perceived power and ability is translated into actual ability through traditional training and organizational policy and design. As an example of the latter, several metanoic organizations limit the size of divisions so all employees can accept personal responsibility for their actions and see their own contribution to the entire division's performance.

The effectiveness of this viewpoint is well demonstrated by the case of a large division in a highly traditional manufacturing organization. Operating within a non-growth market for discrete semi-conductor components, the division had lost money eight out of ten years, when a new general manager of one of the division's plants began to alter prevailing attitudes. The plant manager believed that "People can produce results beyond what is thought possible if given an opportunity to fully express themselves and be responsible for their collective productivity." He instituted a variety of methods for encouraging self-expression focused on plant productivity, including actively-managed suggestion systems, brief but frequent meetings at all levels, and extensive opportunities for managerial and personal growth training. Through such additional activities as customer line tours, graphic displays of progress on key goals, and acknowledgments for truly outstanding performance, he made people believe that their actions mattered — that they personally could make the difference in overall results. Within a year, the division was operating at a profit. It has been making money ever since, and profits over 10 percent have become standard. Turnover and absenteeism have also declined dramatically.

By contrast, people in many organizations feel that they do not make a difference. They see themselves as victims of external forces beyond their control. This is true at the individual level (subordinates feeling controlled by

Figure 3. Personal power.
Any steps to develop the capacities and abilities of individuals in an aligned organization (A)
contributes directly to organization results. In an unaligned organization (B), any steps to develop
people's individual power often exacerbates underlying conflict.

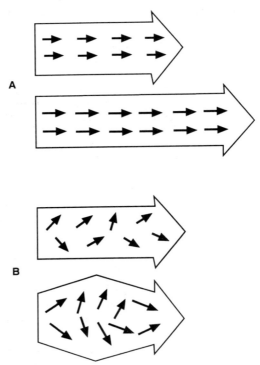

their boss), at the department level (managers feeling manipulated by other departments), and at the organizational level (executives frequently blaming competition, government regulations, or the economy for corporate failings). This "powerless" point of view pervades the organization and easily becomes a self-fulfilling prophecy. For example, a manufacturing department may feel burdened by a growing number of engineering change orders. Rather than providing the engineers with a better understanding of how manufacturing works, this department fills the orders while privately complaining that engineers do not know what they are doing. The lack of useful feedback to engineering results in still more change orders, and a greater sense of powerlessness on the part of manufacturing.

Aligned organizations particularly value personal power, because when people are fundamentally committed to the same direction, the increase in their individual power increases the total power of the organization (Figure 3-A). By contrast, increasing personal power in an unaligned organization tends to increase organization conflict and thereby create additional dissatisfaction and failure (Figure 3-B).

Results/Process

Because they recognize the power of people to achieve what they focus on, metanoic organizations place primary emphasis on results rather than on the processes for achieving results. Any process that is effective and consistent with the higher values embodied in the organization's purpose is considered appropriate. Moreover, these organizations acknowledge that it is impossible to determine the "right" process in advance, because the environment is inherently complex and unpredictable. Hence, they stress experimentation: Do something and adjust it, while always focusing on the desired result (Figure 4).

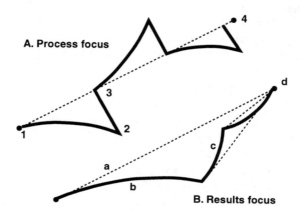

Figure 4. Focusing on results.
When people who place primary emphasis on process (A) identify a desired result (4), begin to work toward it, and find themselves off course (2), they frequently try to get back on the original course (3). In other words, they attempt to use the original process, instead of focusing on getting to the desired result from where they are. Results-focused people (B) realize that reaching the desired goal (d) without deviating from the original process (a) is an exceptional occurrence. When they are pulled off course (b), they change course (c) toward the original desired result, rather than returning to the original process.

In contrast, OD developed as a profession in which process was the major expertise. It grew, in part, out of a reaction to scientific management's emphasis on results — an emphasis that seemed to belittle and dehumanize people. OD practitioners have tended to develop and overemphasize particular processes (such as T-groups, team building, and quality circles) rather than focusing on the higher results such processes were intended to serve. Moreover, many practitioners did not recognize that process obsession tends to produce more and more process. For example, T-groups developed positive feelings, and an awareness of how people function in groups, that often were not translated into action. As a result, many managers have come to view OD as a "soft" profession not aligned with their interest in results.

The strong humanistic values sought by a focus on process are more effectively realized by focusing on the purpose and vision that embodies these values. People then naturally seek results consistent with these values, provided they have the opportunity to experiment in creating processes to achieve those results.

System Structure/Individual Behavior

Inspired, high-performing organizations evolve organizational structures appropriate to their vision. They recognize that vision, alignment, and personal power are quickly dissipated in a poorly designed organizational structure (Figure 5-A). In contrast, well-designed structures, policies, and procedures allow the individual energies developed by alignment and personal power to effectively translate into collective results (Figure 5-B).

It is generally recognized that structure influences behavior; thus, restructuring an organization is a common intervention.[10] We typically limit our structural interventions, however, to several traditional elements, such as authority, role relationships, and reward systems. Moreover, we tend to treat these elements independently. For example, we try to introduce quality circles into a highly authoritative organization. We have largely ignored the majority of underlying interdependencies in a complex organization.[11]

A more common problem is that many people forego structural change in favor of less effective interventions designed to change behavior directly. For example, human resource development departments generally devote more resources to training designed to alter individuals' behavior than to developing the organization. Behavioral change is emphasized because it is easier to understand and manage. When role ambiguities or conflicting policies hinder a person's ability to succeed, but are not recognized or cannot be influenced, managers often blame poor performance on personal incompetence.

Figure 5. Organizational structure.
Often, structures and policies are not clearly thought out (A), and people become frustrated. Consistent sets of structures and policies (B) allow individual effort to effectively translate into collec-

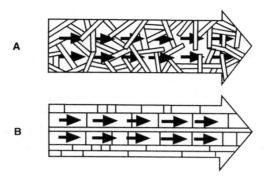

Leaders of metanoic organizations tend to work with organizations as complex, whole systems. They recognize that:

1. Organizations atrophy when they lower their goals to match substandard performance, or become too dependent on outside intervention.

2. Effective action often involves worsening short-term behavior prior to long-term improvement.

3. There are many places to intervene to try to effect change; however, only a very few places will produce system-wide movement in the desired direction. Moreover, such leverage points are often obscure and far removed from the obvious symptoms.[13]

Underlying the principle of leverage points is an appreciation that the best way to manage complexity is to create simplicity. Frequently, this results in a highly decentralized structure guided by a central source. In Kollmorgen, an organization of about 4,500 people, the corporate staff numbers 25, including secretaries, while the remainder work in divisions closely connected to the marketplace. This arrangement integrates clear overall direction and philosophy with a highly responsive, responsible, and productive group of local units.

When leaders appreciate the organization as a complex system, they are more likely to seek flaws in organization design than to search for scapegoats, and to incorporate many structural elements into an overall design that promotes strong individual performance.

Integration of Intuition and Reason — Rational Analysis

The final characteristic of these organizations is their use of intuition as well as reason. Intuition plays a vital role in creating the organization's vision, developing alignment, and thinking about organizational design. The source of a captivating, workable vision lies in the underlying purpose of the enterprise combined with insight into the future. Intuition mediates this purpose and insight. Intuition is equally important for alignment; highly aligned people function in easy, almost unconscious, synchronization with each other. Furthermore, organization leaders use intuition extensively to understand and design structures. At the same time, reason helps reinforce or test intuitive conclusions, clearly communicate the basis for decisions to others, and design the processes by which decisions can be best implemented.

The observation that intuition contributes significantly to organizational performance is supported by studies suggesting that successful executives use intuition more effectively than other managers.[13] The executive's need to make difficult decisions in a complex and changing environment demands the use of intuition, which can gain access to information not usually available to the rational mind, and process it in an inductive, non-linear way. When too much information can be as paralyzing as too little, intuition helps identify truly essential information. Intuition also works quickly, which is important since executives devote a short time to most decisions.[14]

By contrast, rational analysis alone cannot cope with the magnitude of existing complexity and change. Respected management scientists are sometimes the first to acknowledge the limitations of their approach. Even highly-regarded management constructs such as the "7-S" model introduced by Pascale and Athos[15] fail to explain precisely how key variables should be integrated. Leaders develop a unique interplay between intuition and reason. They use intuition to guide their analysis, and they continually subject their intuitive insights to rational examination.

TWO APPLICATIONS OF THE NEW PARADIGM

Over the past four years we have incorporated this new paradigm into programs for leadership and team development. Participants have included senior executives, influential managers, and product development groups. Many of the participants were people who already had proven ability to achieve results, and wanted to realize a more comprehensive organization purpose. The results have been excellent, in terms of both quantitative and qualitative impacts lasting two years and more. We offer them to encourage others to design the new paradigm into different technologies, such as management by objectives or conflict resolution, and perhaps to create entirely new approaches to personal and organization effectiveness.

One program is an advanced seminar for senior executives on the art as well as the mechanics of leadership. It is designed to develop the abilities that leaders of metanoic organizations have to:

1. Create and communicate a personal and organizational vision to which they are wholeheartedly committed.
2. Catalyze alignment around a common vision.
3. Revitalize and recommit to the vision in the face of obstacles.
4. Understand an organization as a complex system whose structure may enable or thwart realization of the vision.
5. Empower themselves and be the sort of people whose presence empowers others.
6. Develop intuition as a complement to reason.

Participants achieve several results in this course. Some build on their current success to develop strong commitment to a new direction. Others rediscover and reaffirm an old vision that they had lost in details and everyday pressures. Many get their jobs done with greater ease, with increased ability to inspire and empower themselves and others, to better understand and work with complex forces in their organization, and to be more intuitive. Finally, people who have never fully appreciated the reasons for their own success learn to transfer what they know to new situations and other people.

The second program is an in-house training and consulting program for management and other functional groups who want to excel in achieving a common task or purpose. This program deepens the alignment of group members around a common purpose, develops their personal effectiveness, and enables them to create structures that translate their individual energies into collective results.

The program includes many familiar techniques integrated in a certain format: developing agreement on a common purpose; identifying strategic objectives necessary to achieve the purpose; clarifying roles and role relationships; decision making; and managing meetings. It also includes new processes designed to deepen alignment, instill personal responsibility, and empower group members individually and collectively.

Where operating results are measurable, participating groups report increased sales of more than 50 percent per year, and 50 percent reductions in time invested in new product development. They achieve improved working relationships and higher personal satisfaction that last for two years and more. Finally, evaluations conducted prior to and six months after formal completion of the program indicate an average increase of 33 percent in such key performance indicators as role clarity, problem-solving and decision making effectiveness, and cooperation.

The new paradigm works, and clearly merits further experiments and applications.

SUMMARY AND CONCLUSIONS

It is possible to create organizations that have the inspiration and ability to produce outstanding performance while enabling members to realize their highest aspirations. These results naturally emerge from placing primary emphasis on several potent variables: purpose, vision, alignment, personal power, results, system structure, and the integration of intuition and reason. While challenging traditional emphases on problem solving and process, the new paradigm also opens new doors to realizing what is more important to us as practitioners.

Knowing that we can create what we truly want, each of us has the opportunity to rediscover and reaffirm our own vision of organizational greatness. Rather than burdensome problems to be solved, current organizational circumstances can be viewed simply as indications of how far we have come in the creative process. We can use our vision and the new paradigm to accelerate this process. Obstacles become vehicles for learning, rather than enemies that destroy our efforts.

We can support others in organizations from a new perspective. We can, as one CEO said, "teach people how to build a new City Hall, not just cope with the old one." This may involve engaging people in the process of creating a vision. It may require working with many complementary visions, and helping people discover the common purpose that aligns them. We can support people to believe that they can create what they want, reach for what they truly value, and take personal responsibility both for their vision and for existing circumstances.

Understanding that a vision without foundation is only a daydream, we must ensure that the vision is grounded in clear action steps with measurable outcomes. We need to work systemically and focus on results. We can help communicate our organization's purpose and values to employees, incorporate management philosophy into the training process, and bridge the key gaps between organization purpose and practice. We can also design new organization and management development approaches using the new paradigm, always ensuring that each new process serves a higher end.

Within every organization lies the potential not only for success, but also for greatness. As practitioners, our commitment to the highest in ourselves and others remains the vital difference in nurturing this greatness into reality. Guided by this vision, every technique becomes a vehicle for infusing spirit, rather than simply a mechanism that succeeds on its own. More than anything else, spirit enables people and organizations to produce results in ways consistent with our most deeply held values.

Notes

[1] See Chapter 5, Charles F. Kiefer and Peter M. Senge, "Metanoic Organizations."

[2] See P.F. Drucker, *Management: Tasks, Responsibilities, Practices* (New York: Harper & Row, 1973). See also R. Beckhard and R. Harris, *Organizational Transitions: Managing Large Systems Change* (Reading, Massachusetts: Addison-Wesley, 1977).

[3] Richard T. Pascale and Anthony Athos, *The Art of Japanese Management* (New York: Simon and Schuster, 1981).

[4] Thomas J. Peters and Robert H. Waterman, *In Search of Excellence: Lessons from America's Best-Run Companies* (New York: Harper & Row, 1982).

[5] Daniel Yankelovich, *New Rules* (New York: Random House, 1981).

[6] See D. Berlew, "Leadership and Organization Excitement," *California Review* 17:2 (1974), pp. 21-30.

[7] Reported by D. DeLong, "Changing the Way We Think," *Boston Globe*, 10 February 1981.

[8] See Russell Ackoff, *Creating the Corporate Future* (New York: John Wiley & Sons, 1981).

[9] See, e.g., Rosabeth Moss Kanter, *Men and Women of the Corporation* (New York: Basic Books, 1977).

[10] J. Galbraith, *Designing Complex Organizations* (Reading, Massachusetts: Addison-Wesley, 1973).

[11] See "Development in an Era of Paradigm Shifts, Changing Boundaries, and Personal Challenge: A Dialogue with Robert Tannenbaum," *Training and Development Journal* 36:4 (1982), pp. 32-42.

[12] D.H. Meadows, "Whole Earth Models and Systems," *CoEvolution Quarterly* 34 (1982), pp. 98-108.

[13] See L. Schroeder, S. Ostrander, D. Dean and J. Mihalasky, *Executive ESP* (New York: Prentice-Hall, 1974). See also R. Rowan, "Those Business Hunches are More Than Blind Faith," *Fortune* 99:8 (1979), pp. 110-114.

[14] See H. Mintzberg, "The Manager's Job: Folklore and Fact," *Harvard Business Review* 53:4 (1975), pp. 49-61.

[15] Pascale and Athos.

11

Myth, Transformation, and the Change Agent

CHANDRA STEPHENS
SAUL EISEN

Comments on the Second Edition

It has been more than a decade since we wrote the paper on mythology, transformation, and the change agent, and we appreciate this opportunity to reflect on what we wrote then. What has changed in our world, and how, in this new context, do we now see the role of the change agent?

Several large and small myths that were then either in embryonic stages or just below the surface seem to us to have emerged and crystallized; others have changed dramatically. One of these is certainly the collapse of the USSR and the consequent reduction (at least for now) in the threat of a nuclear holocaust. A second development is globalism — the awareness of the Earth as a whole system, within which jobs, worker populations, capital, and information are distributed and moved around to achieve various economic or personal goals. Along with this global linking of resources comes the growing awareness of interdependence — that we all really live together in a very small lifeboat. A third development is the frenzy of re-engineering and downsizing of organizations, spurred perhaps by the new competitive pressures of the global environment, but leading all too often to what some have called "dumb-sizing," due to the loss of seasoned, experienced staff and to the collapse of loyalty and trust among employees who survive the blood baths. A fourth is the proliferation of computer technology and networked global interconnections, evoking metaphors like "electronic superhighway" and "global nervous system." A fifth, as we approach the year 2000, is a growing sense of transition from one age to another. In corporate environments, vast sums are being spent on modifying computer systems so they will understand that "00" refers to the year 2000, not 1900. At the level of human experience, there is the feeling of impending — even foreboding — change. Some psychotherapists are jokingly using a new diagnosis: "PMT" (pre-millennial tension).

In a charming and incisive analysis, Walter Truett Anderson has characterized the transition we all are experiencing in terms of the social construction of reality. While large myths — or in his terms, social constructions — have been changing since the dawn of civilization, the current shift seems to be a second-order one: not just from one belief system (or myth) to another, but to a new belief system about beliefs — one that acknowledges that human societies consensually create beliefs. "Reality," he concludes, "is not what it used to be." In organization development, David Cooperrider and Suresh Srivastva have pioneered a change strategy called appreciative inquiry, based on the premise that organizational participants can transform the workplace by co-constructing it on the basis of their highest visions, rather then by focusing on problems.

In several recent papers, Saul Eisen has built on these ideas, as well as *gestalt* psychology, and especially the human systems perspective pioneered by Bob Tannenbaum, articulating a comprehensive framework for understanding the role of the change agent:

When members of human systems (relationships, teams, organizations, etc.) experience difficulties and decide to ask for help, they tend to present the figure situation that is troubling them, and for which they have despaired of finding a solution. The work of consultants is most aptly defined in terms of the assistance we may provide members of the client system to regain awareness of the ground within which that figure has emerged, and then to facilitate processes that generate new ways of construing and working with the figure situation, the contextual ground around it, and the relationship between the two. This is the essence of the Human System Redesign process.

As change agents, then, we are called upon to trust and support the self-organizing and evolutionary dynamics of human systems as they resolve the tensions between small, middle-sized, and large myths. When we are true to this task, we catalyze profound transformation.

— Chandra Stephens
Saul Eisen

The fundamental transformation of individuals, organizations, and cultures requires new understanding and skill on the part of the change agent or facilitator. The emerging emphasis on transformation denotes a quantum leap in the scope of our practice. We are learning to acknowledge the significance of beliefs, archetypes, and myths, as well as their nested structure within the operating mythology in the larger society. This perspective provides a new meta-framework for our work. It may be that as we move toward transformational work with our clients we are participating in transformational change in the larger culture.

We are creatures of our own myths. What we think is what we are and what we create. The context, myths, and environments that we place ourselves in tend to determine our behavior, attitudes, and self-concept. As a society, we are in a crisis of vision in which our institutions and organizations are lagging woefully behind the evolutionary challenges of energy, population, food, political power, and so on. This is creating a real split between our personal, psychological, and mythic experiences, and the consensual reality with which our societal structures demand that we daily contend.

The myths and beliefs by which we live are necessarily an interface between personal experience and cultural norms.[1] They explain what is real. When we bring a set of beliefs to any given situation, that is the lens through which we perceive and experience it. Thus our beliefs become "real," and we integrate that "evidence" into our minds, programming ourselves habitually to experience similar future situations through the same belief-structure lens. The intensity and structure of our beliefs, reinforced by our "experience," set up a resonance field that then sets off "sympathetic vibrations" in others. Thus, we reinforce and even amplify similar beliefs in those around us.

Rupert Sheldrake[2] postulated a revolutionary and revelatory new theory about the basis and structure of reality. Very simply put, he suggested that all manifestation is brought into being through the influence and direction of what he called morphogenetic fields — fields of resonance beyond the confines of space and time. These "M-fields" organize the structure of reality — genes, memories, trees, laws of physics, etc. — into habitual or usual ways of being. M-fields can be changed by a different resonance being brought to bear upon them. Nothing is absolutely determined; it is possible to change anything. This theory provides a conceptual basis within which to understand how our thoughts and belief structures influence reality.

COMPETING BELIEF STRUCTURES

If we lived in a stable and homogeneous society, the question of belief structures would be unimportant. Although each generation within any culture must be taught to perceive and believe the consensually accepted way, in a stable society those beliefs are more or less homogeneous. A few mavericks and philosophers push the boundaries, but the vast majority contentedly conform to the general view. However, we are now living in a decidedly transitional era, and our belief structures are constantly colliding with each other, to the general discomfort of almost everyone. What has worked in the past simply works no longer as we move from an industrial to an information society. The discomfort becomes even more acute when we take an even larger perspective and see that the majority of the world's population still operates from an agrarian economic base, and hence from that consequent belief structure. Yet, many nations yearn to enter the industrial age (with its world view) just when others are struggling to give birth to a post-industrial society. Furthermore, the influence of mass telecommunications media, multinational corporations, and the threat of global nuclear holocaust transcend traditional geographic and political perspectives.

This global situation brings belief and power structures to bear that are not indigenous to the culture they affect. They have not evolved out of the culture, and so are not grounded in the deep unconscious mythic understandings of the local society. This must unintentionally yet decisively widen the gap between competing belief structures. These multifarious world views and belief structures do not mesh gracefully.

The mythic level is the next step beyond belief structures. It takes hard and soft "facts" that we have attempted to measure, codify, or understand, and places them into a broader context of values, attitudes, and a larger purpose. This leads to ways of understanding that are created from and based on our belief structures, and which, as they become more pervasive in the culture, take on the quality of myth. Myth is the story that we tell to explain the nature of our reality. It is a whole picture constructed out of the particular pieces of our attitudes and beliefs. Myths become our touchstones to what is "real," and what is "important." They encompass the most basic, fundamental, and ultimate. They are the "truths" to which we look when trying to decide how we should conduct our lives, what we should actually do, and how we should think and feel.

CONGRUENCE OF MYTHIC LEVELS

One of the most difficult incongruities faced in every society is the conflict between mythic levels, between the small myth and the large myth. The small myth asserts what is everyday, tangible, practical, and explicit (e.g., going to school to prepare for a future job). The large myth encompasses overall pattern and background, is usually abstract and implicit, and provides the context within which the small myth is played out (e.g., being aware that the world population is exploding, thus increasing competition for everything). If the small myth and the large myth are congruent, there is little discomfort in the system. If they are incongruent, however, there is a flashing back and forth between the larger and smaller mythic realities where neither can be experienced as wholly real, and great dissonance is felt. Examples of this are our continuing patterns, both culturally and personally, of consumption and economic expectations. The small myth is that if we just work harder or "luck into" the right job, which pays a huge salary, then we can buy our dream house, have our sailboat, travel to our heart's content, etc. This myth is uncomfortably nested in the larger myth of increasing scarcity of resources, changing economic bases, pollution of the environment, etc. This, of course, always has been true in any culture, to some extent. Death — the largest myth — always has been the background against which we play out our daily lives — the smaller myth — and therefore the human condition, to one degree or another, always has had to contend with mythic dissonance.

Yet stable societies have necessarily encouraged as much congruence between mythic levels as possible. Our times have just increased the complexity of competing realities. Through education and telecommunication, we are not only aware of the incongruities in our own personal lives and cultures, but we are usually at least tangentially aware that other cultures experience a similar magnitude of incongruity. When the smaller myth collides with the larger one (e.g., studying for the future while believing you'll be killed by a nuclear bomb), mythic dissonance sets in and the mind retreats to a lower order of integration. Unless the person can find a way to disengage from habitual/cultural modes of thinking/believing and develop a new lens — new large and small myths — the level of personal and societal functioning diminishes. Thus, the discomfort of a smaller myth colliding with a larger myth becomes either an evolutionary or a devolutionary (regressive) catalyst.

The societal and attitudinal context within which we experience this clash of mythic levels influences how we process and react to it. The prevailing social attitudes subtly and explicitly direct us toward either struggling to find new conceptual boundaries and new myths to live by, or closing down our minds to new ideas. This has very practical implications for personal, organizational, and social planning. The attitudes we bring to a situation really matter. The social environments and support systems in which we choose to put ourselves really matter. Referring back to Sheldrake and his morphogenetic fields, the resonance created by the prevailing small myths in relation to the larger, implicit ones constellates what actually happens in a life, organization, or culture. Thus, it behooves us to examine and to be aware of the nature of mythic structures — and whether or not they are congruent — in any system we engage.

MYTH AND THE CHANGE AGENT

On the organizational level, the vision of executives and other organizational participants affects the prevailing resonance to lean toward new ways of being or toward status quo and regression. If the environment resonates with fear, negativity, scarcity, or deception, it will strongly influence the individual to feel defensive, narrow perspectives and to become manipulative with others. Some individuals, by their own choices, can focus themselves to not succumb to the general resonance, and they can move beyond it; it is not easy. Individuals within an organizational or societal context can choose which larger myths to focus on and align with, and thereby extend the power of choice within small myths.[3]

The usual stance when experiencing mythic dissonance is to fixate on the small myth and disregard the large myth. In order to manifest on the individual, particular level (e.g., manufacture a product or love an individual person), we need to be able to focus on the particular, to act from the smaller myth. Trying to act in specific ways from the perspective of the larger myth can lead to very messy manifestations, if the smaller myth isn't taken into account (e.g., we're living under the threat of nuclear annihilation and must put all our energy into stopping it, so we'll worry about earning money for this month's rent later). Similarly, taking only the smaller myth into account and disregarding the larger one leads to a very limited scope of action and experience (e.g., all that matters is meeting the production schedule, or paying this month's rent) and sets the stage for the larger myth being relegated to the unconscious. This, of course, is a set-up for the larger myth to sabotage whatever we try to do within the smaller scope. Therefore, it is essential that we have the capacity to hold simultaneously both the large and small mythic perspectives. We need to be able to hold the specific focus so that we create what we intend, yet we need to detach from the limitations of immediate concerns and see the larger whole.

Part of the dilemma in which we find ourselves is that we know the old forms do not work, but the new forms haven't emerged yet. We are still operating within the institutional structures and attitudes which were appropriate for the industrial society, and we are trying to do a relatively superficial overlay of the new perspectives n the old structures. This does not lead to very satisfying results. We now have a newly emerging, larger mythic context within which to act, but we have not yet developed specific ways — smaller myths — that are appropriate to this context. Yet, still programmed by the old industrial myth that we must do something, we all madly try to do just that.

CREATING THE NEW MYTHS

Ruben Nelson,[4] a Canadian futurist, has discussed the crucial need for individuals and society to be responsible for what we do. Good intentions are not enough — we can't get ourselves "off the hook" that easily. In order to heal or transform, we must first accurately diagnose a situation and then carry out the appropriate intervention. While the new small myths (e.g., consensual decision making) are slowly beginning to emerge, the prevailing resonance is still based on the old myths of hierarchy, competition, and scarcity.

One way to begin dealing with this dilemma is to identify very closely the myths at work in our own lives, and then in the social institutions with which we are involved. Both individually and later with groups and organizations, we can identify the issues, events, problems, and people that have the most positive and the most negative intensity for us. As this list emerges, we can use our metaphoric faculties to recognize patterns and groups of issues that are related. Then it will be time to become storytellers. We need to weave a mythic story out of those related, emotionally charged issues to see what form they take, and whether they are large or small myths. This transition from personal identification to the epic proportions of mythic stories helps us to disengage from the emotional charge of the moment and to move to a more transcendent perspective,[5] thus changing the prevailing resonance. The most constructive approach that we can take as agents of transformation may be to become identifiers and teachers of the new myths. We need to actively, internally struggle with the ambiguities, paradoxes, and conflicting world views, grapple with the larger myths, but avoid acting prematurely. We need to ferret out the ways old myths dominate us. We can teach people in organizations what we are beginning to understand about myths and how they affect us, and we can help them to recognize and identify their own operational myths.

We are all beginners in this new way of being. No one has been here before. As individuals, we need to learn to have an impeccable awareness and understanding of the mythic contexts in which we operate. Setting up study groups to provide supportive resonance for this learning process can help. We are the myth-makers, identifiers, and disseminators. We can do this without giving in to the temptation to particularize specific forms prematurely. This is a time of seeding and sowing, not a time of harvest. We can try different approaches with each other, create networks, struggle, work, laugh, and be patient. It is important to trust and honor the process of evolution. We see some of the big picture — the large myth — but the small myths require time to sprout and flower in their season.

Notes

[1] See O.W. Markley and W. Harman, *Changing Images of Man* (New York: Pergamon Press, 1982). See also F. Polak, *The Image of the Future*, trans. Elise Boulding (San Francisco: Jossey-Bass, 1973).

[2] R. Sheldrake, *A New Science of Life: The Hypothesis of Formative Causation* (Los Angeles: J.P. Tarcher, 1982).

[3] M.B. McCaskey, *The Executive Challenge: Managing Change and Ambiguity* (Marshfield, Massachusetts: Pitman, 1982).

[4] R.F.W. Nelson, *The Illusions of Urban Man* (Ottawa: The Ministry of State for Urban Affairs, 1978).

[5] Jean Houston, *Life Force* (New York: Dell, 1980); Jean Houston, *The Possible Human* (Los Angeles: J.P. Tarcher, 1982).

IV.

TRANSFORMATIONAL

TECHNOLOGIES

12

Achieving and Maintaining Personal Peak Performance

JOHN D. ADAMS

One is limited when one is conscious of limitation.
— Hazrat lnayat Khan

One who wants to become that which one is supposed
to be must leave that which one is now.
— Meister Eckhart

Comments on the Second Edition

During the almost 15 years since this chapter was written, things have speeded up immensely. Cycle time reduction has become a priority in many industries — most notably the high-tech electronics industry — as an essential focus for maintaining a competitive edge. Products, such as a new line of computers, are designed, developed, introduced, marketed, and "end of lifed" in less than a year. Those who cannot sustain high performance in such environments are encouraged to move to other lines of work.

Magazines such as *Fortune* and *Business Week* chronicle the breakthrough achievements of the high fliers in business in every issue.

On reflection, I trip over the idea that now, more than ever before, companies are taking whatever level of performance they can engender from their employees; and if someone burns out along the way, they are cast aside and replaced with a younger and more vigorous replacement part. I have little evidence that the average corporation, in the U.S. at least, has any interest in nurturing and sustaining its human resources. The message seems often to be "Bring your body and most of your mind into the workplace — that's all we are renting from you. Leave your spirit and emotions in your car!"

When this chapter was originally written, the average difference between the salary of the CEO of a large corporation and the front line employees was 47 to 1. At this time, 15 years later, the discrepancy has risen to over 200 to 1. Following the leveraged buyout fad of the late 80s and the reengineering drive of the early 90s, a large portion of the workforce is today somewhat cynical about their employment, and more willing than at any time in the past to advance their own personal situation by quitting and moving on to another company. After being treated as pawns in a drive for shareholder equity over the last decade (with the senior executives of most profit-making companies having huge holdings of their company's stock), loyalty to the firm is understandably rather low in many corporations.

So today I have some ethical issues with teaching people to achieve and sustain high levels of performance, and I will continue to have them until the whole person is invited to work in companies that make long range sustainability of both the workforce and the larger "economic engine" a priority.

It is still true that every individual performs to an unwritten "script" or pattern. With enough exploration, one can not only find the qualities that drive her or his high performance, but one can even identify the generic sequence which one tends to follow — usually unconsciously — whenever one is generating outstanding results. It also is still true that workgroups have analogous high-performance qualities and patterns.

Identifying these qualities and patterns can be a very valuable discovery during periods of rapid change when high performance is called for. For example, it is not possible for a rapidly growing company to close down its business while it expands into new quarters and adopts new technology operating tools and management practices at the same time. In order to sustain high levels of performance during such a transition, knowledge of one's innate high performance qualities is as necessary today as it ever was.

— John D. Adams

Organizations undergoing transformation need to evoke high levels of performance from their employees, both individually and as work groups. Personal Peak Performance is explored as a function of the individual's belief systems and her/his level of well-being. Both PPP's and belief systems are thematic with each individual, and techniques are described for helping people to identify these themes. Techniques are also presented for assessing the level of well-being. With awareness of this information, one becomes more able to achieve and to maintain higher-than-normal levels of performance.

S weeping social, economic, and ecological factors are increasingly interacting with each other around the world, pressuring organizations to make fundamental changes in how they relate to both their employees and their environments. These fundamental changes in organizational outlook and organizational behavior are entering management thinking with the title of Organization Transformation (OT). Just as organization development (OD) has evolved to help organizations develop toward their potentials, OT is evolving today to help these same organizations undergo needed fundamental changes in their very natures.

The transformation of an organization's fundamental purpose and outlook requires that its individual members must also undergo some very basic changes (or personal transformations). Indeed, it could be argued that a "critical mass" of individual members need to undergo personal transformations before their organizations can undergo system-wide transformation. Organizational systems, through their formal practices and procedures, and through their informal norms and myths, steadfastly attempt to maintain the status quo. To alter that status quo, it is necessary for individuals to perceive and act in new, perhaps unfamiliar, ways.

With increasing turbulence, transience, and complexity in our society, both organizational and individual excellence will be at a premium. High Performing Systems, as described by Peter Vaill[1] will be at an advantage. These High Performing Systems will need to attract and keep members who are able to evoke and maintain their own Personal Peak Performance (PPP).

The focus of this chapter is on PPP and on two of the factors I view as critical for achieving and maintaining PPP: individual belief systems and whole-person wellness. The chapter will be of interest to anyone who is experiencing the transformative pressures mentioned above. It also should be of special interest to would-be facilitators of OT, for whom personal transformation is a prerequisite to serving as a key resource to organizations and organizational members experiencing transformations. For these practitioners, the chapter provides both guidelines for their own personal work, and suggestions for working with others.

THE REALM OF ORGANIZATIONAL TRANSFORMATION

The dynamics of achieving and maintaining PPP can be embedded in an overall framework for Organizational Transformation. As can be seen in Figure 1 on the next page, this view of OT emphasizes interactions among the organization and its purposes, the organization's external environment, and the individuals who populate the organization. Each of these domains —

Figure 1. The realm of organizational transformation

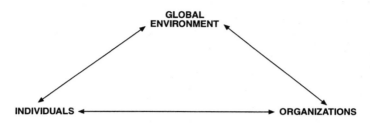

organization (system), environment (suprasystem), and individual (subsystem) — influence and are influenced by the other two.

Figure 2 adds detail to Figure 1, providing a performance focus to the interaction. The environment provides an overall performance ethos which, at least in the United States, encourages people to do their best and rewards organizations for superior productivity. This performance ethos has arisen from a variety of myths about the moral virtues of hard work and persistence. Similarly, the prevailing "world view" suggests that performance will reach its peak if people will use the scientific method and logical analysis to understand situations and solve problems. Many argue that this world view is giving way to a more systems-oriented, holistic approach to understanding and problem solving — reductionist to expansionist; analysis to synthesis; deterministic to teleologic.[2] This new paradigm will surely generate new myths about performance and alter the performance ideal, or ethos, in our culture.

Transitions occurring in the global environment are, to some extent, being generated by organizational successes (*e.g.*, technology) and excesses (*e.g.*, acid rain). In turn, these sweeping changes are exerting tremendous pressures on organizations, leading to the decline of many traditional "bread and butter" industries and the meteoric rise of new, high-technology industries. Both decline and rapid growth create tension. As is well known, organizational systems tend to be persistent in their form and function. Their internal norms (the unwritten rules or expectations about "correct" behavior) and myths (the "oft-told tales") provide both status quo maintenance and membership boundaries on an informal level. The organization's procedures and "rituals" provide the same pressures for persistence on a more formalized level.[3] Equilibrium is maintained without much difficulty until external pressures for change arise from the environment and/or from organization members. When this happens at a significant level, system performance falters until new internal procedures and rituals are adopted that are more in

Figure 2. The realm of OT—performance focus

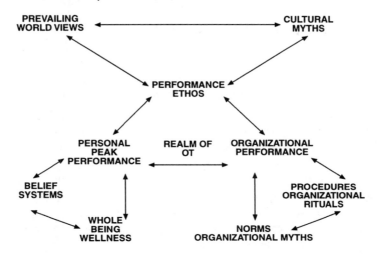

tune with the times. The norms and myths can be expected to provide a continuing drag or resistance to these needed changes. The myths will change very slowly unless they are worked with directly to speed their adaptation.

No organizational system can perform at its peak unless enough individual members are willing and able to perform at their peaks. Even if the organization's norms, myths, rituals, and procedures are aligned with its purpose (assuming the purpose is clear), individual performance may not be high. The performance ethos provided by the external environment may work against performance (*e.g.*, "I work in order to afford the play style I want, and no harder"), as may the person's own level of well-being and basic belief systems. Poor physical health can impair performance, as can underutilization of capabilities and the absence of emotional and spiritual supports. Likewise, personally limiting beliefs such as "I am an innocent bystander in the universe," "We must restore the good old days," and "I am inferior" have an obvious adverse effect on one's performance.

PERSONAL PEAK PERFORMANCE

Over the next few decades, organizations will highly value people who can achieve and maintain excellent, or peak, levels of performance. While much work needs to be done with organizational and work team variables that have a clear effect on people's performance, this alone will not be sufficient.

Attention must be paid to individuals, and support must be provided to facilitate their personal transformations.

Let us first explore the nature of PPP. I have asked participants in a large number of seminars and workshops to describe what the experience of PPP has been like for them — how it feels and some of the defining conditions. The words most often used to describe PPP have been: energized, totally focused, enthusiastic, exhilarated, inner peace, attuned, confident, resonance, powerful, alert, flowing, and automatic. Such feelings are closely aligned with Abraham Maslow's notions about peak experiences.[4] It may be that PPPs are nearly always accompanied by peak sensation or emotion; however, the reverse is not necessarily true.

Based on my own and others' explorations, I have identified six conditions that evoke and sustain excellence in performance. These six conditions, as seen in Figure 3 below, are not innate and can be learned or adopted by anyone. Unfortunately, many organizations today operate in ways that stifle many of these conditions.

Commitment

One condition that is common to several explorations is a strong sense of commitment. A University of Chicago research team[5] found that a high level of commitment protected people from the adverse effects of high stress levels and heavy workloads. Vaill[6] similarly hypothesized that large investments of both "time" and "feeling" are necessary ingredients if one wants to generate high levels of performance in a work group. In interviews with over 1500 peak performers, Charles Garfield found primacy of internal goals and intrinsic rewards

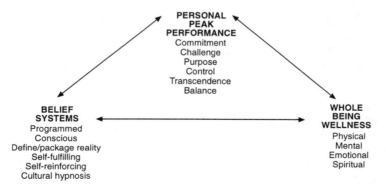

Figure 3. Some key considerations in achieving and maintaining personal peak performance

---

CONDITIONS THAT STIMULATE PERSONAL PEAK PERFORMANCE.

Commitment
— Investments of feeling and time
— Primacy of internal goals and rewards

Challenge
— Moving out of comfort zone
— Developing worst-case scenario and
  taking calculated risks
— Focusing on results, not perfection
— Mental rehearsal of desired outcomes

Purpose
— Clear and accepted focus for effort

Control
— Balance of autonomy and direction

Transcendence
— Overcoming self-limiting beliefs
— Focusing on process, not barriers

Balance
— Work and nonwork
— Time for family and friends
— Regular relaxation habit
— Managing stress and protecting health

---

was a widely shared characteristic.[7] Garfield's peak performers also were working on tasks they cared a great deal about.

Challenge. A second major condition for stress resistance and peak performance identified by the University of Chicago team was a sufficient level of challenge. Garfield also described his peak performers as continually moving out of their "comfort zones" to take calculated risks. When peak performers are faced with a challenge, they consider the implications of failure and ask themselves, "Can I live with them?" If the answer is yes, they move ahead. Garfield also found that peak performers meet challenge by focusing on results (rather than on being perfect) and on solutions to problems (rather than on placing blame). Finally, Garfield found that peak performers use imagery in a focused way to mentally rehearse the various facets and feelings associated with the challenge.

Purpose. A third condition for maintaining excellence in performance is purpose. Several chapters in this book emphasize the importance of working with a clear sense of purpose, and Peter Vaill[8] has suggested that alignment with a clear focus or sense of purpose is necessary for maintaining high levels of performance. Peak performers need to know what the mission or purpose behind the performance is, and they need to agree that it is the right one.

Control. A fourth condition identified by the University of Chicago team is sufficient control over our approach to a task. This means having enough discretion to exercise our judgment, while not being left without guidance or standards. Garfield found that his peak performers regularly both sought and provided a balance of autonomy and direction, to provide the appropriate amount of control in any given situation.

Transcendence. A fifth condition that Garfield found common among peak performers was the person's drive to transcend previous performance levels. Our presumed limits are usually erroneous and rooted in self-limiting beliefs. Regular peak performers are able to concentrate on the process of functioning, and not on artificial barriers. For example, the four-minute mile was once widely believed to be an insurmountable athletic barrier. Shortly after track star Roger Bannister transcended his own previous performance — and this "barrier" — many other milers began to break the barrier.

Balance. A sixth condition for sustaining excellence in performance, balance, is further explored below in the section on whole-being wellness. Garfield found that his peak performers were hard workers, but they were not workaholics. They maintained a balance between work, family, friends, and other pursuits. They knew how to relax and to take steps to manage their stress and protect their health.

CONSCIOUSNESS OF PERSONAL PEAK PERFORMANCE EXPERIENCES

Our experiences of PPPs are not lost in our unconscious, but are filed in a perhaps forgotten part of our consciousness. Thus, we can bring them forward for investigation. When we do, we discover that our PPPs cluster into themes. If we become aware of the thematic nature of our past PPPs, of the described feelings accompanying PPPs, and of the basic conditions necessary for them to occur, then we become able to consciously evoke peak performances. A second characteristic of this consciousness raising process is that on different occasions — perhaps reflecting different emotional states — we are likely to recall different experiences of peak performance, and to discover new themes. Thus, recollection should be undertaken periodically, rather than being viewed as a "one shot" activity. Awareness of the thematic nature of our PPPs can help us to identify our "vocation," or core purpose in life.

An Activity: One very good way to bring these PPPs forward is to divide your life into significant periods. The periods you select will be different from those selected by others. Once this has been done, spend about 15 minutes reflecting on the PPPs you can recall from each of the identified periods. Some PPPs may occur in more than one period; some periods may not yield any PPPs (a significant event for you to ponder, should this occur). Stay with the task even if you feel finished, for some of the most significant PPPs are recalled after "plateau" periods. Try to avoid self censorship. After 15 minutes, review the recollections in a search for themes. This process is enhanced if you work with one or two partners, since the feedback/helping process often uncovers new material for both the helper and the helpee.

After the review is complete, continue together to explore how, when, and where PPPs might be consciously evoked both on and off the job.

Two factors that affect our PPPs are the level of overall well-being, and the nature of our personal beliefs. If we choose to work toward whole-being wellness, and if we work to alter or replace self-limiting and self-defeating beliefs, we can further enhance our prospects for evoking PPPs.

WHOLE-BEING WELLNESS

Obviously, limitations in our physical, mental, emotional, and spiritual well-being can inhibit our evoking PPPs. Conversely, it is likely that high level well-being can enhance the level of performance possible. Thus, efforts to enhance overall wellness are important. Most illnesses these days are caused by a multitude of factors that interact in complex ways. These factors include stress, the environment, our genetic predispositions, our previous health experiences, the nature and quality of our health care, and our daily lifestyle choices.

The U.S. Center for Disease Control in Atlanta estimates that the risks to one's health are about 20 percent biological, 20 percent environmental, 10 percent medical care, and 50 percent lifestyle. The majority of the risks to our health are determined by our everyday choices about how we live.

The primary issue in health protection, then, is to address those factors that are controllable (lifestyle plus portions of the environmental and medical care risks). The following list contains measures to control risk factors generally recognized by public health educators:

- Nutritional habits — avoidance of sugar, salt, fats, white flour and rice, and caffeine; plenty of complex carbohydrates
- Moderation in the use of alcohol
- Not using tobacco
- Not using drugs (including prescription drugs)
- Sufficient restful sleep
- Regular relaxation/meditation habits
- Regular exercise (aerobic, stretching, and recreational)
- Recommended body weight
- Positive psychological outlook
- Good personal relationships

- Seatbelt use and safe driving habits
- Moderation and self-control of Type A Behavior[9]
- Control of blood pressure and cholesterol
- Avoidance of unnecessary stressors and effective coping with unavoidable stressors
- Healthful and appropriate expression of emotions.

Numerous studies have shown that the more of these habits we practice, the better our day-to-day health will be, and the longer we can expect to live.[10]

Unfortunately, during prolonged periods of high or peak performance (as well as during periods of high stress), many of us give up these positive health habits. The periods when we most need to protect our health are the very times when we ignore controllable risk factors. Fortunately, there is a way to tell how much the high performance period or other stressors are "getting to us." The following list itemizes some of the most frequent "strain" symptoms I have identified — indicators that the risks to our health are rising to significant levels:

- Feel slow, sluggish, weak
- Tire easily
- Rapid weight gain or loss
- Gastrointestinal problems
- Difficulty in concentrating
- Changed eating patterns
- Smoke/drink more than usual
- Sleep disorders
- Headaches, stiff neck and shoulders
- Nervous, apprehensive
- Depressed
- Irritable, easily angered
- Cynical, inappropriate humor
- Withdrawal from supportive relationships

These conditions are warning signals, and the first step to protecting and enhancing our well-being is to become sensitized to our own unique strain symptoms. Second, we must reflect on the controllable risk factors, especially as the strain symptoms become manifest, and make improvements as needed.

An Activity: First, review the symptoms of strain listed above. Make an assessment of how many you currently or recently have been experiencing. The more you can identify with, the greater the present risks to your health. Second, see if you can find those symptoms which regularly occur as early warning signals for you among the items on the strain list. It is very important to know what these are and to pay attention to them when they occur, since they are biofeedback messages telling you that your body is likely to break down soon if you don't begin doing something differently. Third, go back to the list of measures to control risk factors, and make an appraisal of your present life style. Identify potential projects for improvement. Finally, honestly answer these seven questions:

1. Are there present situations in my life that I should avoid or unhook from?
2. How, and how well, am I coping with unavoidable stressors?
3. Am I making responsible choices to reduce unnecessary risks to my health?
4. What am I doing well that I should continue doing?
5. What should I be doing less of, or stop doing?
6. What should I be doing more of, or start doing?
7. What kinds of support, guidance, or direct assistance do I need? From whom?

These four steps — overall strain assessment, identification of warning signals, overall risk factor assessment, and responding to the seven questions — are suggested as an effective way to protect and enhance your overall level of well-being.

When needed changes are identified, one is often inclined to attempt all of the desired changes at once. This usually does not work, since the magnitude of the needed changes, when taken all at once, often becomes overwhelming. A more successful approach is to take relatively small actions one step at a time. This approach, of course, makes whole-being wellness into a life-long learning process.[11]

An important dimension of whole-being wellness is our beliefs about health and well-being. Basically, if we believe ourselves to be "well", we will be "well." In their ongoing work with cancer patients, for example, Carl Simonton and Stephanie Matthews-Simonton[12] have had some major successes and some major disappointments in using self-hypnosis and visualization techniques in conjunction with more traditional modes of treatment. One of their conclusions is that visualization activities work if the patient believes they will work, and they do not work if the patient does not believe. The next section explores this critical dimension.

BELIEF SYSTEMS

Just like past peak performances, our belief systems are contained in our conscious minds, and are therefore directly accessible. This permits us to easily bring them forward in our consciousness for review and possible change.

To further extend the idea that our beliefs have a direct effect on our health, consider the case of mass hysteria and the use of placebos to successfully treat certain symptoms. During late 1982, several people died after taking over-the-counter pain relievers that someone had intentionally contaminated with cyanide. These poisonings received a great deal of coverage in the media, and virtually everyone in America was well aware of them. Shortly after this, a spectator at a high school football game became ill after drinking a soda. As a result of the widespread poisoning anxiety, about 200 other people attending the game — who had drunk the same kind of soda — exhibited poisoning symptoms and were hospitalized. The symptoms of several people were so severe they remained hospitalized overnight for observation. No poison traces were ever found in the soda.

If our beliefs can have this effect, they certainly can have equally powerful positive effects, if we can understand the process better. Our beliefs also directly affect our performance since they define our reality for us. They help us to focus and to relate to the world, and they provide boundaries on what we are sensitive to, cutting us off from a great many alternatives. For example, if one believes oneself to be systematic, logical, analytical, and thorough, one is likely to be a good problem solver who never overlooks details. The limitations that accompany such beliefs are that one is likely to overstructure, to draw premature boundaries, to be rather inflexible, and to resist contradicting information. As another example, if one's beliefs are intuitive, spontaneous, holistic, and relativistic, one is likely to be able to find the meaning behind situations and to step back and see the broader issues. The limitations that accompany such beliefs are that one is likely to be impulsive, ungrounded, and impatient with structure. Clearly, each system of beliefs has its assets and its liabilities as related to performance. With awareness of the self-limiting beliefs we hold within our belief systems, we have the opportunity to alter them, or to add new beliefs, in order to reduce our limitations and enhance performance.

What Are Beliefs?

Put most simply, a belief is something that one accepts as true without needing supportive evidence. It is a statement of fact one makes to oneself. Beliefs, however, do not constitute reality, though we usually take them for reality. They are only statements about reality. They cause us to filter out or transform certain information from all that is available to us, and they package our experience.

We are utterly convinced by our beliefs. While every belief we hold has served a useful purpose at some time, it is likely that we each hold beliefs that we no longer use. If we do not examine our beliefs from time to time, we become increasingly limited by those beliefs that no longer serve a useful purpose.

Initially, our beliefs come to us as messages from our environment (especially during our preadolescent years), which receive continual reinforcement. The environment, of course, is the culture in which we are socialized, complete with all of its myths and rituals. Thus, to a very great extent, we are hypnotized by our cultures. As we grow up, our patterns of conscious thought reflect our beliefs. These patterns are made more conscious by our "self talk" — our inner dialogues, which serve both to reflect and to reinforce our beliefs.

If our experience runs counter to one of our beliefs, we are likely to have an emotional response. For example, if one is habitually angered by rush hour traffic and by long lines at the bank and the airport, it may be because one has the (unexamined) belief that one should never be made to wait. Thus, another way to become conscious of our beliefs is to pay attention to those things that regularly trigger emotional responses in us.

Beliefs Are Self-Fulfilling and Self-Reinforcing

Our experiences may not always follow our desires, but they do reflect our beliefs which, as statements of reality to ourselves, are strongly self-fulfilling. They provide a constant and powerful hypnotic suggestion, causing us to acquiesce to any idea that is reinforced by our own self talk, and to reject any idea that runs counter to it.

One commonly experienced example of this is whether or not one expects to learn something from a given "educational" event, such as a lecture or a group discussion. Those who come to the event with the expectation that they will learn something new nearly always do. Those who expect it to be a waste of time nearly always find that it is. If members of either group are "surprised," it is because there is another (also unexamined), competing belief operating.

Collective Beliefs

Our families, our organizations, and our communities all operate to reinforce a "correct" system of beliefs. Since we must react from the frame of reference of our own beliefs, we resist changes in beliefs that others in our family, organization, or community make. We either try to get the person or organization to revert to the old collective belief, or we reject them.

These collective beliefs tell us what is "good" and what is "bad," what is acceptable and what is unacceptable. The more strongly we accept the collective beliefs and receive reciprocal acceptance, the better we feel. For example, there was once (and still is, to a certain degree) a collective belief in the United States that the most successful, influential, intelligent, and wealthy people are males whose families originally came from a few European countries. People who did not exhibit these characteristics (women, blacks, Latinos, Native Americans, Asians, etc.), but who did accept these collective beliefs about themselves, seldom experienced success, influence, "intelligence," or wealth. Instead, they often experienced depression and frustration, and they perennially accepted a second-class position in the society. These groups generally have not "progressed" in the U.S. culture until they have collectively altered their beliefs to be more supportive of their own characteristics.

Collective beliefs in an organization are reflected by the myths of the organization. As Harrison Owen[13] points out, these collective beliefs, as expressed in the myths, have a strong effect on the performance of both the individuals and the overall organization.

Of many possible futures, the one that does occur will be a manifestation of interacting collective belief systems operating around the world.

Changing Beliefs

The first step to changing our belief systems is awareness. Inaccurate and self-limiting beliefs continue to be accepted until we examine them and make an effort to change them. Since we often can see beliefs in others they cannot see in themselves, it is helpful to examine our beliefs in an interactive setting.

In formal hypnosis, we accept the hypnotist's reality and suspend our own beliefs. Subjects have readily developed blisters on their arms in response to a hypnotist's suggestion that they have been burned. In order to "dehypnotize" ourselves, we must first learn to hypnotize ourselves intentionally. To change a belief means to work against messages from authorities, the patterns of our thinking, our "self talk," and our emotional triggers. Thus, we need to assume the authority of the hypnotist ourselves, to visualize new beliefs and to create intentional self talk.

Clearly, with unexamined beliefs, the power is in the past and beyond our control. When we examine and work with our beliefs, the power is in the now, and under our control.

An activity: To increase your awareness of your belief systems, you must first get in touch with the consistent messages you received in late childhood — roughly between the ages of eight and twelve. Allow yourself to become relaxed and attentive and then spend several minutes recalling messages you once received from each of these sources: parents, teachers, friends, significant others (e.g., grandparent, neighbor), the "community," and role models. In some cases, messages may not arise in your awareness so much as images of the actual people. Exploring what these people represent can help identify further messages.

The second place to look for beliefs is in recalling the really significant events that have occurred since childhood, since your recollection process is also focused by your beliefs. Third, make a list of those situations that regularly trigger emotions (joy, anger, excitement, depression) in you. Fourth, make a list of the most frequent topics in your self talk, or internal dialogues. It is this self talk that reinforces beliefs and makes them persistent. Finally, imagine what the future will be like, and list the images that come to mind. Our expectations and predictions also are strongly influenced by our beliefs.

With these five lists, you are now ready to look for themes and, out of these, to list your basic beliefs by looking at the themes contained in the lists. This step is often most effective if done with another person, since both of you are likely to discover additional beliefs from the sharing process.

After you have established an awareness of your basic beliefs, you can easily review them with a focus on your overall wellness and on your personal performance. You undoubtedly will find that some of your beliefs contribute to your wellness and/or to your performance, and that others detract from them.

Finally, as you become aware of beliefs you wish to change, identify actions you can take to validate new, more desirable beliefs.[14] Establishing new, deliberate self talk messages can be most helpful. Developing clear visualizations that represent the new or altered beliefs is also important. For example, if I conclude that one of my beliefs is that "I am not an effective public speaker," and if making formal presentations is a necessary aspect of my job, I can begin to alter this belief by identifying some safe ways to practice making speeches. I can begin telling myself "I am an effective speaker." I can visualize myself making a superb presentation. This visualization can be enhanced and made even more effective by actually rehearsing the body language part of the speech in front of a mirror.

Notes

[1] See Peter B. Vaill, "The Purpose of High Performing Systems," *Organizational Dynamics* 11:2 (1982), pp. 23-39.

[2] See Russell Ackoff, *Creating the Corporate Future* (New York: Wiley, 1981); F. Capra, *The Turning Point* (New York: Simon and Schuster, 1982); Marilyn Fersuson, *The Acquarian Conspiracy* (Los Angeles: J.P. Tarcher, 1980); John Naisbitt, *Megatrends* (New York: Warner Books, 1982).

[3] See Chapter 13, Harrison Owen, "Facilitating Organizational Transformation: The Uses of Myth and Ritual."

[4] Abraham Maslow, *Eupsychian Management* (Homewood, Illinois: Richard D. Irwin, Inc. and The Sorsey Press, 1965).

[5] M. Pines, "Psychological Hardiness: The Role of Challenge in Health," *Psychology Today* (December 1980), pp. 33-44.

[6] Vaill.

[7] See E. Larsen, "Why Do Some People Outperform Others? *The Wall Street Journal* 21 January 1982; E. Larsen, "Why Are Some Managers Top Performers? *The Wall Street Journal* 21 January 1982.

[8] Vaill.

[9] Meyer Friedman and R.H. Rosenman, *Type A Behavior and Your Heart* (New York: Knopf, 1974).

[10] See, e.g., N Belloc and L. Breslow, "Relationship of Physical Health Status and Health Practices," *Preventive Medicine* 1 (1972), pp. 409-421.

[11] For a more detailed exploration of the concept of whole-being wellness, see John D. Adams, *Understanding and Managing Stress* (San Diego: University Associates, 1980); John D. Adams, "Health, Stress, and the Manager's Lifestyle," *Group and Organization Studies* 6:3 (1981), pp. 291-301; John D. Adams, "Planning for Comprehensive Stress Management" in *Coping with Stress at Work*, eds. J. Marshall and C.L. Cooper (Aldershot, United Kingdom: Gower, 1981).

[12] Stephanie Matthews-Simonton, "Psychological Aspects of Healing," presented at "Healing in Our Time" Conference, Washington, D.C. (October 1982).

[13] See Chapter 13.

[14] For a further exploration of the nature of personal belief systems, see J. Roberts, *The Nature of Personal Reality* (Engelwood Cliffs, New Jersey: Prentice-Hall, 1974) and Woolfolk and Richardson, *Stress, Sanity and Survival* (New York: Sovereign, 1978).

13

Facilitating Organizational Transformation: The Uses of Myth and Ritual

HARRISON OWEN

Comments on the Second Edition

In 1983, when this chapter was first written, words like organizational trans-formation appeared as a total oxymoron, for everybody knew that transfor-mation happened only at the level of the individual. Indeed most people never thought about transformation at any level, leaving such esoteric thoughts to the gurus and psychotherapists. Today, of course, the notion of organization transformation, or transformation in organizations, is almost banal. Virtually no day passes without reference to this phenomenon in such esoteric publications as *The Wall Street Journal* and *Barron's*. How things have changed.

It would be lovely should those of us who have contributed to this book be able to claim great prescience, based on careful research. Speaking only for myself, it was more like a blinding flash of the obvious. The flash was occasioned by a landslide of curious books: *The Aquarian Conspiracy, Future Shock, Megatrends, In Search of Excellence,* and for me the most crit-ical, Ken Wilber's *Up From Eden.* Suddenly my experience in organizations was seen in a new light, and as the circle of that illumination expanded, I found other aspects of my experience included. Way back when, I thought I was going to be an Anglican (Episcopal) priest, with a life devoted to under-standing the mythology and ritual of the ancient Near East. Things happened, and that life work never occurred, except that it came back to haunt me in a strange new way: I found that the stories people told (their mythology) and the acts they performed (ritual) not only described their present and emerg-ing self-understanding, but in many ways created it. This has always been so, I think, but in days characterized by surging megatrends and crashing third waves, keeping track of what was going on was more than a little difficult. But somehow, things seemed to become clear and possible if you just kept track of the stories.

The present moment makes the turbulence of the early 80s look like a calm day at the beach. It is even harder to keep track of what is going on and learn to ride the changing tides — otherwise known as surfing. But the central stories and acts (myth and ritual) continue to provide necessary clues to a world in transformation. At least that has been my experience.

— Harrison Owen

Owen uses an understanding of mythology to diagnose the underlying rhythms and cultures of organizations and to facilitate transformations in those organizations. Once the key myths and rituals have been identified, the positive ones can be accentuated and the negative ones dismantled or allowed to atrophy. After defining what he means by myths — stories that embody the givens in a group's life — Owen presents a case study of transformation in a complex system in which these concepts played a central role. He then goes on to answer some of the key questions regarding the use of myths in OT work, and discusses ways of diagnosing, creating, and changing myths in organizations.

Turbulent environmental circumstances emerging today are forcing the fact of transformation upon all organizations. The choices are both clear and stark: organizations must either modify their forms and structures (transform) in ways appropriate to the emergent environment or, over a period of time, cease to exist. Contemporary organizations are not all "bad," but, rather like the dinosaurs, their anatomy and physiology are simply inappropriate to the emergent world. Facilitating the process of transformation — midwifing the birth of new organizational forms — is therefore critical to organizations' survival.

Much of the effort currently devoted to transformation only amounts to what I call "tinkering." It is hoped that some minor, or perhaps major, adjustment to the organizational structure and technology will permit passage into the "new world." However, the experience of the automobile industry, for example, suggests that the degree of environmental change is such that tinkering will not suffice. Automobile makers simply cannot do more of what they have always done. The world really has changed, and those corporations that will survive are literally inventing a whole new way of being, doing business, and relating to their worlds. All of this suggests that structural and technological improvement alone, while necessary, do not go deep enough to effect the required adaptation.

How deep into the fabric of organizational life one must be prepared to go is suggested by Peter Vaill's work on high-performing systems.[1] When he reported on this work in 1978, the concept of organizational transformation did not exist, but the phenomenon he discussed was, I believe, the transforming organization. He observed, as have others, that some organizations "really have it" — despite — or perhaps because of — the fact that they don't play by the usual rules, or organize themselves in accordance with "standard practice," whatever that might mean. By any objective standard, these organizations consistently meet or exceed their objectives. Faced with change, high-performing organizations see opportunity and seize it. To outsiders, such organizations appear mysterious and perhaps chaotic, for just as their form and function is defined, it transmutes into a new form to meet change and opportunity.

Why such "superstar" organizations should exist is more than an interesting question, and then, what the differences are between them and the also-rans. In Vaill's view, the significant variables turn out to be such things as the "charisma of the leader" and the "rhythm of the organization;" both variables seem more appropriate to the cogitations of a poet than to the writing of a distinguished management scientist.

As non-traditional as Vaill's view may be, his work moves to the very center of the concern for transformation, to describe those organizations that, regardless of their structure and management procedures, really get the job done — presently and in the emergent future. But, one may ask, how do you get there from here? Clearly, it is desirable for also-rans to become high-performing systems.

At least part of the problem involved in applying Vaill's observations is the difficulty of developing a suitable conceptual framework within which to view the organization and its components. The conceptual problem relative to large complex systems is how to get your mind around a mind-boggling entity. In this regard the concept of the organizational culture is a promising possibility. Attention to the culture of an organization focuses on both the internal and external relationships of the total organization.

Perhaps more importantly, the idea of culture makes us think in active, fluid terms — synergistic terms — rather than in static, concrete terms. However, after we have assessed the culture and enumerated the bits and pieces of organizational life, and even put them together in some working semblance of the total organization, we come back to first principles. We must ask: what drives the culture; what gives it its character, *joie de vivre,* or *élan;* or, why aren't those things there? Once more we return to Vaill's terms "charisma of the leader" and "rhythm of the organization."

Although this discussion may seem circuitous, viewing an organization in overall cultural terms is a very workable and useful approach, if only because it forces one to think about an institution as a whole, in addition to thinking about its constituent parts. Another level of viewing is required that takes into account the important, though perhaps intangible, elements of which Vaill wrote. Furthermore, Vaill's flights of poesy, though non-traditional, are by no means casual in terms of substance (what he says) or method (how he says it). The critical mechanisms in the organizational culture — from which its drive and excitement come — are exactly in the domain of the poet and, in fact, are the organizational myths and rituals.

DEFINING MYTH AND RITUAL

The significant differences between similar organizations (i.e., with the same resources, structure, procedures, and so forth) in terms of function and performance are the intangibles such as charisma, rhythm, and "feel." The "carrying mechanisms" for these intangibles are the myths and rituals indigenous to the organization. The manager desirous of high performance can better understand the organizational culture, and potentially enhance it, through sensitivity to the local myths and rituals.

Popular usage tells us that myths are quaint stories from another time or place, that may be historically interesting or aesthetically pleasing but certainly are not true or useful for anything. My understanding and usage of myth is quite different. Myths are a body of likely stories that emerge from the life of any group, and enable a group to understand its past and present, and thereby project its future. Quite the opposite of untruths, myths embody the *a priori* givens for a group's culture.

Myths are the stories of a group's culture that describe its beginning, continuance, and ultimate goals. Whether or not the stories actually happened is unimportant. What *is* important is that these stories are so much a part of the institutional fabric as to define that fabric and the institution. To know the myth is to know the institution in a way that balance sheets and organizational charts can never impart.

Ritual also has suffered common misinterpretation. Popular usage defines ritual as an activity done for its own sake, with little real significance, as in the phrase "mere ritual." I view ritual in a very different way: as the dramatic reenactment of a myth. In a ritual, the group acts out its central stories in such a way that members experience really being there and participating in the original event. Rituals are typically the means the group uses to get new members into the "old history." Rituals always look strange to outsiders and have little apparent meaning to them. That, however, is precisely what makes an outsider an outsider. To the insider, the rituals are real and valid.

As an example, the following institutional case study highlights how an understanding of organizational myths and rituals identifies organizational culture and leads to institutional strategies for change and development. My work with the institution is ongoing, so lack of long-term results and concerns for confidentiality constrain the presentation. This organizational situation, however, exemplifies a number of points and provides a useful introduction to the broader discussion of the uses of myth and ritual that follows.

CASE STUDY: THE STORY OF EVMA

Background

The Eastern Virginia Medical Authority (EVMA) is a curious institution in the Tidewater region of Virginia, a growing metropolitan area with 1.3 million residents. Externally, EVMA looks very much like a modern health services center. Legally, it is a regional authority serving several municipalities. Its charter requires it to enhance the quality of health care for the citizens of the Tidewater area of Virginia, although the charter does not specify how such "enhancement" is to be accomplished. Governance is exercised through a board of commissioners appointed by the seven municipalities served by EVMA. Historically, these seven municipalities have been fierce rivals.

EVMA consists of: a medical school, a graduate school, a mental health center (with its own separate board), a rehabilitation institute, and working affiliations with 28 local hospitals and seven institutions of higher education. EVMA began about 1966 as an idea, or dream, several community leaders had that there should be a medical school in their area. At that time, the quantity and quality of available health care were deficient. Citizens with any serious malady often traveled up to 140 miles for treatment — provided they could afford it. The community leaders felt this to be an unacceptable situation for an area the size of the Tidewater.

They reasoned that if they could start a medical school, it would act as a catalyst and produce a more sophisticated level of health care. The medical school opened in 1973, and EVMA was created by state law as the legal vehicle to support the school.

From the beginning, EVMA was an experiment. By design, EVMA (and the medical school) was conceived as a community-based organization, like the "university without walls" concept. The situation, however, is not without its problems. First, there is a lack of institutional definition. Although there is a campus of sorts, much of the authority's activity takes place elsewhere; the vast majority of its faculty do not work on the campus. The very amorphousness of the institution has led to numerous perceptions as to what it is.

Members of the pre-existing health care community (small hospitals and physicians who were not positively predisposed toward the creation of EVMA) could view the authority as the great amorphous "they," out to do all sorts of evil. As one outsider remarked, "I don't know what EVMA is; but whatever it is, it's bad." Further, management instability characterized the authority during its formative period; it had a succession of presidents, deans, and other administrators.

Despite the problems and incongruities, EVMA has worked. In fact, the level of health care — both quality and quantity — has improved dramatically. Outstanding specialists have been attracted to the area. Citizens ceased having to journey elsewhere for good medical care. Young physicians from the area are being trained and, perhaps most important, are choosing to stay in the Tidewater area to practice.

While one might not yet call EVMA a "high-performing system," it is the only game in town and it is doing the job. The critical issue is how to keep it together and improve its overall function.

My association with the authority began with the arrival of a new president, whose charge was to address the problems of institutional maintenance and improvement. As consultant to the president, I assisted in the creation of a coherent, formalized support environment for EVMA. This environment should do for EVMA what a university structure would do for any other health sciences center. We reasoned that by bringing some publicly identifiable definition to the institution we could create sufficient stability to permit other organizational problems to be resolved. As this process developed, we could focus on raising the level of organizational performance.

Approach

The approach followed two tracks. On one track, we designed and instituted a formal strategic planning process in which the objective was to articulate mission and goals statements for EVMA. The 44-member planning group met over a nine-month period, with members representing every significant internal and external constituent group of the authority. (The majority came from the outside.) The group moved through four phases in its deliberations: 1) an identification of health care needs of the region; 2) an outline of possible approaches and appropriate institutional roles that might be performed by any of the several organizations of the region; 3) an identification of specific roles for EVMA; and 4) development of mission and goals statements.

The second track was the creation of an independent "picture" of the culture in which the authority operated, in order to provide the president with some strategic options he might pursue to enhance the function of his institution.

I interviewed 100 individuals in the Tidewater region, including all participants in the planning group, the board of commissioners, other influential citizens from the financial, medical, commercial, and government communities, and a small group that had been intimately involved in the creation of EVMA. The central concern of the interviews was to find an answer to the question, "What are the myths?"

I wanted to discover the commonly told tales about this institution. To what extent did certain tales limit themselves to certain groups? How did the tales vary from group to group? What variances related to which group? At the risk of being misunderstood, I was less concerned with historical truth — what actually happened — than with the corporate or community memory of historical occurrences. As suggested above, myth becomes reality.

Obviously, the interviews would have been very short had the respondents been asked, "What's the story?" — or worse, "Please tell me your myths." Two more-specific questions were asked: "What is EVMA?" and "What should it be?" Almost without exception, the respondents began in a very "objective" way, describing the organization, function, charter, and so on. In a very short time, they began telling stories by way of illustration. While the respondents may have considered these stories incidental, they represented, in fact, my central concern.

Two basic stories emerged, which might be titled EVMA the Omnivore and EVMA the Unifier.

EVMA the Omnivore described EVMA in very negative terms, almost as a cancer spreading capriciously and destructively through the health care industry of the region, devouring or taking over the competition. In telling the tale, respondents frequently referred to the fact that while EVMA started as a medical school, it quickly acquired a variety of other institutions (e.g., the medical health center), and was obviously well on its way toward becoming the super, all-inclusive health maintenance organization for the region.

The second story, EVMA the Unifier, was quite different. According to this story, the most significant thing about EVMA is that it represents the first continuing example of intra-regional cooperation. It recounts how a small group of dedicated citizens conceived the idea of a medical school and set off, against overwhelming odds, to bring that idea to fruition. Although the initial membership of the group came primarily from only one of the region's municipalities, it was enlarged, carefully and by design, to represent the whole region. One of the centerpieces of the story involves what can only be described as a very high-stakes civic poker game, in which the leadership of the region anteed up over $1 million during the course of a luncheon meeting. That was the beginning. From there the leadership fanned out over the region, gathering additional support.

Once a month for two years, the leaders gathered in the private dining room of an old hotel to plot strategy and to support the cause. According to all sources, nobody would miss a meeting; and if catastrophe should force an absence, the missing person would immediately check to find out what had happened.

At the conclusion of the interviews, two observations were made. First, given the tale of EVMA the Omnivore, it was not at all difficult to understand why the institution had been subject to an incredible amount of internal and external turbulence since its inception. Whether the myth accurately reflected the behavior and intent of EVMA was almost impossible to determine.

The second observation related to one of my original purposes as a consultant: to create a coherent supportive environment for EVMA. It would seem that this, to a degree, was an unnecessary goal, for EVMA already had a very supportive environment — the leadership of the Tidewater region had been and continued to be deeply involved in its support. There was still a need, however, to make that support more coherent and relevant to the new kinds of demands EVMA would face.

Based on the analysis of these stories (myths) of EVMA, I suggested the president's strategy should be: "Accentuate the positive —eliminate the negative." The story of EVMA the Omnivore was clearly a very destructive element in the environment. If this story could be neutralized, the chances for organizational survival would be improved. One neutralizing approach would be to refute the story each time by saying that EVMA had no such "imperialistic" plans; and indeed this was done. But such direct denial could have had the undesired effect of simply confirming the "omnivore" myth in the minds of those who already believed it. One of the key characteristics of a myth is that, once accepted, it becomes "truth," and the mechanism or means by which all occurrences are viewed and interpreted.

A more promising approach was to emphasize the positive aspects of EVMA the Unifier. One concrete way in which this was done was that the regional character of the strategic planning group was emphasized and heightened whenever possible. To help the group function effectively as a symbol of EVMA's interest in and power to enhance regional cooperation, a three-part strategy evolved.

First, the group was asked to begin its deliberations with an overall consideration of regional health problems, irrespective of any role that EVMA might have or undertake. This made sense from the planning perspective because it provided the broadest possible base from which to move. Of equal importance, in terms of the "mythic" concern, all participants in the planning process were placed in areas with which they were comfortable and knowledgeable. It also gave the participants an opportunity to interact with their colleagues and to educate them as to what was happening in other areas of the region. During the first several sessions of the planning process, EVMA as an institution was scarcely mentioned. The most commonly expressed experience of the participants was that they had learned more about their fellows and about the problems of the region than ever before.

The second step came under the heading of "time and colleagueship." Had the sole objective been the production of a mission and goals document for EVMA, this could have been done in half the time, with one-tenth the people, simply by hiring a consultant group that could have done some interviews and then drafted such a document. In fact, seven months passed, with six meetings, each one lasting about six hours and concluding with dinner. The primary objective was to create a regional group — which was accomplished.

The third element of the strategy involved ensuring the openness of the planning process. We were determined that all points of view should be expressed by all possible constituencies, even if such viewpoints apparently ran counter to the perceived self-interests of EVMA as an organization. This approach makes sense as a planning procedure. It also was essential to the neutralization of the myth of EVMA the Omnivore.

Did we succeed? The only answer is that time will tell. Some early indications are promising. First, there has been a marked improvement in the relationships between EVMA and a number of regional health organizations and institutions. Obviously, factors other than the strategic planning process also may have led to this improvement, but the fact remains that the planning process itself has been cited with approval by these organizations. An interesting, though not statistically significant, remark was made by one of the participants who had been cool toward EVMA in the past. He said, "You know, I came to these meetings thinking I was going to plan for EVMA. I now realize that in a very real sense we are EVMA, and we are planning for ourselves."

Q: Why did you take us through all that verbiage about myth and ritual when what you ended up doing — strategic planning — looked pretty much like what an intelligent planner would do? What's so new in that?

A: In many (perhaps most) cases, an understanding of organizational myths does not affect what you do so much as how you do it. An understanding of the mythic elements of an organization's culture permits one to see standard functions and procedures of an organization in at least two ways: what they are, and how they function as organizational symbols. If nothing else, one might avoid the non-productive situation so often encountered in personal relationships, wherein what you are speaks so loudly that what you say can't be heard.

Q: What material advantage did the president realize from the undertaking?

A: In this particular case, the president is a skilled administrator who, if he has a fault, tends under pressure to move out of the policy area back to the organizational "nitty gritty" in order to "get things done." He is, in fact, demonstrably competent to do that. But when he does so, institutional policy-making tends to get clouded by the day-to-day happenings. We call this the "forest-and-trees syndrome." By laying out the myths, a broad-based vantage point is established, from which to view the more technical operations and assess their potential impact. In our discussions, the code word for this was "presidential distance" — which does not mean non-involvement with technical matters, but rather sufficient detachment to be able to call an elephant an elephant rather than a tree, a rope, or fan.

Q: You discerned two basic myths (stories) related to EVMA. What would happen if you were wrong?

A: Either nothing, or disaster. Had we been so totally wide of the mark as to be irrelevant, no harm would have been done. On the other hand, had the mythology been significantly misread, the situation could have been quite difficult (e.g., if the story of EVMA the Omnivore had not been identified).

The myth approach has a number of internal and external checks that serve to limit error. First, the number of people interviewed must be both large and representative. Second, a single telling of a tale is not sufficient to give it "mythic" status. When one hears the story over and over, however, with only slight variations, one develops a degree of confidence.

MYTHOLOGY AND WHAT IT'S GOOD FOR

It is hoped that the central thrust of this chapter is now clear, having been grounded in some organizational reality. A more systematic look at myths and ritual follows, as a means of understanding the organizational culture and as a potential mechanism for increasing performance.

A myth is easier to see, and to perceive as such, when it is not one's own. Hence we readily apply the word "myths" to the literature of Greece and Rome. We are less comfortable using the word relative to early Judeo-Christian literature. We are quite shocked if we see the word used to describe the activities of science or the capitalistic system. Something inside us insists that the Hellenic myths are mere fables, and the stories of science are *truth*. We tend to forget that the Hellenic myth, for the Greek, was true — as is the Torah for the Jew, the Bible for the Christian, the Koran for the Moslem, and so on.

On the contrary, myths are common, essential, and powerful mechanisms of human communication that are used whenever deeply held beliefs or values are expressed. To the extent that contemporary organizations have such values that require expression, they do have and employ this mechanism.

The Creation of Myths

Myths are built from the happenings of history (or that which could have been history), but myths are rarely, if ever, literally true; but that is not the point. That the story has the capacity to powerfully communicate a central value is the point.

For example, in the myth of EVMA the Unifier, there is the story of the high-stakes civic poker game. That tale has been told and elaborated upon so many times that it is almost impossible to tell precisely what happened. But in a very real sense, that doesn't matter; in the corporate life of EVMA, the story does communicate the excitement, dedication, and commitment of those civic leaders who brought EVMA into existence. It serves as an effective model for the kind of behavior one would hope for in the future.

Given the high performance of the community leadership, one almost would have to invent such a story, if it did not exist, to demonstrate the values and spirit of this group. Typically, myths are narratives, and must be "likely" events.

Myths arise through the assemblage of narrative material descriptive of a community and its leaders. This assemblage may be only partially conscious — certain stories may "bubble up" from the group leadership as being especially descriptive of the group. Once assembled, the myths create a "narrative environment" in which the group lives, and into which new members may be drawn.

A body of myths functions very much like a novel. A good novel draws the reader in to confront directly the reality the author had in mind. Rarely, if ever, does the novelist say, "This is my point." Rather, the novelist creates situations in which the point is made manifest. The point is made through encounter, not through argument. A novel becomes "true" because it is felt as such — it is immediately self-validating. Its truth and power derive from the story's compelling nature, not from someone telling you it was good or arguing its position.

A myth is a good story that grips you, creates a world, and, to some significant degree, transforms and interprets the "real" world. Working with or in a given myth is like living in a good novel. The difference is that you can't put the myth down: A myth not only reflects life, it becomes life.

Myths Evolve

Myths have a life cycle: they are born, grow, and even may die. For example, the myths of Greece and Rome continue to persist as somewhat esoteric literary allusions, but one will look far before finding a present-day believer in Zeus, Athena, and the rest.

Another body of material comes from the same time, but from a different group. The tales of Israel and the ancient Near East continue to exist, not only as historical curiosities, but as relevant and valid mythologies that inform and shape the world of their believers. Why Israel and not Greece? The believer's answer is, of course, that the former is "true," and the latter wasn't. A more objective answer would be that somehow the Judaic myths have been constantly reinterpreted so that they remain vital today.

The life of EVMA has perhaps been too short for us to see changes in the myth. However, such mythic transformation is quite apparent in the broad American corporate scene. The tales of the "Robber Barons" — J.P. Morgan, John D. Rockefeller, Andrew Carnegie, *et al.* — dominated the values of rising young executives for more than a generation. The historical circumstances changed, and today these stories seem distant, possibly heroic, and also somewhat in bad taste. The stories have been successfully replaced by tales of Henry Ford, Charles Erwin Wilson, Charles T.R. Wilson, Robert MacNamara, and the "Whiz Kids." One might profitably ask, "What's the story today?"

Myths Can Be Changed

While generally it is true that myths seem to "bubble up" out of a group's experience, and therefore are largely subconscious or unintentional, it is also true that in the hands of certain people at certain times, myths can be created or radically changed by design. One can point to significant moments when fundamental mythical shifts occurred. For example, one may view the recent and continuing civil rights battles in the United States simply as a struggle between Negroid and Caucasian people. It certainly is that, but more: It is a struggle between *black* people and *white* people. In the mythology of the Western world, *black* epitomizes all that is evil, sinful, dreadful, and fearful. It is the opposite of *white*, which represents goodness, truth, purity, and beauty.

In a mythological interpretation, the civil rights battle becomes caught in the historic dualism of the Western world. The feelings expressed are not only those of one race against another, but of order against disorder. Nobody intended that it be this way; it is a matter of historical accident. What makes matters worse is that Negroids had generally adopted the Western myth, and so their situation was twice damned. Not only were they seen as *black* by whites, but they also thought of themselves in the same terms as whites did. Black was evil, albeit *black people* may be good. That was a very difficult intellectual juggling act. It is very difficult to achieve a positive self-image if the very words one uses to describe oneself connote sin and death.

By serendipity or design, Stokely Carmichael, representing a long chain of activists, communicated a new myth: *Black is beautiful!* From the point of view of established Western myths, that phrase made as much sense as "water is dry," or ice is hot." Yet, by juxtaposing those two powerful mythic words — "black" and "beautiful" — Carmichael and other leaders created a new mythic reality in which Negroes could claim their *blackness* with pride. It will be a long time before the full ramifications of this move are perceived. In any case, Carmichael's statement was a watershed. To be sure, it did not stand alone; and a great deal of cultural change prepared the conditions for such a statement. But the point remains: myths change, and they can be changed intentionally.

The Power of Myths

Adolph Hitler represents perhaps the best (or worst) example of a man who manipulated the mythic world to his own ends. No matter what Hitler may have been or done, he had an exquisite sense of the mythic underpinnings of Germanic culture. His creation of the Third Reich and his own rise to power began with the isolation and articulation of the mythic powers of blood, iron, and race, which permeate the Germanic myths. He and his associates resurrected the myths and gave them a new form. The stories weren't new, nor were the ideas. However, Hitler told them in a new way and gave them institutional form. The mythic world is something to conjure with — carefully.

RITUAL — THE ACTING OUT OF MYTHS

The active side of myth is ritual. When there is a myth, there is usually a ritual. Ritual is nothing more nor less than the dramatic reenactment of the myths. It is the re-presentation of the myth in present time. For those who own these myths, the attendant ritual may be the most real thing that happens. For Catholics, the mass is participating in the life, death, and resurrection of Christ (transubstantiation). Protestants actually hear the word of God.

Rituals, like myths, usually grow out of commonplace activities; the mass (Lord's Supper) originally was a meal. The common activity becomes a ritual activity when it assumes some special meaning or significance in the life of a group. In some cases, rituals become very abstracted from their original setting and use. This is particularly true with old rituals. The Christian communion service is an excellent case in point. New rituals retain much if not all of their original form and function. Hence it may seem to an outsider or casual observer that the group's members are merely doing what they are supposed to do, and the ritual "overlay" is not at all apparent. For example, at a regular staff meeting it may turn out that all the participants always sit in the same place. An outsider would see no difference, but woe to the new staff member who sits in the "wrong" place.

Signs that an ordinary activity has become a ritual are the presence of specific acts for which there is no immediate rationale, such as always leaving one chair vacant (for a departed member).

The real meaning of a ritual usually only becomes clear when one has the story — the myth — that explains, justifies, or describes what is going on. At this point, the connection between myth and ritual not only becomes clear, but essential.

The power of ritual resides principally in its ability to communicate nonverbally. The participant really does not have to think or understand anything. It is more a matter of ambience and feel.

The importance of sensitivity to ritual in organizational life is twofold. First, it provides an added dimension for understanding the myths. One actually may see the group doing what it tells stories about. Second, the rituals themselves may be reworked to generate positive change in the environment of the organization. A very limited example of this was the structuring of the strategic planning process in the case study.

WHAT MYTHS AND RITUALS DO

The central function of myths in organizational life is to create a narrative world through which the values of the group are preserved and communicated, primarily to the members of the group, but also to the external world. Myths also:

Define groups. To the extent that you know the story and it is — or becomes — your story, you are a member of group. The high-stakes civic poker game in the case study is a good example. The original attendees at that luncheon tell that story with considerable pride and relish. During annual fund-raising for EVMA, the story is told again, and new members participate in it vicariously. It becomes their story.

Initiate new members. As new members are brought into the group, after they have passed through the formalities (personnel forms, etc.), some senior member will almost inevitably start telling "war stories" about how it was "in the old days." This tale-telling can be viewed as a pleasant interlude of no particular consequence, but in fact it may be the most important thing that occurs. Every vital organization has its myth-tellers, whose titles and positions have nothing to do with this function.

Sustain the group. In bad times the myths and rituals constitute the bedrock to which the group returns. They contain the history of past disasters overcome, and provide assurance that the present troubles can be dealt with. If Chrysler Corporation "makes it," and then gets in trouble later, one might expect to hear a harried executive say, "Back in '81 Lee Iaccoca really did it!"

Challenge the group. Myths contain not only the history but also the future expectations and aspirations of the group. The myth of EVMA the Unifier records the story of how things got started, but it also includes the hope for tomorrow: an end to inter-municipal feuding and the creation of a sophisticated health care system. Each time the story is told, it challenges the group to become the dream.

THE USES OF MYTH AND RITUAL IN THE MANAGEMENT OF ORGANIZATIONS

I contend that the quality of an organization's culture is a pivotal concern to its management, particularly when the issue of enhanced performance is central. Specifically, the culture should permit and encourage the effective synergism of each organizational component. A prerequisite for such synergism is the competent performance of the various components. Also needed are environmental conditions that are as free as possible from destructive organizational turbulence, supportive of clearly defined organizational goals and values, and charged with a level of excitement that urges creativity and demands excellence. The prime mechanisms that affect the atmosphere of the culture are the organizational myths and rituals. To the extent that a manager is aware of these elements, he or she is at least in a position to identify and understand some of the major operative forces. At best, the manager may utilize these forces strategically in the development of the organization.

Some Points to Consider

The following suggestions are offered for uses of myth in the management of institutions. The suggestions are not exhaustive, nor should they be viewed as a panacea. The material is divided into two parts. First, there are five points that a manager should bear in mind while considering the institution and its mythology. Second, some more direct comments relating to institution building and institutional change are introduced.

Identification and attention to the myths. This should be obvious. Each organization has its own myths, and being aware of their nature is a necessary first step. How one does this may be problematical. In the case of formal religions, the problem is solved in part by the collection and publication of the myth, as in the Bible or Koran. Political systems also tend to collect and publish their myths, as in the cases of *Das Kapital, Mein Kampf* and the Declaration of Independence. Other social structures, such as corporations, are less formal in this regard, but no less controlled by the operative myths. The problem is to identify them. If the myths aren't published, they still show themselves in predictable ways:

Heavy words. Each organization has certain words that are laden with meaning over and above their usual use. In Christianity such words as "redeem," "save," "judgment," "bread," and "wine" have this status. For a medical school words like "science," "rigor," "excellence," "patient," "professional," "instrument," and "healing art" appear to assume the same status. These "heavy words" are the building blocks from which institutional myths are created.

Central personalities. Almost by definition, every organization has a founder and a succession of important figures. The importance of these figures is not dictated by position so much as by impact and remembrance. The stories that are passed along in the institutional memory about these individuals almost inevitably form a central part of the operative myths.

Ritual events. Many events in the life of an organization are adapted. All schools, for example, have a "graduation." Some events, however, are peculiar to an institution and may have more significance. Such things as special award celebrations, initiation rites, founder's day, and annual conventions are examples.

Mythological coherence. Given an identification of the operative myths, an important question is: How coherent are they? Do they all go in the same direction, or are there alternative versions that can be destructive? Such mythic dissonance was obviously a major factor in the case study; myths of EVMA the Omnivore and EVMA the Unifier are mutually contradictory. Organizational health is related in important ways to the degree of mythological coherence.

Congruence of myth and ritual. Most myths have a ritual, and vice versa. Under ideal circumstances, the myth explains the ritual, and the ritual demonstrates the myth. It occasionally happens, however, that this relationship is disturbed, and what one says and what one does end up being two different things. The organizational dissonance resulting from this can be very destructive. A painful example of this occurred in the late 1960s and early 1970s when "traditional" parents watched their offspring make a shambles out of high school and college graduations. For the parents, graduation had been a respected ritual marking an important point of passage. For the children, graduation simply highlighted the disparity between their beliefs and values and those embodied by the "system." Put somewhat simplistically:

Same Ritual + Different Values (Myths) = Turbulence

Congruence of myth and organizational structure. In most organizations, there seems to be an internal (implicit-informal) and an external (public-formal) organization. The external organization is for the world to see. This distinction is most obvious in some West African societies where the whole world of myth and ritual is kept secret and available only to the initiates. What the external world does see is the village governmental structure (chief, elder, and so on). In virtually all cases, the roles of chief and priest are separate, though highly interrelated. At times, however, the relationship between the operative myth-and-ritual and the external structure is strained and/or broken. The internal world of traditional myth-and-ritual then goes underground and may disappear, while the external structure develops a new myth-and-ritual that gives it new meaning. In a general way, one might view the history of Europe since the Reformation as an example. The rise of secularism is the result, and it constitutes not the abolition of old myths, rituals, and religions, but rather the creation of new ones. Sometimes the reverse takes place, as in Iran, where tradition is seeking to replace innovation. The delicate relationship between the world and personalities of myth and ritual, and the external structures of an organization is critical to institutional life. Sometimes both worlds are united, as in a theocracy; they are usually separate. Whenever they are estranged, there is turbulence.

Congruence of myth and the world. This observation is, in a sense, only a variant of the preceding one. Just as the relationship between the internal myth and ritualistic structure of an organization and the external structure is critical, so also is the relationship between the myth and the world, or external environment. Myths die when they are no longer useful to interpret a changed world. For example, as the power of Rome faded, its great myths just didn't seem to fit, for they referred to a world that no longer existed.

Some Practical Applications

Institution Building and Mythological Awareness. As an institution is developed, and particularly when substantial organizational change is anticipated (such as when a new center or department is being created), close attention to the ambient and operative myths is essential. Under the best of circumstances, the new structure should be presented as the natural, expected response to the current myths. Ways of doing this include:

- cloaking the new structure in the "heavy words"
- appealing to tradition ("The founder said that one day we should do such and such")
- providing a meaningful place for the new institutional structure in the ongoing ritual of the organization.

Institutional Transformation and the Transformation of Myths. It may happen that the necessary organizational change is at such variance with the operative myths as to be unacceptable. For example, several years ago it became apparent to many in the American health care system that there was a real shortage of general practitioners, and an overabundance of specialists. As a result, medical schools around the country were encouraged to start departments of family practice and community medicine. These new departments were grudgingly accepted into the medical school structure, and to this day, generally have had difficulty. There are a variety of practical reasons for this, but in my judgment there was one overriding reason: There was no place for these departments in the operative medical school myths. Most of the narrative tales on the medical school campus related to acts of derring-do performed by heart surgeons and other "high priests" of medicine. A second strong body of myths celebrates the prowess of the biomedical researcher. The general practitioner just doesn't "fit in." Given the odds, this organizational change perhaps should not have been attempted. Alternatively, one might seek to change (transform) the myths. This is a difficult and dangerous business. The possibility for success is enhanced if the following points are kept in mind:

- Myths are very powerful, and very conservative. If outright "war" is to be avoided, they should not be attacked directly.

- Indirect manipulation of the operative myths may be accomplished in two ways: One may identify those elements of the myths that are the closest to supporting the proposed change, and subtly develop and enhance them. An alternative would be to identify another myth also current with the group that more closely matches the organizational need, and then seek to institute the proposed change through this myth. In the case of the medical schools just cited, that alternative would be the somewhat dormant myth of the caring personal physician (who, of course, makes house calls).

The role of myths and rituals in organizational transformations is critical, for they shape and form the culture, which in turn provides the power, purpose, and values of the organization. Profound change in the environment that requires equally-sweeping organizational change cannot be accomplished by "tinkering" with structure and technology alone. In order to facilitate the emergence of new organizational forms, one must look to the "depths" of an organization that support the technology and structure,. While there can be no substitute for good, traditional management practices and approaches, these alone are not sufficient. Organizations cannot live by myths alone. However, organizations cannot live without them either. Those who are concerned with the facilitation of organizational transformation will carefully attend to the realm of myths and rituals — for the new organizational forms will have new stories, appropriate to new ways of being.

Note

[1] Peter B. Vaill,"Towards a Behavioral Description of High-Performing Systems" in *Leadership: Where Else Can We Go?* eds. Morgan McCall and Michael Lombardo (Durham, North Carolina: Duke University Press, 1978).

14

High Performance Programming: A Framework for Transforming Organizations

TYLER NELSON
FRANK L. BURNS

Comments on the Second Edition

In our original paper describing the High Performance Programming model, we confidently predicted that high performing leaders would use new on-line networking technologies to create self-managing networks of highly fluid, self-managing teams. We may have been inaccurate in our prediction about when this would happen, (though the U.S. Army was already using these tools when we developed the High Performance Programming model). But what we have seen in the last couple of years has strongly reinforced our belief that cyberspace is a key factor in the development of high performing organizations. Applications of the Internet and the World Wide Web have exploded, and our organizations are being transformed by these new technologies in profound ways.

We need to understand the deeper benefits of the Internet and its human system applications — intranets, extranets, deltanets, and metanets. We who pretend to be smart about organization and community transformation need to understand that this new geography of cyberspace has deep implications for our field. All of us should be taking advantage of these applications of cyberspace tools in our large system change and organization development strategies.

Time doesn't "work" on the World Wide Web in the same way as it does in "real" space. The "click" that takes me from Chicago to Atlanta takes no more nor less time than the "click" that transports me from Washington, D.C. to the Galapagos Islands. The profound implication for OD and HRD of the arrival of distance-less and time-less space is that these rapid clicks can connect me to my teammate across the hall *and* my teammate in Hong Kong. And it doesn't matter whether my teammate is "in" my own organization or in a "virtual" organization of "virtual" teams we may have conspired to create. We need to understand the vocabulary of this new organizational terrain.

Internet. The Internet is best understood as nothing more than a set of protocols enabling computer networks to interconnect and pass information back and forth. The World Wide Web is currently the fastest growing subset of these protocols, and what's important about the Web is that its standards permit connected computers and computer networks to share multi-media files, in addition to the text.

Intranet. An Intranet is an arrangement of computers and computer networks internal to an organization, using Internet protocols and standards, to serve internal organizational purposes. Large corporations and large government agencies developed most early applications of Internets. Recently, more and more small and medium organizations have developed Intranets to serve their own internal organizational purposes.

Extranet. An Extranet's purposes is to improve the quality of communication between a "sponsoring" organization and the external organizations and constituencies that are important to its success. For example, manufacturing organizations are building Extranets for communicating with their distributors, dealers, suppliers and end customers.

Deltanet. A Deltanet takes its name from the Greek "delta," which is used to indicate "difference." Deltanets are networks based on Internet protocols that are designed to make a difference for an organization. They are therefore one of the more interesting applications of Internet protocols for everyone involved in transforming the world of work. Virtually all Intranets and Extranets are designed for the purpose of achieving some kind of "difference," and in this sense perhaps all could be thought of as Deltanets. What is proposed here is that the term "deltanet" be used for those applications of Internet standards and tools that are specifically designed to support organization-wide change strategies of the nature familiar to HRD and OD practitioners.

Metanet. Even less widely used at the present time is the term "metanet," which we propose as a term for applications of Internet tools designed to bring a community of people together who want to share their experiences and learn from each other. On-line communities of practice will be increasingly popular for consultants and managers who want to build high performing organizations.

In this new network of self-organizing virtual teams in virtual organizations and virtual communities, our new professional challenge in transforming work is to practice what we might call VOD: Virtual Organization Development.

— Frank Burns

The high-performance programming model provides a coherent framework for understanding the different levels of functional effectiveness that organizations can attain, and the cultural frames associated with each of these levels. It has been developed from the authors' efforts to understand differences that exist between current and potential levels of performance in organizations — and in parallel differences one sees in the thinking of their leaders. The central implications of the model are that leaders must focus their organizations on the future, and they must also attend to the needs of the present. They can unleash the vast reservoir of human energy that lies dormant in their organizations and also provide their members with a vision of the future that channels their energy toward new opportunities and challenges.

The High Performance Programming (HPP) model illustrates concepts that assist in transforming an organization into a high-performing system. The structure of the model provides a nested framework for diagnosing current levels of performance, and for understanding the potential for performance at the highest levels. Specific methods are outlined for creating the conditions that elicit high performance from individuals, teams, and organizations.

The term programming is used to highlight the proposition that an organization's present performance level is a function of past implicit or explicit "operating instructions" to the system. Similarly, future performance will depend on how the organization's culture is being programmed now. This critical issue is the key to unlocking the performance potential of an organization. Specifically, an organization's future performance is a direct result of its culture and the operative frame of reference supplied by that culture.

This concept is reflected in the series of four frames that make up the body of the HPP model, shown in Figure 1. Each of these four frames portrays a distinct operating frame of reference. With the exception of the reactive frame, these frames are nested to reflect one of the basic concepts of the model — each larger frame builds upon and provides an enhanced cultural context for the frame or frames within it. The proactive frame of reference is an extension and an enhancement of the responsive frame. Likewise, the high performing frame of reference is an expansion beyond the proactive frame and includes both the proactive and responsive frames.

Figure 1. The Framework of the High Performance Programming Model

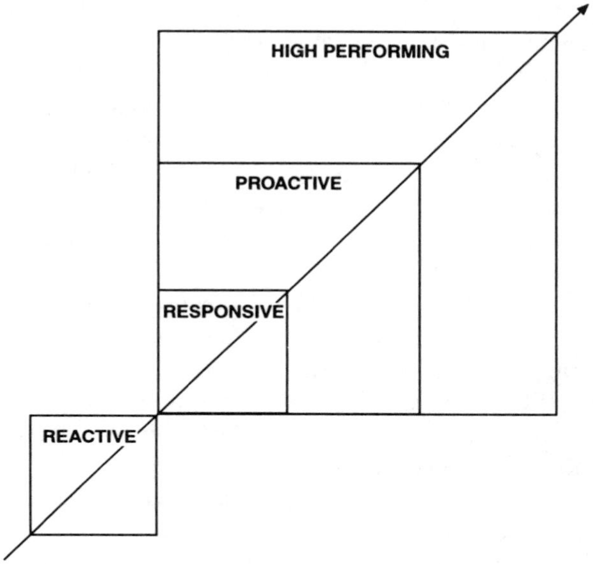

Background

Frames of reference allow us to examine the difference between organizational change efforts that merely re-sort and re-label the organization's sub-elements and functions, and change efforts that truly transform the organization. No matter how dramatic a change effort looks on paper, or how solid the reasoning behind it, actual improved performance happens only if there is also a parallel change in the frames of reference of the people in the organization.

For example, the implementation of "matrix management" in an organization we observed was intended to improve its responsiveness, but the change actually produced an information traffic jam that amounted to gridlock. All eight layers of management, still caught up in old habits of thought, continued to insist that everything go through old channels. Their impoverished frames of reference neutralized the intended outcomes of the matrix strategy.

A second and related issue illuminated by the HPP model is how an organization's culture either allows or hinders its adaptation to accelerating change in its internal and external environment. In today's fast-paced and complex society, change is no longer a choice; it is a given. Research on the functioning of systems suggests that complexity itself is the driving force behind the increasing rate of change: the more complex a given system is, the faster its rate of change, which creates more complexity.[1] Even though change is a given, its direction may take different forms. A system facing increasing complexity will either evolve toward a more connected and integrated form, or drift into an increasingly fragmented state. Organizations, when viewed as systems, can be observed over time to move into higher and more productive states or to devolve into lower, less-organized, and less-effective states.

The following summary describes the organizational characteristics that accelerate disorganization and the techniques and strategies that can move an organization through the responsive, proactive, and high-performing levels of the HPP model. Our intention is to provide leaders and managers, particularly those with executive responsibilities, with new ways of thinking coherently about what they can do to influence the future of their organizations — not merely to ensure their viability and success in a changing world, but to set them on a course for excellence.

We begin with an examination of organizations in which decay and disorganization have already begun.

The Reactive Organization

The reactive state is not the state in which organizations begin. It is the state in which survival itself may be in question. In talking to members of these organizations, one notices an absence of shared purpose or sense of accomplishment. Not only will one get different responses about what's important, one also will be left with the distinct impression that nobody cares much. The reactive frame is the state of disintegration into which an organization devolves when its leaders fail to keep the organization focused on its purpose.

The culture of the reactive organization can be described using the 11 dimensions in Figure 2. The central purpose in a reactive organization has lost its vitality and no longer provides a foundation, leaving a vacuum in which disintegration and disorganization begin to take their toll. Shared purpose and clear goals act as an organization's steering mechanism: without well-focused goals, the enterprise and its members are adrift. Given no focus on the future, people become fixated on the past — a past that no longer exists.

The lack of shared purpose has a telling effect on the structure of the organization. In spite of its neatly aligned appearance on paper, the structure is really a fragmented collection of separate elements, often working at cross purposes and competing for resources and territory. Managers in such reactive cultures lay intricate paper trails, hoping to appear dedicated to detail and thorough in their endless search for problems and faults. This breeds a defensive atmosphere throughout the organization that results in a self-centered perspective on the part of the organization's members, who protect themselves by "looking out for number one."

The purpose of planning is similarly debased. Instead of planning the future direction of the organization, managers carry out huge paperwork drills designed to defend the status quo. Rather than being pulled by a vision of future achievements, the organization is driven by the fear of not being able to justify its continued existence.

People caught in a reactive organization seem strikingly similar to persons suffering from paranoia. They have little enthusiasm for anything but survival, and they are chronically cynical, pessimistic, and distrustful. They

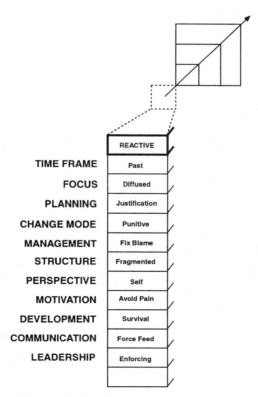

	REACTIVE
TIME FRAME	Past
FOCUS	Diffused
PLANNING	Justification
CHANGE MODE	Punitive
MANAGEMENT	Fix Blame
STRUCTURE	Fragmented
PERSPECTIVE	Self
MOTIVATION	Avoid Pain
DEVELOPMENT	Survival
COMMUNICATION	Force Feed
LEADERSHIP	Enforcing

Figure 2. The Culture of the Reactive Organization

are trapped in what psychologists call a "negative reinforcement environment," in which the avoidance of painful consequences reinforces behavior. This distortion in the organization's reward system causes individuals to become obsessed with staying out of trouble; sticking one's neck out is viewed as tantamount to getting it cut off.

Symptoms of a punitive environment are when managers behave as if taking care of problems means finding someone to blame, when change takes place primarily through punitive and corrective means, and when communication takes the form of a force-feed system of directives rolling down through the fragmented hierarchy — complemented by paperwork fighting its way back up.

Another lethal symptom of reactive cultures is the unwillingness of subordinates to tell their bosses bad news unless it no longer can be hidden. The bosses, for their part, rarely praise their people for good work, thinking — and saying — "That's what they get paid for."

One of the primary reasons for confusion and lack of clarity in reactive organizations is the prevailing norm against the subordinates asking questions of their bosses. Not only are supervisors never asked questions that might challenge the merit or wisdom of their decisions; they are rarely even asked questions for clarity.

The leadership style observed in reactive organizations is usually immature, and frequently abusive. We have seen many a "nice guy" revert to this "leader-as-obedience-trainer" style upon entering a reactive organization. Though this might not be their preferred style, it is the style that appears to them to work, at least in the short term.

As many supervisors and managers have discovered, getting work done in reactive organizations takes a lot of kicking and shoving. In painful environments people become withdrawn and insensitive in order to survive. Many managers have been co-opted by these environments and develop a "punishing- dictatorial" style just to get the attention of subordinates, who have become immune to all but the most direct and demanding sorts of instructions.

Members of reactive organizations are also among the least willing to risk change, because of the terrifying potential that the "rules of the game" will change — rules that have been learned through hard experience. Thus these low-risk and painful organizational climates are actually perpetuated by the very persons suffering the most from them. They at least know what not to do, and the unknown only invites trouble and threatens one's ability to predict.

Building the Responsive Organization

To move the culture out of a reactive state and into a responsive one requires a carefully balanced approach that involves both patience and leadership. Change must occur in the frame of reference of individual members, and in the organization as a whole. Leaders must clarify the organization's goals and purposes and build a bond of mutual trust between the leaders and the led. A well-established set of techniques designed to revitalize and re-energize the organization by renewing its focus on goals and internal cohesion is shown in Figure 3.

The most important revitalizing step is to re-focus the organization on clearly defined goals that build a sense of shared purpose among the organization's members. The goals can extend across a year, or can be targeted on major projects. They should be specific enough to clarify the outputs that are to be produced, by whom, and when.

Goal-setting and action-planning sessions are the most effective means of gaining the understanding and commitment of those who will be accountable for carrying out necessary tasks. Those people must participate in developing the goals and the plans designed to achieve them. The whole process goes down the proverbial drain when managers form goals and plans in isolation, and merely pass them along to their subordinates. Goal-setting and action-planning sessions in which both managers and subordinates contribute

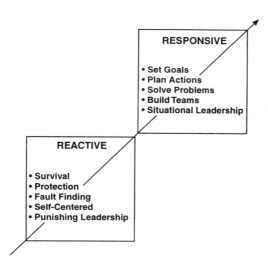

Figure 3. The Responsive Frame of Reference

are the best builders of shared purpose, understanding, and commitment. They provide a basis for building the trust and clarity that are critical to motivating the individual and instilling *esprit de corps*.

Once goals and plans are established, slippages and unexpected problems can be identified before they become crises. Good problem-solving strategies are available to promote effective participation and better solutions. As with goal-setting and action-planning, improved understanding and follow-through are achieved when the team members responsible for carrying out the solutions participate in the problem-solving process. This process, used so effectively by Japanese managers in their quality circle programs, not only has the advantage of training personnel to solve problems, but also helps them to be on the constant lookout for potential problems.

It is up to the leader to carry out these processes competently and in a manner that is responsive to people's needs. We suggest leaders follow the guidelines provided by the Situational Leadership model when moving their organization from a reactive to a responsive state. Developed by Hersey and Blanchard,[2] this model emphasizes that leaders must adapt their style to fit the maturity level (knowledge and experience) of the follower. While the new employee needs direction and structure, the more experienced employee requires less "telling" and more "selling" behavior by the leader. Mature followers work better in a participative mode with the leader. Those who are most highly experienced and qualified can accept delegated responsibilities. Movement toward a responsive state, in summary, has to begin with a leader who is responsive to the needs of adults to be treated as adults.

The Resulting Responsive Culture

Provided that the above set of management and leadership practices are carried out, the responsive organizational culture will reflect the characteristics shown in Figure 4. Team members are focused on producing outputs in the present through activities planned to achieve near-term goals. Management keeps team efforts coordinated and responsive to changing needs and conditions. Since members help develop the goals and plans of action, they know what output leaders expect, and what activities are to be performed. They work as cohesive teams, able to adapt as they identify and solve problems. This environment fosters a team perspective rather than a self-centered one, and results in team members looking out for each other and for the good of the organization.

The boss is a leader and coach who motivates group members by rewarding high performance through positive feedback, awards, and pay increases based on merit. The boss keeps the team efforts coordinated and

Figure 4. The Culture of the Responsive Organization.

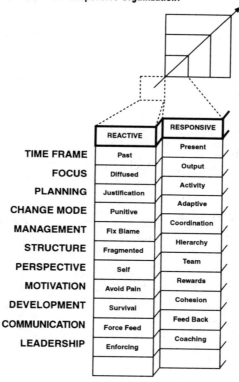

	REACTIVE	RESPONSIVE
TIME FRAME	Past	Present
FOCUS	Diffused	Output
PLANNING	Justification	Activity
CHANGE MODE	Punitive	Adaptive
MANAGEMENT	Fix Blame	Coordination
STRUCTURE	Fragmented	Hierarchy
PERSPECTIVE	Self	Team
MOTIVATION	Avoid Pain	Rewards
DEVELOPMENT	Survival	Cohesion
COMMUNICATION	Force Feed	Feed Back
LEADERSHIP	Enforcing	Coaching

focused on the goals through planning, evaluating progress, and promoting team cohesion.

While the responsive state is productive and beneficial, and it certainly is far superior to the reactive state, it is also the operational level of a larger cultural frame of reference that is proactive as well as responsive.

To maintain high levels of responsiveness and adaptability, the organization needs a more expansive frame of reference that supplies the guiding philosophy and vision around which individuals, teams, and departments become an aligned and attuned whole. This larger context is the proactive frame.

Strategies for Developing the Proactive Organization

A *proactive* frame of reference requires looking to the future and taking the initiative. It is a frame of reference from which the future is seen as a choice to be made, rather than a given with which to cope. It incorporates a way of looking at the world in which the future is viewed as something to be chosen, worked for, and realized.[3]

The first critical factor in moving beyond the responsive frame of reference lies within the value system of the organization. The chosen future must be a widely shared vision that is attuned with the values of members of the organization and which serves as an attractive and compelling force for them. The power of NASA's original mission statement, "A man on the moon by the end of the decade," is an excellent example of the motivational force supplied by an attractive, compelling vision of the future.

Second, the vision must communicate that the organization values people highly. People do not put forth personal effort beyond being responsive unless they feel the organization is "theirs," and that it values them personally and professionally. The success of Japanese management in producing high-quality products is largely due to the message conveyed to the workforce that management genuinely values and wants their ideas.

Third, the future vision must reflect a commitment to human values that give people a deep sense of personal meaning and satisfaction. High purpose, to be achieved, must be based on higher-order values. It is this point that companies that focus solely on the bottom line fail to take into account. High purpose cannot be counted or quantified because it addresses emotional qualities rather than material ends.

Strongly held values and the norms of behavior that flow from them serve an often overlooked role. Values are normative beliefs held by individuals as to what is good and desirable. They provide standards that influence people in their choice of actions. The clearer and more widely shared the organization's value system, the more it provides direction for individual behavior, and the less need there is for formal policies and rules and regulations. Thus, an enormous amount of energy that might otherwise be tied up in developing, perpetuating, and enforcing official rules — which can eventually immobilize an organization — is released to work on attaining the desired future state.

Although a widely shared set of organizational values is necessary to propel the organization into the proactive frame, the values selected are critical. Certain types of values are needed. For example, values that reinforce one's sense of interdependence with the environment are important in developing a commitment to producing results valued by the larger cultural system, e.g., the customer. The Matsushita Corporation, one of the most successful companies in the world, rose from a one-person bicycle shop to an $11 billion industrial giant with a corporate philosophy aimed at producing results valued by the larger system. The underlying foundation of Matsushita's management genius lay in the deeply held conviction that Matsushita must contribute to improving the standard of living in the larger society.

Figure 5 shows the types of strategies that foster proactive organizational cultures. These include establishing values-based and results-oriented mission statements, and developing the long-range plans to accomplish them. To maintain progress and to ensure that future results are achieved, decision-makers need to establish performance-feedback systems to keep themselves informed on significant changes and performance trends. This does not mean that executives should bury themselves in endless briefings and reports, but that they should identify a few critical performance indices and manage them intensively.

Clearly stated and widely shared organizational values are the cohesive glue that holds the culture together. These values, embedded in the corporate philosophy and manifested every day in how it operates, determine whether the organization will exist mechanically, adding to or subtracting from its collection of functions, or live organically, developing a sense of community in which work teams are knitted together to form the larger cultural fabric. It is the leader's role to shape and mold the values that provide positive meaning and value to the members' lives.

This style of values-based leadership can be called transformational. Transformational leaders engage their followers at the values level, as opposed to merely activating them at the material level. Transformational

Figure 5. The Proactive Frame of Reference.

leaders relate to the full person of each of their followers by looking for ways of developing their potentials and satisfying their higher needs.[4]

Genuine transformation leadership demands a resolute commitment to fundamental ethics and integrity, demonstrated through congruent behavior. Transformational leaders understand that true development can only take place as a function of the co-development of themselves and others. Thus, values for the transformational leader are the basis for developing the human potential of the organization as a whole.

The Resulting Proactive Culture

The results of these management strategies are presented in Figure 6, along the same 11 dimensions previously used. Future-oriented, firmly rooted in a values based philosophy, the organization is pointed toward long-term results, and strategies for achieving them. Change is planned for and used by

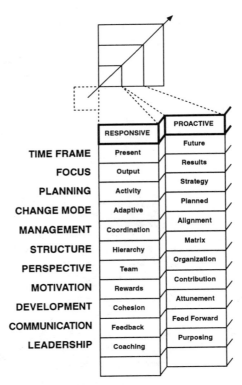

	RESPONSIVE	PROACTIVE
TIME FRAME	Present	Future
FOCUS	Output	Results
PLANNING	Activity	Strategy
CHANGE MODE	Adaptive	Planned
MANAGEMENT	Coordination	Alignment
STRUCTURE	Hierarchy	Matrix
PERSPECTIVE	Team	Organization
MOTIVATION	Rewards	Contribution
DEVELOPMENT	Cohesion	Attunement
COMMUNICATION	Feedback	Feed Forward
LEADERSHIP	Coaching	Purposing

Figure 6. The Culture of the Proactive Organization.

leaders to keep the organization clearly focused on its purpose. Communication is also focused on the future, and on how the current state affects future plans.

Management ensures the alignment and integration of sub-organization objectives within a total whole. Members are motivated by the opportunity to make a contribution toward achieving a future they value, and to work as cohesive teams aligned with and attuned to the larger perspective of the organization.

The role of leadership in proactive organizations is to keep the organization focused on its purpose and well-tuned. Leaders must think strategically and act systemically. Their style is critical to producing and sustaining the proactive, innovative culture of the organization; to promote its future orientation, they must welcome risks as opportunities for further growth and development. This requires leaders who are able to develop an atmosphere of trust and mutual support with their followers, so that potential problems can be identified before they become crises. Reciprocal loyalty and mutual respect are the hallmarks of the leadership climate created by leaders in proactive organizations.

META-STRATEGIES FOR PROGRAMMING THE HIGH PERFORMING ORGANIZATION

The more progressive perspective afforded by the proactive frame of reference is nevertheless still insufficient to generate truly high-performing organizations. The phenomenon of corporate excellence is characterized by a high level of energy that unleashes human spirit and results in markedly improved productivity.

To generate these highest levels of performance, leaders need to operate from a frame of reference that sustains and enhances the proactive level of performance. They also shape the cultural conditions inside the organization that breed the high spirit seen in high-performing systems.

Our observations of high-performing organizations have led us to many of the same conclusions reached by others who have written on this subject. Peter Vaill[5] has pointed out that sometimes the energy level in such organizations is so high that their activities seem frenetic and confusing to the outside observer. Yet to the members of the high-performing organization, these activities seem quite natural and not at all incoherent. (Vaill also pointed out that sometimes the reverse is true: calm appearances may mask the commitment felt by members of a high-performing system).

The leaders of high-performing organizations may not all have the same way of eliciting high performance from their people. But they all seem to have found a way to manage the flow of energy in their team or organization. They "see" energy patterns and the human spirit these energy patterns release; they attend to these indicators with a dedication that equals and usually exceeds their dedication to the more ordinary indicators of performance, such as profit.

Although not all leaders of high-performing organizations use the same words to describe how they elicit the spirit and unleash the energy of their people, those who become acquainted with our work invariably report that the HPP model helps them make sense of and think coherently about what they already do with their intuitive grasp of "what's right." Invariably they become interested in understanding themselves and the possible reasons for their success. This fact — their immediate interest in their own potential as leaders — has provided us with a major clue about the nature of high-performing leaders and high-performing organizations: They have an almost insatiable curiosity about their own potentials, and actively seek out those challenges that they believe will activate these potentials.

Figure 7 shows the elements that constitute the enhanced frame of reference required for high performance. As noted, the frame of reference in high-performing organizations must be oriented on scanning for potentials — for what might be possible. It is from this understanding of the organization's potential that leaders and managers make choices about the organization's mission and purpose.

Figure 7. The High Performing Frame of Reference

The high-performing organization's choices about strategy are based on an underlying philosophy and folklore that give meaning to the organization's long-range plans. The task becomes one of strategically navigating the organization along an established path in the long-range plans. Likewise, the performance management system that is required for a proactive organization finds extra meaning in a high-performing organization, because it includes designing the plans for the organization's evolution within which its actual performance can be more effectively monitored.

Another key feature of the high-performing frame of reference is the emphasis on developing metasystems as well as formal systems. Metasystems such as quality circles, executive boards, and excellence networks, serve to shape the cultural milieu throughout the high-performing organization's structure.

The kind of leadership required to achieve and sustain organizational high performance is what we suggest be called "holistic," because high-performing leaders appreciate the larger roles played by their organizations as instruments of change in adjacent and higher systems in the environment. They look not only into their own organizations to help develop their potentials and that of their people, but to the outside as well. They see their own organizations as contributing actors in the general drama of human development, and they use their organizations to make contributions to the human communities and the culture in which they reside.

The Resulting High Performance Culture

Figure 8 shows the shifts that occur along the same 11 dimensions previously used to describe these nested frames. In high-performing systems, the focus is on achieving high standards of excellence by identifying new potentials, seeking out new avenues of opportunity, and activating the human spirit. To do this, leaders must have a frame of reference that extends beyond identifying the results to be achieved. They must look for ways of achieving the rich potentials in the future. This enhanced frame of reference expands the operative time frame to one that bridges and flows across time.

Leaders operating in this state of "flow" are able to sustain for themselves and communicate to their members an appreciation of the rich legacies, proud traditions, and positive legends that are the valued roots of the organization's past — and sustain and communicate an in-depth knowledge of the present state, and sustain and communicate a high-resolution vision of the future they want to create.

This extended time sense allows managers to plan a smooth, continuing evolution of the organization toward an even more promising future. They view change in the organization not as a threat to the survival of the status quo but as a natural process that allows new dreams and offers new opportunities

The planning process in a high-performing organization is a tool for conscious evolution rather than something done once a year, in a frantic way to get something down on paper. The change mode is "programmed," meaning the requisite conditions for high energy, creativity, and innovation are consciously built into the organization's operating values and cultural norms.

Management in high-performing organizations focuses on the strategic navigation of the total organization. The breakthroughs announced daily in the new world of electronic communication now permit forms of human structures

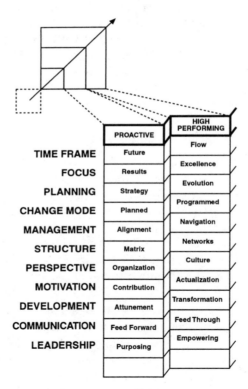

	PROACTIVE	HIGH PERFORMING
TIME FRAME	Future	Flow
FOCUS	Results	Excellence
PLANNING	Strategy	Evolution
CHANGE MODE	Planned	Programmed
MANAGEMENT	Alignment	Navigation
STRUCTURE	Matrix	Networks
PERSPECTIVE	Organization	Culture
MOTIVATION	Contribution	Actualization
DEVELOPMENT	Attunement	Transformation
COMMUNICATION	Feed Forward	Feed Through
LEADERSHIP	Purposing	Empowering

Figure 8. The Culture of the High Performing Organization

to be designed as key tools for the long-term navigation of complex organizations. Networks that are focused on the pursuit of high performance and human excellence can be "electrified" by linking network members together with a common electronic mail and computer conferencing system. When these internal "excellence networks" also include senior executives and other leaders in the organization, the ideas for action generated by the network have a direct connection into the decision-making mechanisms that exist at multiple levels in the organization.

Metasystems such as networks already exist in all organizations. Sometimes we call them "old boy networks," "interest groups," "constituencies, or infrastructures." High-performing leaders are beginning to realize that the advantages of quality circles can be amplified — that the principles of design and operation that enable quality circles to serve an organization's purpose can be implemented on a much larger scale. Interest groups, constituencies, infrastructures, and other metasystems can be developed and linked by computer to form a distributed "think tank" for new ideas, for keeping members informed of breakthroughs in their fields of specialization, for scanning for trends and future opportunities in the organization's field of operation, and for advising decision-making boards.

As suggested so vividly by Marilyn Ferguson,[6] while bureaucracies are always much less than the sum of their parts, the synergistic efforts activated by the rich information flow natural to networks makes them many times more efficient than the formal human structures through which they weave.

The perspective of leaders operating in the high-performing frame of reference includes the culture of the organization. As well as developing strong, cohesive teams and integrated organizations, high-performing leaders look for ways to consciously strengthen their organization by building a strong corporate culture. They understand the uses of ceremony and ritual in creating and perpetuating the positive folklore, legends, and myths that give each member of the organization a strong and proud heritage to maintain and reinforce. This attentiveness to the culture of the organization enables the leaders to act in ways that fortify the efforts of individuals to pursue their own actualization within the organization, rather than seeking individual fulfillment only in outside activities.

The focus of development in the high-performing frame of reference is on continuing transformation and renewal. This is accomplished through communication that links the positive heritage of the organization with its potential for excellence in the future. Not only do leaders in high-performing organizations have the unique ability to think far into the future and to keep their organization aligned around a great vision, they have the parallel ability and courage to give their people the freedom to pursue it. These leaders lead through their ability and willingness to empower their followers, to push power down into the hands of people so that they have the energy and freedom to seek adventure, creativity, and innovation. Most importantly, they lead by virtue of caring deeply for their followers, which produces the mutual bond of strong emotional commitment and reciprocal loyalty that are the wellsprings of spirited performance.

CONCLUSIONS

Given that we are already well into a new age of rapid change and transformation, higher-order models such as the one shown in Figure 9 are vital. Organizations that approach the challenges ahead with impoverished ways of thinking will be caught at the "shear line" of conflicting paradigms. They

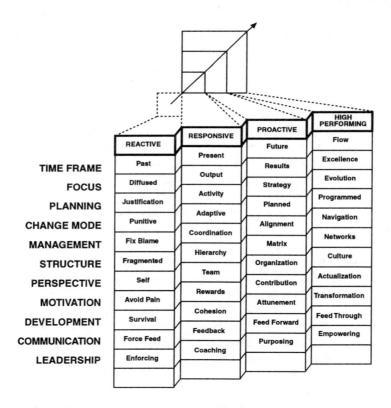

	REACTIVE	RESPONSIVE	PROACTIVE	HIGH PERFORMING
TIME FRAME	Past	Present	Future	Flow
FOCUS	Diffused	Output	Results	Excellence
PLANNING	Justification	Activity	Strategy	Evolution
CHANGE MODE	Punitive	Adaptive	Planned	Programmed
MANAGEMENT	Fix Blame	Coordination	Alignment	Navigation
STRUCTURE	Fragmented	Hierarchy	Matrix	Networks
PERSPECTIVE	Self	Team	Organization	Culture
MOTIVATION	Avoid Pain	Rewards	Contribution	Actualization
DEVELOPMENT	Survival	Cohesion	Attunement	Transformation
COMMUNICATION	Force Feed	Feedback	Feed Forward	Feed Through
LEADERSHIP	Enforcing	Coaching	Purposing	Empowering

Figure 9. Nested Frames of Reference for Programming High Performance

can anticipate increasing difficulties as the pace of change continues to accelerate, and as their habits of thought fall further and further behind the realities of an increasingly complex world.

We find that the overall picture is bright. We see a new generation of leaders emerging during this age of transformation. With their enhanced cognitive models of what must be done to achieve excellence in human systems, these leaders have the capacity to shape the manner in which their organizations deal with the turbulent times. They and their organizations are at the threshold of great opportunity, for these new leaders also possess the quality of spirit that they know to be the source of excellence and high performance in all human activity. They have the capacity to infect others with this high spirit and high purpose, and in doing so, to release the high levels of human energy required for extraordinary human achievement.

Notes

[1] I. Prigogine, *From Being to Becoming* (San Francisco: Freeman, 1980).

[2] Paul Hersey and Ken Blanchard, *Management of Organizational Behavior: Utilizing Human Resources*, 4th Edition (Englewood Cliffs, New Jersey: Prentice-Hall, 1982).

[3] S. Beer, *Platform for Change* (New York: John Wiley and Sons, 1975).

[4] J.M. Burns, *Leadership* (New York: Harper & Row, 1978).

[5] Peter B. Vaill, "The Purpose of High Performing Systems," *Organizational Dynamics* 11:2 (1982), pp. 23-39.

[6] Marilyn Ferguson, *The Aquarian Conspiracy* (Los Angeles: J.P. Tarcher, 1980).

15

Fast-tracking the Transformation of Organizations

LAWRENCE H. de BIVORT

Comments on the Second Edition

Looking back, I am startled — and pleased — by how well this essay has held up since 1984. Published in *Transforming Work*, it took on a life of its own, triggering a steady call for copies and pointing the way to successful organizational change and high performance for a slew of companies and a few governments.

Today, the essay still satisfies me. There is little that I would change or add to it. Since 1984, we have gained much experience with fast-tracking organizational development and transformation, but the new insights have been operational and tactical in nature, rather than strategic. The intervening years appear to have affirmed the accuracy of the discussion presented in the essay.

At the same time, in re-reading the essay now, I am swept by a certain sadness. At the time I wrote it, I hoped and expected that organizational transformation and fast-tracking would, within a relatively few years, become the norm. After all, why would an organization *not* pursue fast-tracked transformation, when it would achieve better results, faster, with greater reliability, and at lower cost than conventional approaches to organizational performance? Yet most organizations today remain stranded in trivial expectations for themselves, in modest visions of what they can achieve, in slow incremental change, and in chancy change initiative. They remain mired in a belief that organizational change *must* be slow. This belief expresses itself persistently, for example, in the assertion that changing an organization's culture must take many years, or the argument that it is safest to solve one problem at a time. Even today, the expectations of these organizations have not kept up with the technical ability we now have to raise organizational performance to very high levels.

I still hope and expect that fast-tracking and transformation will become organizational norms, as familiar to company executives, employees, shareholders, board members, and citizens as they are to today's high performance companies and organizational performance specialists. We know how to put organizations on the fast-track to high performance. That is no longer difficult.

For now the question remains, "How can we fast-track the world's understanding of the bright future that lies ahead for organizations that pursue high performance levels aggressively and rapidly?" Given the competitive pressures that are building up on organizations from the powerful forces of globalization and technology, it is a question that demands an answer. Given the growing dependence of individual well-being on the success of organizations, it is a question that directly or indirectly affects everyone.

— Lawrence de Bivort

This chapter reports on techniques developed specifically for the successful transformation of organizations. Lessons learned by the author over a five-year period and their implications are discussed. Emphasis is placed on the role of the Evolutionary Manager, who has the lead responsibility to develop a "meta-perspective" on the process of transformation and to serve as a catalyst, initiating and then guiding the transformation of the organization. The key elements covered are vision-goals, evolutionary managers and their skills, node points, internal communications, and slough-off strategies.

For those with a sense of urgency about the state of the world, a sense that a world that works must be built as a matter of the highest priority, the concept of transformation takes on a special meaning. No longer do business-as-usual, incremental, or accommodative strategies for organizational development seem adequate. Rather, transformation suggests a highly positivist, vision- and action-oriented strategy, in which activist visionaries, or what we will call "evolutionary managers," transform an organization quite deliberately, using high-level skills and techniques.

During 1978–1982, the advantages of and obstacles to fast-tracking the development of organizations were studied by the author, who was then Director of Corporate Development of Flow General Inc., a major multinational research and development corporation. During that period, fast-tracking strategies and tactics were developed and applied to a large number of affiliated companies. Collectively, results over the three-and-a-half year period were quite dramatic, as measured by conventional indicators: revenues multiplied by 2.3 times; net income by 4.5 times; and total assets by 4.9 times. The number of shares outstanding multiplied by 2.4, while the share price multiplied by 14. 7 times.

The conclusions presented here are based on that and subsequent experience with private and public sector organizations when the author became CEO and Director of the Evolutionary Services Institute.

For those with both a sense of urgency and high-level vision and action capabilities, anything less is likely to seem tentative and ultimately inadequate. Assertions that "transformation takes time" are viewed more as tacit admissions that their authors lack the requisite skills, technique, or experience than as accurate assessments of intrinsic organizational dynamics.

From this perspective, the following propositions on transformation and fast-tracking are considered.

Transformation

Transformation requires at least some basic structural and procedural change in at least some of the basic systems of an organization. Transformation, as used here, includes the notions of metamorphosis and transmutation, suggesting an elemental change in structure, process, or habit, marking a development from a lower to a higher order. Transformation requires breaking through existing belief structures.

How would one recognize transformation in an organization? Indicators that organizational transformation is occurring, as distinct from incremental or accommodative change, include the following.

1. The process of transformation results in a radical enhancement of the basic capabilities of the organization, particularly in the areas of:
   - access to and use of energy and material resources,
   - productivity, or the ability to aggregate resources,
   - generation and use of information,
   - creativity, or the ability to identify and pursue alternative development strategies.
2. The process of transformation leads to an alignment or linkage with larger systems and larger objectives than those in the past.

3. The process of transformation may be characterized either by strong vision and development capabilities, or by a sense of things being out of control, or a combination of both.

Fast-tracking

Fast-tracking involves the conscious acceleration of the transformative process. In true fast-tracking, the premium value is full achievement of pre-specified transformative objectives as rapidly as possible. Time is considered the resource in shortest supply. Saving time is a priority second only to achieving the transformative objective.

Fast-tracking requires the highest level of evolutionary management skill if things are to stay on track. When done with evolutionary management skill, fast-tracking can bring an organization to extraordinary levels of capacity in extraordinarily short periods of time. Such levels are measured in terms of:

- conventional values (such as sales, profits, stock price),
- intermediary values (such as leadership, research and development, and product value),
- transformative values (such as whole-systems integration, process flexibility, and socio-psychological elan).

If taken to the limit without adequate evolutionary management skills, fast-tracking can create process-related strains such as the misuse of resources, mis-synchronization of efforts, and a sense of trauma or burnout.

How would one recognize fast-tracking in an organization? Indicators of fast-tracking include the following:

1. A highly ambitious, highly attractive set of strategic/transformative/evolutionary goals is present in the organization. The goals may be stated in quite abstract terms, designed to conjure up visions of possibilities, or directions to move in, rather than providing specific descriptions of end-states.

2. A very rapid achievement (by conventional standards) of the goal, usually taking observers by surprise.

3. A coherent evolutionary management capability is present in an individual, a team, or an action network, which "holds" the goals; it causes, monitors, and guides the processes of transformation.

4. A sense of enthusiasm and commitment among the immediate catalysts of the transformation process is evident. It is picked up by

other individuals in the organization who understand and align themselves with the transformative activity. It also may be opposed by some, who fear that change will affect them negatively, or who fear uncertainty more than they are attracted to high- level empowerment.

5. During the transformative process, instability within the organization may be visible. It is mitigated by the natural resilience of the organization — a resilience strengthened, if necessary, by the evolutionary managers.

KEY ELEMENTS IN FAST-TRACKING

A number of key elements seem to mark every successful fast-tracking effort: vision-goals, evolutionary managers, evolutionary manager skills, focus on node points, internal communications, and slough-off strategies. The more complex an organization, i.e., the larger its number of semi-autonomous subsystems, the more essential these requirements become.

Vision-Goals

The strong, well conceived, and highly attractive vision of what the organization is seeking to become is the cornerstone of a fast-tracking transformative effort. This vision becomes the single "master template" through which all participants in the transformative process can, singly and collectively, assess their undertakings; it provides coordination and synchronization. To many, inside and outside the organization, the magnitude of the vision-goals will prove attractive in and of itself, a chance to accomplish something of larger significance without a massive or debilitating commitment of time — a chance to test and further develop one's deepest abilities. To others, the vision-goals might seem unreasonably ambitious; the abstraction with which they are described allows people to see specifics in the goals that are appropriate to their own view of the cutting edge of possibility.

The central vision-goals can spin off many secondary visions. People in the organization may find themselves more attracted to a secondary vision-goal than to the primary one. Identifying the mutual congruence of the vision-goals permits fast-tracking to proceed coherently; full agreement is not a prerequisite.

The most coherent vision-goals are crafted by a relatively small number of people, but it is important to share these goals with as many others as possible within the organization, so that they may influence, redefine, and come to view the goals as their own. This identification is critical to freeing the usually immense personal energies and capabilities that lie fallow in most organizations. These energies and capabilities are essential in fast-tracking, providing both the momentum for change and the resilience to overcome inevitable glitches.

In a large, publicly held, high-tech corporation that went through a successful fast-tracked transformation, the vision-goals were stated as follows:

The Metadevelopment of [Company A]
The purpose of the [transformative] effort is to enable the Company to benefit from, and take a position of leadership in the evolutionary [transformation] movement. The goal is to make [Company A] into a world-class company by turning it into an "evolutionary manager," that is, a catalyst and guide of the [world-wide] evolutionary development effort.

Criteria of Evolutionary Development
In effect, to become an evolutionary manager, [Company A] will go through an evolutionary development [process] of its own, involving the same characteristics that all evolutionary activity has [when it is] successful . . .

The Metadevelopmental Program for [Company A]
Three areas [will] be emphasized:
- participation and prominence in the evolutionary technologies
- management and guidance of the applications of the technologies
- development of evolutionary management and leadership capabilities to help guide the general evolutionary development effort and to provide for effective two-way interaction with the . . . environment.

First-order implications [of the Metadevelopmental Program]: a world-class Company
- rapid growth in financial size and well-being
- global venue and perspective
- visibility and influence
- leadership, initiative, and responsibility at the center of the global evolutionary development effort, for the directions of society, and the creation of a beneficial environment.

For a large biochemical company, which was seeking to commit one of its divisions to a high-risk, high-return development strategy, the vision-goals were summarized as follows:

> By initiating the development strategy with the electrophoretic purification payload on the [space] shuttle, we are taking our first step toward the next frontier — space — and demonstrating our long-term interest in all human and technical development in space, including the certain, if eventual, establishment of space-based industries and human colonies.

For a small manufacturer of particle sensors, the vision-goals were stated in this way:

> The world we seek to build is one in which all information is openly available to all, in which knowledge or knowing about the state of the world is as much a right as are life and liberty.

> By focusing its present efforts on the development of cheap, reliable multiband sensors, and upon eventual merger with telecommunications and [automated data analysis capabilities, this company expects to make a substantial contribution to building this kind of world, while attracting to itself the financial resources and well-being that will allow its stakeholders to thrive.

Vision-goals such as these require considerable thought, emotion, and deliberation. They galvanize the energy of an organization to fast-track its transformation and so to position itself to make a reality of its present vision-goals and others it will develop later.

Ironically, some of the best candidates for fast-tracking are companies that are having difficulties: lost markets, aging plants, or tiring management. The organization, while in a resource and morale slump, knows something dramatic has to be done. A transformative vision-goal may be precisely the thing to mobilize the remaining energy and imagination of the organization and to provide a coherent scheme within which to make the inevitable and painful moves involved in a turnaround.

Companies that have become accustomed to success may become complacent, and so enshrine precisely the methods and ideas that will someday prove inadequate as the world moves on more rapidly than they. The greatest threat to an organization may not be the inadequacy of its capabilities, but the paucity of its imagination and its ambition.

Evolutionary Managers

By whatever name, organizations that fast-track successfully typically do it with the immediate assistance or guidance of a designated "evolutionary" manager. This individual, or team of individuals, takes the lead responsibility in generating the momentum needed for fast-tracking, ensures that it remains on track, and anticipates or responds to the inevitable problems which emerge along the way.

The key requirement here is that the evolutionary manager be semi-independent of the main line operations of the organization — independent enough to have a metaperspective of the organization and its vision-goals, and yet sufficiently part of the organization to have a deep understanding of its history, people, capabilities, culture, and belief structures. The meta-perspective is essential to providing calm, objective leadership and assistance to the fast-tracking organization. The deep understanding is essential to pulling together, with high-level precision, economy, speed, and predictability, the resources and efforts of the organization as it fast-tracks. This evolutionary management capability is both "of" the organization and somewhat removed from it. Being by definition a complete system, an organization cannot readily or fully generate its own transformation — its own transcendence of paradigms. A semi-independent "metacatalyst" is needed for this, one that can see beyond the self-restricting paradigms imbedded within the organization.

The "ideal" evolutionary manager often turns out to be a team — composed of three or four highly skilled, highly enthusiastic insiders in middle or upper management who become wholly committed to fast-tracking and the vision-goals. They are often the primary originators of the draft vision-goals. Additional team members may be one or two outside specialists in fast-tracking, the organization's president or chief executive officer and, most desirably, a handful of directors and other key officers and operations managers. As the fast-tracking effort begins, others join in the effort, and the evolutionary management team eventually can become quite large and diffuse. Ideally, everyone in the organization becomes part of the evolutionary management team. Regardless of how many people in the organization "join" the team, the initial key people typically continue to identify themselves as a small, somewhat closed, "core" group. They monitor the fast-tracking process, catalyze what needs to be catalyzed, guide all fast-tracking efforts to ensure synchronization, and provide any services that are needed that would not otherwise be available. In the process of holding these responsibilities, they develop among themselves their own camaraderie, rituals, and myths (i.e., the glue of social cohesion and effectiveness).

But there is another element without which even the most enthusiastic team will not be able to fast-track an organization successfully: skills.

Evolutionary Management Skills

Successful fast-trackers have high-level skills in three basic areas:

- Interpersonal effectiveness
- Business development
- Technical development

The latter two skill areas are fairly well understood; business development means maintaining and enhancing the financial viability of the organization, and technical development means research and product (or service) development. The major breakthroughs in skill levels used by fast-trackers lie in the area of interpersonal effectiveness. Disciplines such as evolutionary biology, cybernetics, linguistics, and living systems theory have opened new doors and led to the development of extraordinary new standards of interpersonal communications effectiveness and influence. These provide the primary tools for creating fast-tracking in organizations. They provide for the creation of effective vision-goals coded to the culture of the organization. They enlist assistance, empower others, build cohesion, overcome reluctance, resistance, or friction, and ensure high-level feedback and communications through all segments of the organization.

If the core people in a successful team do not have advanced instinctive ability in these areas already, it is certain that they should receive formal training in high-level interpersonal effectiveness skills and patterns, preferably before the fast-tracking program is launched in an organization.

Node Points

One can imagine an organization simply as a medium through which knowledge, authority, and resources flow unevenly. Where these three intersect, a node point is formed — a high-level leverage point where fast-tracking can be introduced by the evolutionary management team. After the initial vision-goals have been prepared, the evolutionary management team has been identified and trained, and the high-level development strategies have been determined, the node points are then approached simultaneously, with precision and inter-node cohesion. The organization hits the ground running. Fast-tracking is under way.

In one company that was interested in fast-tracking its development, the CEO was concerned that many line managers would oppose the effort. Although the company was well-off, the CEO could see strategic difficulties ahead (in this case, new federal regulatory policy). It would be difficult, however, to convince all key line managers of the need to make some product changes — fast — and the CEO feared that open discussion might harden opposition rather than dissipate it.

The fast-tracker team, still in its embryonic form, was instructed to proceed, but discreetly. It did so by segmenting portions of the development strategy until it applied specifically and appropriately to each separate node point. Then, in an intensive two-day period, the fast-trackers, using high-level interpersonal skills, interacted separately with the people involved at each node point, bringing about a *de facto* fast-tracking developmental cohesion and synchronicity. The overall development strategy was later discovered by the line managers at the node points, who were by then quite pleased with the rapid development they were experiencing, and equally delighted to find that their fellow line managers were also up to some interesting things.

Successful fast-tracking evolutionary management teams learn a key truth swiftly: All transformative efforts are done through the node points. Any actions directed elsewhere (that is, to a point where knowledge, authority, or resources are lacking) are strictly of secondary importance.

Internal Communications

Fast-tracking strategies depend largely (some might say solely) on the exchange of "symbols" — those nebulous items to which human beings, with varying degrees of enthusiasm and precision, attach meaning. Fast-tracking lies in the area of new hopes and endeavors, rather than in ingrained habits, so it particularly depends on the richness, speed, and accuracy with which symbols — words, pictures, sounds — are transmitted and used.

Most organizations, particularly the larger ones, have communication patterns that serve key individuals rather than the organization as a whole. One of the first items on the agenda of an embryonic evolutionary management team is communications: communications within the team, and the team's communications with the full organization. The communication system has to be capable of informal, off-the-record exchanges as well as formal, recorded ones.

The main communications problems usually arise from encrusted, hierarchical communications patterns, in which information flows up and down hierarchies based on organizational position, rather than freely between people based on need. Loosening the old patterns is a key objective of the evolutionary managers.

If the organization is located at a single site, face-to-face meetings with provision for thought-provoking memoranda and documentation should be sufficient. If the organization is dispersed geographically (e.g., a multinational corporation), the challenge of building an organization-oriented communications system, as opposed to a key person-oriented system, is compounded by the intrinsic weaknesses of the communications media. Mail is slow and receipt is not usually confirmed. The telephone requires the other party to be available, and does not provide an automatic record. The telex is ponderous and expensive. Travel is time-wasting and expensive. A growing, useful communications medium is electronic mail and conferencing. Combined with the telephone and some travel, the appropriate electronic mail system provides communications with features that are similar to fast-tracking itself: rapid, precise, supportive, non-hierarchical, flexible, social, and discreet.

Slough-off Strategies

People who don't know organizations well are often surprised to find out that caring about people is, ironically, one of the ways organizations can get into trouble. This is as true of the most hard-nosed, profit-oriented "megabuck" machines, as well as the cuddliest nonprofit groups. Inevitably, in the natural life of an organization, individuals and programs lose their vitality. This process is aggravated in an organization that is undergoing transformation. The evolutionary management team almost inevitably must address this issue at some point. Most only do so when it arises. The issue is always the same: are resources to be committed to assuring the continued presence of a non-contributing operation or employee? Courage, compassion, and respect for the values being sought in the vision-goals may come into uncomfortable, irreconcilable conflict with this issue. An essential element of fast-tracking is to face this issue, as it comes up, with grace, speed, and effectiveness, lest the transformative effort itself be undercut. It has happened before, and will undoubtedly happen again, though all the other elements needed for fast-tracking were present.

CONCLUSION

Vision-goals. Evolutionary managers. Evolutionary manager skills. Node points. Internal communications. Slough-off strategies. These are the essential elements in fast-tracking the transformation of organizations.

Fast-tracking is an adventure — perhaps the most important adventure we can pursue. The true new frontiers are not geographic or in the world of materials; they are social and psychological, having to do with the vast, unexplored, untapped regions of human capability. Learning how to get there is as much the objective as getting there. Once there, we may discover fast-tracking possibilities of even greater magnitude, and if this proves so, learning how to learn will prove to be the real payoff of our fast-tracking efforts today.

16

The Fusion Team:
A Model of Organic and
Shared Leadership

LINDA S. ACKERMAN ANDERSON
DIANA K. WHITNEY

Comments on the Second Edition

As we reflect over the past decade, a time of great social innovation and change, we realize that the principles and practices of Organizational Transformation have come of age. Much of what was written in the first edition of *Transforming Work,* including the idea of the Fusion Team, are now "best practices" in organizations around the world.

In our work and that of colleagues, large group interventions have become an intervention of choice for global organization change and community development. As a change acceleration strategy that builds wide-scale commitment through participation, large group interventions are being deployed throughout business, in government, in the public sector, in education and in communities. The success of these interventions, which often include meetings of 100 to 1,000 or more people, depends on the ability of a core team, as it is often called, to manage the complexities of design, logistics and varied human needs. In addition to overseeing large group events, the fusion team also serves as the focal point for monitoring the process and generating, receiving and communicating information to influence the change strategy.

In our work, the core team resembles a fusion team even though it may be called by other names, such as the Vision 2002 Project Team, the Taos Summit Planning Team, the Culture Council or the Vision Realization Team. We have found that organizations and communities use fusion team concepts and adapt them to fit their intentions and needs. For example, one of the most exciting applications of a core team is in the Appreciative Inquiry approach to change. In these situations, it is the core team that creates the conditions for active inquiry and guides the organization in the discovery and design of a better future.

The principles and practices of the fusion team have withstood the test of time in the form of these change management teams. They are made up of diverse individuals from across the organization or community. They serve to organize highly complex processes while ensuring participation and innovation. They operate with a sense of shared leadership, adaptable roles, and self-empowerment. And they terminate once their effort is complete, or matures to the point of being integrated into the organization's daily practices.

Some of the benefits that our clients have experienced through the use of fusion teams have included the building of diversity and the establishment of cooperation and co-creation as ways of operating to produce quick and integrated results across functions, businesses, processes and levels of the organization. As we reflect on the potential uses and benefits of fusion teams to organizations in the new millennium, we see the use of such teams to oversee complexity and to produce results in an accelerated and integrated manner. We see the fusion team structure increasing personal responsibility for outcomes, and decreasing the dependency that workers and managers often have on their executives.

We also hope that the spirit within which the fusion team was born can continue to thrive and grow in businesses and communities around the world. We hope that the fusion team might be used more fully as a vehicle for attending to the emotional, spiritual, and physical well-being and morale of organization members as they produce results. It is our belief that fusion teams can continue to serve as a model for engaging people in meaningful ways, for ensuring that work be enlivening and nurturing, and for managing large-scale organization and community transformations.

— Linda S. Ackerman Anderson
Diana K. Whitney

The fusion team is a model for shared leadership structure and process useful in situations where a large and diverse group of people is brought together for an intensive, innovative, or change-oriented project. It does not replace traditional hierarchies; rather, it works within them with special "license" to enhance learning, synergy, and product development. Fusion teams are usually conceived to reflect the values of positive vision, the release of human potential, group cohesion, and individual responsibility. The authors develop the fusion team concept and describe how it has been used successfully in a variety of settings.

Current work in organization transformation focuses on the collective attitudes, beliefs, values, and style of organization members — in essence, the culture. Strategies for transforming work involve altering elements of culture by purposely shaping those aspects of an organization that transmit and maintain it. One of the primary vehicles for the transmission of culture is an organization's structure — the way people arrange themselves to accomplish important tasks. Leaders must therefore be aware of the relationship between the way individuals think about themselves and their contribution, and how they organize physically and psychologically.

For instance, if people feel the structure of their organization is cumbersome and controlling, they will reflect this in the slowed output of work. Likewise, if they feel their organization is set up to assist and support them, they will perform with much greater efficiency.

Unfortunately, not many executives today spend time reflecting on the direct relationship of their organization's structure to the productivity and emotional health of their employees. However, implicit in the form of an organization — its chart, policies, and physical layout — are very strong messages about how work is to be conducted. Control promotes constraint; freedom promotes creativity. The purpose of this chapter is to introduce a model in which the relationships among structure, culture, and outcome are explicit.

This model of the fusion team is useful under circumstances that require a focused working environment to produce accelerated innovation. It does not replace the traditional hierarchy; it works within it to meet the unique demands of intensely creative or change-oriented projects.

What the Fusion Team Is

By design, a fusion team (usually consisting of about nine members) guides and oversees the coming together of a large group of people to perform a complex or innovative task. It is founded on the principle that both individual and collective potential should be recognized and used at the highest rate possible. Webster defines fusion as "the process of melting together; a merging of diverse elements; a coalition; the union of atomic nuclei to form heavier nuclei with the release of huge quantities of energy." It is for this energy (creativity), released from the merging together of diverse people (collaboration and synergy), that the fusion team is designed. It is a form of group management that looks after the creative process, balancing the needs of people with the requirements of the project, budget, and timetable. It is an organic body — changing shape, membership, and focus to assist the larger project group to fulfill its charge.

To accomplish a task involving a multitude of activities and expectations, it is necessary to attend to all possible demands. This attention, or caretaking, is called stewardship. Any time stewardship over a complex project and people is required, a fusion team can be used to great advantage. Fusion teams are best suited to situations in which the following conditions exist.

- A large group is brought together to accomplish an innovative and complex project over a period of time.

- There is a great variety among the people, their backgrounds, their expertise, the information they bring, and the values they hold.

- There is a desire for synergy, and to maintain and expand variety in order to accomplish the task in a creative way.

- There is a willingness to delegate responsibility within the group to ensure commitment to the task and a fuller utilization of leadership resources.

- There is the desire to build cohesion among the total group while recognizing, valuing, and utilizing the unique contribution of each member.

- The effort is legitimized by the larger organization and protected from traditional methods of operating for the interim of the project.

Examples of fusion team applications include designing and implementing a major organizational change; running a conference or a campaign; creating an "information product" such as a book, report, or media event; or

The Formation of a Fusion Team

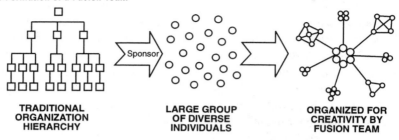

| TRADITIONAL
ORGANIZATION
HIERARCHY | LARGE GROUP
OF DIVERSE
INDIVIDUALS | ORGANIZED FOR
CREATIVITY BY
FUSION TEAM |

developing and managing a new strategic and operational plan. When an executive group decides it needs to pursue one of these efforts, it selects a sponsor to oversee the project. The sponsor then identifies the most appropriate members of the organization, and outsiders or consultants, to participate full- or part-time. Once everyone is brought together, this diverse group of individuals forms a fusion team that then oversees the endeavor. The figure above graphically represents this structuring process. It demonstrates that the fusion team helps transform a more static hierarchy into a dynamic, productive network. This structure, coupled with the unique cultural dynamics of the fusion team philosophy, paves the way for a successful outcome.

Unique Values of the Fusion Team

As previously mentioned, specific values are implicit in any organizational form. The fusion team is built upon seven core values and beliefs.

1. The *pursuit of excellence* enables people to fulfill their highest potential.

2. *Synergy* brings talented people together to create an outcome greater than the product of any subset of the group and, at the same time, contributes to individual growth.

3. *Productivity* stems from caring for people's physical, mental, emotional, and spiritual needs within the work setting.

4. Organizing to support a *creative process* enables an optimal balance of flexibility and control.

5. *Shared leadership* enhances the experience of personal responsibility and group effectiveness and optimizes group resources.

6. *Personal responsibility* enables each member of the project, participants as well as fusion team members, to take care of his or her own needs while supporting the needs of the overall group.

7. Creating an environment where *focused work* is perceived as fun is a great facilitator and accelerator of learning, synthesis, and creativity.

The operative culture within the project group is often radically different from the culture of the traditional organization within which it exists, as these values may demonstrate. It is for this reason that the group's sponsor plays a very important and unique role.

Organizational Sponsorship

Once the project is legitimized by the organization, a sponsor is chosen. The sponsor selects the large body of expertise needed for the project out of the larger organization, ensuring that the best resources are available full- or part-time. External resources such as consultants also may be included. To establish the appropriate context for the project and a fusion team structure, the sponsor then obtains the "license" for the fusion team and group to operate outside the normal organizational culture if necessary. To do this, he or she may have to act as a political buffer, managing the interface between the two organizations. The sponsor keeps the larger hierarchy well-informed, and protects the project's autonomy.

Once the project group is brought together, the sponsor clarifies its mission and task, and sets the expectations for how it will work. A high level of energy and enthusiasm at the launching of the project and the fusion team is critical to its success. The sponsor clarifies the need for commitment to the mission, the core operating values, and the general function of the fusion team. He or she provides encouragement, clarification, and guidance, and creates the sense, real or imagined, that the entire process is well-supported and directed. Most importantly, the sponsor sets the stage for the formation of the fusion team.

Membership on the Fusion Team

Membership on the fusion team is usually voluntary. Any member of the large group, regardless of title, rank, educational level, expertise, sex, race, or technical knowledge can volunteer to serve on the team. The boundaries between the fusion team and the large group are flexible, so the team is established with a norm of open membership. During the life of the project, members of the larger group may join the fusion team as appropriate to the needs of the effort. There is an attempt to keep the team size under nine active participants. Others may observe or support, but when the team meets to make operating or strategic decisions, having more than nine people often complicates the process.

It is assumed that those who volunteer their participation on the team do so out of commitment to the project's success. Open volunteering over the life of the project establishes the norm of self- responsibility — a key ingredient for fusion team success. Individuals join because they feel they have a contribution to make. They carry out this contribution by gracefully balancing what they have to offer with the needs of the fusion team and the larger group. Once the fusion team is formed, several key functions must be handled to get the group off to a healthy start.

Dynamics Within the Fusion Team

Of primary importance is leadership, which within a fusion team is dynamic, situational, and shared. The traditional mode involving one leader and many followers is not the norm in a fusion team. In this setting, leadership often changes hands or is shared simultaneously for different activities. Leadership varies according to what is to be done and who is best suited to do it. For instance, different individuals may take the lead on specific decisions, communications, administration, or discrete tasks.

Leadership is best described as emergent and contingent upon needs. The notion is to create a group filled with leaders, not a group without one. Individuals volunteer to step into leadership roles for particular activities, and they freely release leadership upon completion of their tasks. Individual members must be able and willing to let go of the power associated with their regular organizational titles and positions, and to step into the forefront when their unique skills and ideas are needed.

It is not uncommon that a fusion team develops this way of operating over time, as the members become more comfortable with the process and more trusting that it will work. The urge to take over, to push decisions, or to act in other counterfusion ways may be felt by team members initially. However, to be successful, open leadership must be clearly understood and accepted. The sponsor can help guide this if necessary.

Planning for fusion team activities is highly flexible, depending on the needs both of the large group and the fusion team members. In the meeting, team members begin the planning process by sharing their individual hopes for both the outcome and the group's process. Ultimately, a collective vision forms and focuses all fusion team members in a common direction.

This collective vision of both the desired results and the steps needed to reach them becomes the general planning guidelines for fusion team activities. Next, the work needs to be organized.

Initial Questions to Be Considered by the Fusion Team

The following are some key initial questions that help shape the desires of the fusion team:

1. What do the people involved need in order to do an excellent job, to enjoy doing it, and to feel super about the result?
   - How should we best organize ourselves?
   - What should we provide for these people?
   - How should we relate to these people?

2. What do we need to do to facilitate, support, encourage, allow, and create the following?
   - high performance
   - innovation
   - new information
   - cohesion
   - energy, excitement
   - self-regulation
   - results

3. What can we do that will allow each person to contribute in a way that best suits him or her, and will at the same time get us to the desired project outcome?

Division of labor within a fusion team occurs on a voluntary basis, guided by the norms of self-expression and self-responsibility. Once the vision is formed, tasks are identified and ordered, including both large areas of responsibility as well as detailed administrative activities. Team members then discuss their preferences and skills, each taking responsibility for some part of the work that needs to be done. Once the general dynamic is set, the team then organizes its work from meeting to meeting, as well as deciding how the larger group sessions will be run. Often the team is only a few hours ahead of the larger group in knowing the next step.

Fusion team members volunteer to do what they enjoy and want to do. The result is a high-quality outcome, which emerges from the optimum use of the skills and abilities of all team members. Just as the leadership role changes within a fusion team, so do other roles. Individuals work together in whatever combinations are required by the needs of the large group and the project.

Participation in a fusion team does not automatically exclude one from a role in the large group. Fusion team members decide for themselves how to balance their roles as a contributor to the large group and as a member of the fusion team. One fusion team member may work only on the fusion team; another may be on the fusion team as well as in another role in the large group. Such variation is encouraged and supported, since it allows for the greatest contribution overall.

The team places high priority on building a cohesive group and on looking after its own well-being. This bonding together may take a number of forms, such as:

- sharing personal reasons for volunteering,
- giving each other recognition and constructive feedback,
- creating a unique and supportive environment,
- engaging in social or athletic activities together,
- performing bonding rituals,
- assisting each other to relax, to release stress and pent up emotions.

The experience of caring and cohesion increases fusion team members' commitment to each other as well as to the process and to the task. These are essential aspects of high-performing groups. Once the fusion team organizes itself and bonds together, it then focuses on its interaction with the larger group.

Functions in Service to the Large Group

The fusion team serves the larger group by providing a resource essential to any innovation and organizational change — human energy in the form of action, information, ideas, and material assistance. Fusion team members stimulate, link, and focus the creative energy among group members. They guide the formation of working subgroups and then coordinate between them to facilitate the greatest synergy. Creative working groups linked together provide the key organizing principle used by fusion teams. Supporting this type of subgrouping requires very effective communications.

Communications management within the larger group takes place in three ways. First, fusion team members operate as liaisons between and among various working groups. Communications within the large group ordinarily might be limited by position, title, rank, or organizational status. Fusion team members translate across the boundaries represented by different value sets, ideologies, and perspectives. Such freedom and flexibility of communication enables fusion team members to function as bridge builders, weavers, and catalysts for the flow of group ideas and creativity. As liaisons, or linking agents, fusion team members identify and provide resources and information needed by various subgroups, and represent the group's sponsor.

Second, the team establishes a fusion center, like "mission control," through which a great deal of group communication flows. The fusion center enables group members to exchange information (ideas, events, schedules, messages, requests, needs, data) with one another without having to be in the same place at the same time. Part of the fusion center is an administrative area that provides resources to group members throughout the project as needed. It serves as a home base and a gathering space for the larger group. The structure of the fusion center may vary, depending on the length and complexity of the project, the communication technology available, and the needs of group members. Anything from a centrally located bulletin board to an integrated telecommunications network can serve as the fusion center. It is essential that the fusion center be designed, created, and operated by the fusion team in response to group needs.

Third, the fusion team is accountable for scheduling, planning, and facilitating community meetings for the large group as a whole. Community meetings may be initiated by the group's sponsor, by a need sensed throughout the group, by a subgroup, or by the fusion team itself. Whatever the initial impetus, the fusion team determines the relative benefit of using total group time and schedules whatever events are on the agenda. The large meetings may involve these elements.

- presentations of information by outside experts or organization leaders
- opportunities for inspiration
- progress reporting
- dialogue among group members
- social activities
- pauses in the process to consider where the group is going and how effectively it is getting there

They provide an opportunity to insure that the total group and its process are maximally productive and satisfying. If this is not so, they are then able to correct and move to a higher level of functioning.

The fusion team also looks after morale, productivity, and spirit of the larger group; this is often called energy management. Energy management requires that fusion team members monitor and stimulate levels of positive energy reflected in commitment, enthusiasm, creative risk-taking, self-expression, mutual respect, and caring, as well as group members' physical and emotional well-being. Its goal is to maintain a focus that is collective, creative, and which inspires confidence. This can be demonstrated through words and behavior, such as the collective use of "we," collaboration, brain-storming, visualization, and a positive attitude.

Fusion team members manage the flow of energy by stimulating and connecting resources and by removing constraints. This may take any of the following forms.

- getting people together who have skills or ideas to share
- giving feedback, encouragement, and recognition
- airing and resolving conflicts or confusion
- laying out a plan of activities
- encouraging creative forms of documentation, such as visuals and graphics, rather than just words and prose
- helping people look at an issue from different points of view

Fusion team members also must be sensitive to the group's physical energy level. Stretch breaks and relaxation or play periods need to be scheduled at appropriate times to ensure the balance of mind and body needed for high performance. Modeling these behaviors fosters and supports norms that contribute to excellence.

HOW TO CREATE A FUSION TEAM: IMPLEMENTATION

Successful fusion teams are like dramatic productions. The drama analogy is useful to describe the steps to creating a fusion team. Players, people with diverse resources, are brought together with the expectation of creating an outstanding performance. Technical specialists, humanists, conceptual thinkers, content experts, and pragmatists might all be invited to join. Part of the fun is setting the stage and watching the drama unfold.

The sponsor initiates the scene with a well-crafted, heightened sense of theater. She or he emphasizes the importance of the project, along with the uniqueness of the process being used, the quality of the people involved, and the unfaltering commitment to the project's success. The sponsor goes on to recount the history of the effort, begins to imagine the future, and asks each participant to assume his or her rightful place in the story. With continuity with the past and commitment to the future effort established, the selection of the fusion team begins.

Casting is a volunteer process. Members must choose roles appropriate to themselves and to the culture of the total group. Space is opened up, to be filled by individuals wanting to serve on the team. In essence, a vacuum is created, attracting team members into it. At a conference, the vacuum may be created by a circle of empty chairs. In an organization, it may be slots on an organizational chart or empty office spaces waiting to be filled. This technique, the opening of space to be filled, has a compelling impact that initiates the process with a powerful sense of mission.

The drama is heightened by giving participants time to ponder, "Do I want to serve on this team? What can I contribute?" Individuals must judge for themselves what they are able to give and what kind of experience they want to have. This personal reflection aids their commitment to the effort.

At a given time, people come forward and take a seat or choose a role to play. They are acknowledged by the sponsor and the group as a whole. In some form of start-up ritual, they are empowered with the sense of service and commitment to their function and the mission of the larger group. This initial ceremony enhances the drama and clarifies the purpose and value of the fusion team. It is attention to this kind of process detail, the ceremonial kick-off, that makes this form of management uniquely successful. In an organization, this ritual may be a dinner, a formal announcement, or a specially designed meeting.

Then, the plot emerges. At the earliest appropriate time, the team holds its first meeting. It is here that team members truly join together as a cohesive group. They introduce themselves and state their expectations, visions, and personal objectives. It is suggested that someone record the process and outcome of the team's meeting from the beginning. The team then turns its attention to the needs of the total group. What is required to successfully accomplish the mission? What would success look like? What do the large group, the individual members, the fusion team, and the extended environment (beyond the large group) need? What resources are required and what kinds of technical, managerial, personal, and spiritual support are needed?

The answers to these questions are organized and prioritized. Individuals volunteer for activities and responsibilities based on personal preference and ability. The team organizes itself around when and how often to meet, how to interact with the larger group, and what its own management process will look like. Topics such as sharing leadership, communications, generating excitement, staying focused on the vision, political factors, feedback, and self-renewal needs are discussed. The team monitors both its own and the larger group's energies, looking after production, mental clarity, and emotional and physical needs. It sets up ways and resources to balance these demands over the life of the project.

Orchestrating the effort begins after the team presents its plan and structure to the whole group. Subgroups form and the work begins. The team meets and monitors progress as needed; the large group meets together or in smaller units, as appropriate. Communication, feedback, encouragement, refocusing the effort, and leisure time are all built in and played out. The sponsor, as mentioned earlier, manages the interface with the larger organization, handling progress reporting, changes in plan, requests for resources, or whatever is needed.

As the goal is achieved, the grand finale occurs. This is a time for the group and the team to applaud their efforts. The sponsor, who has monitored progress and supported the fusion team, assists in the closing activities. He or she brings back the drama from the first day, reflecting on the process and acknowledging the team and the large group for its efforts. The team members and participants from the total group have an opportunity to show appreciation, to report personal feelings or learnings from the experience, and to celebrate their accomplishment.

Early Examples of the Fusion Team

The fusion team concept was initiated and successfully employed during the Eleventh Army Delta Force Conference in July of 1982. Lt. Colonel Frank Burns, Director of the Army's Delta Force, and Lt. Colonel Jim Channon first created the concept just prior to that meeting. The Army's Delta Force was a "think tank" whose mission involved bringing people together in conference to generate innovative ideas and strategies to improve or expand Army potential. This particular one-week conference was appropriately called "Creating an Army of Excellence."

About one hundred people came together to generate a book of ideas and visions to be circulated among all army officers. The group consisted of both military and civilian specialists in over twenty fields of expertise.

The sponsor of the conference was the director of Delta Force, Lt. Col. Burns, commissioned to hold the conference by the Deputy Chief of Staff of Personnel. His role was played out with great subtlety in this case, becoming active only at crucial moments in the week, offering a broader perspective on how the task was progressing and how the book might be developed. The psychological benefit of his presence was strongly felt, however. It was clear that he expected the effort to be successful in both process and outcome, since the stakes were so high.

This chapter is written by two members of this original Delta Force fusion team, and is an extrapolation of their experience — what the fusion team stood for, how it operated, and the impact it had. Another member of this first fusion team, Sharon Connelly, reflected upon the experience:

> This process fosters creativity, innovation, adaptability, well-being, cohesion, an open system, leadership, productivity, teamwork, and the possibility of lasting personal and organizational growth. Commitment to a shared task is needed. Sufficient time for the task is needed. Easy access to resources and limited interruptions from the outside world are required. The fusion team is useful for an interdisciplinary or cross-system situation where people are open to the contributions of all comers, good for working on issues where creativity and imagination are likely to contribute to an improved result, and good where task group or think tank members are ready to work hard on results and are not concerned with issues of ego, protocol, or rank.[1]

Other examples of the fusion team concept have been used in the management of large-scale reorganizations and the start-up of a new business line in one of the country's leading communications service companies. In addition, there is currently a fusion team organizing an international relay run around the world in 1986. Another team has been operating successfully for one-and-a-half years to oversee a professional intern program in the field of organization development. One of the world's largest petroleum-related businesses has also initiated the concept to oversee the transformation of that company's culture.

In some cases, the structure has been referred to as a Transition Team or Implementation Task Force.[2] Although the pure fusion team principles have not all been used consistently, the basic concept has held. In most of these situations, many of the non-traditional values and language were not made explicit, but were modeled by the leaders and consultants to the efforts.

The fusion team is a new form of leadership and management structure which we believe has usefulness in transforming the nature of work. Still a young innovation, the fusion team will be refined and adapted over time. Clearly, it will work in some situations and not in others. In the Army's Delta Force experience and some of the other cases, the fusion team has already demonstrated itself to be a management approach that facilitates the achievement of extraordinary results, along with high levels of participation, excitement, and satisfaction on the part of those involved.

Notes

[1] Sharon L. Connelly, "The Fusion Team: An Experimental Group Management Technology" in *An Army of Excellence: Visions of Our Future Force*, ed. L.L. Franklin (Carlisle Barracks, Pennsylvania: Delta Force, 1982).

[2] Linda S. Ackerman, *Managing Complex Change Guide* (McLean, Virginia: Linda S. Ackerman, Inc., 1982).

17

A Formula for Corporate Fitness

ALFRED M. COKE
MICHAEL D. MIERAU

Comments on the Second Edition

The need to be organizationally fit is even more important now than when we wrote the original chapter. The reason is that our understanding of forces that shape and influence our business thinking are shifting to match our new understandings of the universe and natural laws. As we move from the Scientific Management model of mechanistic, rational, and predictable, to a Relationship model of systemic, fluid, and dynamic, our business organizations must be psychologically healthy enough to absorb, process, and apply the changes. They must understand the need to create new ways of doing work based on high-energy, short-term relationships.

We believe that a healthy organization is one that avoids the 90s trap of false management thinking, while building a solid core of interdependent relationships using guiding principles instead of fads. As organizations become lean with re-engineering, downsizing, and rightsizing, the requirement for operational effectiveness is critical. The paradox of giving away intellectual capital in organizational reductions, while maintaining a creative edge using the human potential, has never been more evident.

The effect of this paradox creates stress. How do I do more with less? Will I be the next victim of the downsizing? What is my future with this company? These are common questions being asked by the average person in today's business climate. Trust of management and company loyalty are wishful thinking that disappeared with the passenger pigeon and the dodo bird. Both are extinct because of poor applications of management theories, "Book-of-the-Month behaviors," and quick-fix, solve-all solutions.

In the 80s we saw organizations getting control of stress. Life got better. Things settled down. Then along came a resurgence of mis-applied management models. The greatest stress producer was the misapplication of re-engineering — now synonymous with downsizing. Even highly profitable companies violated the traditional informal contract with employees. That contract was a simple, unwritten understanding: when times are good, there will be no layoffs.

The new century must bring with it not a return to stability, but a new model of managing instability. Chaos will be the model of organizational behavior. It will be a time when every management model we have learned is suspect. Our old ways of thinking about sacrosanct things like organizational structures, job descriptions, and pay will be out the window. However, contrary to the fears of those old-school managers, business will not be left to anarchy. Instead, new patterns of management will emerge.

As new management accountabilites, responsibilities, and authorities evolve, we must manage the associated stress of employees. These will not be easy times, nor will they be casualty free. Management's ultimate responsibility is to minimize loss of human potential, while making maximum use of intellectual capital. Our suggestion is to use Corporate Fitness, which is in fact a systemic model for corporate success.

— Alfred M. Coke
Michael D. Mierau

This chapter describes a concept and series of techniques designed to produce high levels of effectiveness of individuals and work units through the study of stress. It focuses on the elimination of undesirable stressors and the reinforcement of positive stressors. The Corporate Fitness concept first builds individual awareness and capability to deal with stressors, and then focuses on work teams and management issues. Blending these factors together produces an integrated approach that leads to high-level corporate fitness.

Corporate Fitness (CF) as a goal integrates and balances individuals and work teams into a high-performing organization. It systematically reviews how the organization functions under stress (positive or negative), and what actions are required to create high performance. There is a logical sequence of events that produces this. By using certain procedures, management can make choices about corporate behavior based on proven management principles. CF involves two study components:

1. CF itself calculated in terms of the individual wellness (IW) of all persons involved, and

2. The organizational wellness (OW) of corporate management practices.

The formula IW + OW = CF shows the connection between major elements of the interactive procedure, and becomes the basis of our hypothesis. An organization can be transformed if the individual, work-team, and organizational dimensions are viewed with the goal of systematically analyzing these subsystems, determining each system's stress, and correcting states of imbalance using technologies presently available to managers.

CF strives to achieve peak performance from both the individual and organization. Intervention can be further defined as those techniques required to re-balance a system under stress. Stress occurs when corporate values, mission, product, structure, leadership, and resources are out of balance. Building an intervention plan to correct organizational imbalance calls for strategic changes.

Paradigm Grounding

The CF model (Figure 1) indicates movement through a system in multidimensional planes to reach a desired goal. This is a five-part process.

Flow State. Organizations are in a constant state of motion, beginning with the "now state," which is headed toward a "future state." In the "now state," when people and organizations behave ineffectively, people feel pain. Without pain, there would be no call for programmed change. When a business is always in a reactive mode, there is no time to do what is necessary to change the situation. In visualizing the future state, managers develop strategic goals and objectives. Future thinking is absolutely essential to determine the direction the flow state must take. The constant flow from the now to the future is what we must manipulate. Without proper inputs at critical levels, the flow goes forward with no central,

Figure 1. Corporate Fitness Paradigm

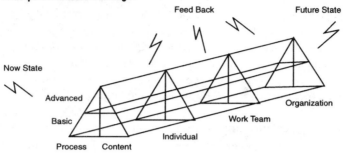

controlled direction. By using CF as a process, people and organizations can determine their futures, manage IW and OW, and make full use of their resources.

Systems Theory. Systems theory applies to organizations of all sizes. The living systems theory regards an office, branch, division, or corporate headquarters as both a part and a whole. Each must be studied as an inter-acting group and as a part of a larger system. Through use of systems theory, stress in the smallest system (the individual) can be extrapolated into the largest system (the organization). If modifications can be made for individual behavior, those modifications will affect the total organization. To achieve CF, we analyze the wellness of the person as an individual, and as a worker on the job. The organization is studied in terms of its subsystems' harmony with the environment.

Hologram. Every sector of a hologram (a three-dimensional photograph) contains information needed to create the entire image. Likewise, a single person reflects the larger system. Therefore, we can systematically study the individual person, then translate that learning to an organization. Any change must likewise follow a simple-to-complex sequence. Beginning the change process at the organizational level is far too complex to deal with. Individual, work team, and corporate targets, however, can be established simultaneously, and momentum can be developed by collecting necessary organizational information. We begin with the individual, progress through the work team, and conclude with the corporation itself.

Process/Content. Change is often focused on the task with little attention devoted to methods. Both process and content are addressed in CF. Interventions must be practical, translatable, and replicable. Managers should relate to what's going on. If they don't see the process in their own terms, there will be confusion, mystery, and suspicion. Finally, they must be able to repeat the process later without outside assistance. Intervention content must relate to the felt need or pain arising from the current behavior. Any materials used for interventions must sound reasonable to the user and be supported by facts that can be easily tested.

Basic and Advanced Skills. Total organizational transformation uses both basic- and advanced-skills training. Using the individual as an example, we find that basic-skills training for stress management isn't enough to promote long-term change. The person tends to return to old habits if there is not reinforcement, or if significant improvement isn't quickly realized. Advanced-skills training is often difficult because people prefer to do the basics and then quit. The novelty wears off and they think there is no need for advanced training. It becomes too easy to build illusions of success from short-term actions or delusions of failure from lack of measurable short-term results. When documented risk factors are presented as indices of stress, the scientific and lay communities take notice. An example is the high level of attention being given to serum cholesterol levels. Little attention is paid to less-obvious factors such as attitude. M. Friedman[1] describes this problem with great clarity in his research on Type A behavior and coronary heart disease. People need an increased level of awareness for development and use of advanced-skills training. Kobasa[2] supported the need for higher awareness in dealing with stress. She found that psychological hardiness (stress resistance) did exist in persons who have challenge, control, and commitment in their lives. We translate this idea to a larger system. An organization can be psychologically hardy if it provides challenge and self-control, and if it stimulates commitment through its operating practices and procedures. To achieve psychological hardiness, we attend to the organization's need for basic awareness training, and also install advanced-skills training.

The five keys described above are not all-inclusive, but represent major points in our approach to instilling a practical organizational transformation.

Corporate Fitness

A full CF intervention consists of six major components, and we recommend using all of them to achieve peak effectiveness. Figure 2 shows a schematic of the six components.

Training consists of three one-day workshops and a cluster of interventions. The first day is devoted to IW (Figure 2, Number 1). We hypothesize that managers can't begin to deal with the stress of others until they have their own behavior under control. The focus on personal stress includes

Figure 2. Corporate Fitness Process

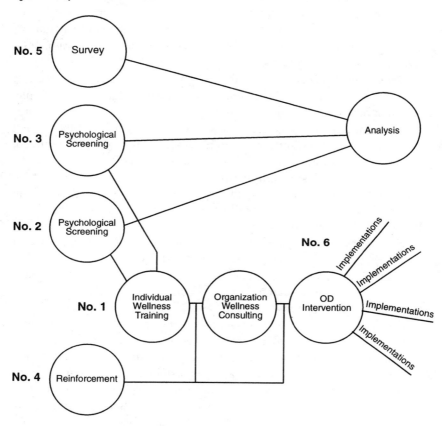

everyone from the CEO to the lowest-ranking person. Spouses are also encouraged to attend the opening day to reinforce the program's goals.

The second day addresses occupational-stress management. It begins with an in-depth review of Type A behavior as it relates to managers. Existing work teams review the work process, not what they do on a day-to-day basis.

The third day confronts managers with the problems of organizational stress. Those responsible for guiding the business meet for operational, managerial, and strategic planning.

These three one-day sessions constitute the basic awareness and skills-building training. The Organizational Development (OD) interventions that follow work on the issues developed during the assessment of the organization and during the training.

Another component of the CF concept is evaluation. Prior to training, all personnel go through a voluntary medical screening for physiological evaluation (Figure 2, Number 2). This is a full physical examination to determine their current state of health. An efficient and easily-administered screening process developed by the U.S. Army Surgeon General's Task Force on Fitness can be used for CF training. It consists of:

- Routine physical examination
- Standardized cardiovascular risk-assessment interview
- Multi-stage, symptom-limited exercise test
- Skin-fold thickness measurement to determine percentage of body fat
- 12-lead scalar electrocardiogram
- 12-hour fasting blood test
- Calculation of the Framingham Risk Index
- Structured interview for Type A behavior patterns

This provides a comprehensive screening of individuals who should be flagged and given prompt medical attention, and of those who exhibit significant risk factors. Another important, parallel evaluation is the psychological screening (Figure 2, Number 3), also done prior to training. Like the physiological screening, this provides individuals with a baseline from which they can establish improvement goals. The psychosocial screening can be done with existing standardized instruments such as the Jenkins Activity Survey, or with instruments developed by the consultant. A fourth major component is reinforcement (Figure 2, Number 4).

After the physiological screenings are completed and the basic workshops have begun, reinforcement must begin. People are suddenly made aware of stress and its ramifications. A reinforcement technique we use is to schedule prominent speakers on a wide range of related subjects that support the training. For individual training, these include diet, exercise, Type A behavior, and meditation; for organizational training, conflict management, strategic planning, problem solving, and others are presented. Other reinforcement techniques include media "blitzes," distribution of information booklets, and participation in field day events. Blood-pressure cuff machines and weight scales may be placed at strategic places within work areas. The key is to keep stress management and health promotion in constant focus. The central themes of self-responsibility and positive attitudes are constantly reinforced.

Management's support is very important for reinforcement. One effective technique to show support begins with a briefing by the CEO to the assembled organization, to explain why the CF program is being adopted. This presentation clarifies many concerns and questions about the program.

Another component of CF is the organizational survey done prior to the training (Figure 2, Number 5). There are many good surveys on the market. Consultants may develop a profile instrument to fit the training model. In our survey, we assess the general organizational structure by studying its subsystems. Indicators relating to the corporate soul, mission structure, and resources are assessed for the harmony of their interactive relationship. Survey data are fed back into the training process. Referring back to Figure 1, data gathering is scheduled at intervals to coincide with the individual, work-team, and organizational interventions. Individuals receive feedback from the physiological and psychosocial screening instruments, while work-team and organizational data come from surveys. Feedback includes observations made during the training sessions. This provides data of the same nature as that generated in group sensing sessions. Data also can be gleaned from other sources not quite so obvious. One method is to keep a roster of people who enroll for training. Rosters of non-attendance provide useful data for further study.

The last component of the CF process is the intervention (Figure 2, Number 6). In this last session, the managers focus on the three levels of planning: operational, managerial, and strategic. Sometimes more than one day will be needed for the planning process.

These six components (training, physiological screening, psychosocial screening, reinforcement, survey, and intervention) constitute the process of CF. The omission of any one component weakens the impact. The complete process becomes an orchestrated flow directed toward a meaningful goal to achieve peak individual and organizational performance.

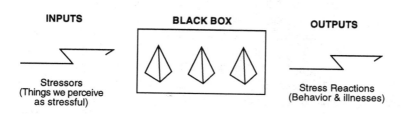

Figure 3. Stress Models and Systems Theory

The Content

CF has two systems models. The first is for individuals and the second applies to the occupational setting, with special emphasis on the work team. There are also organizational issues to be dealt with. We use the individual as a frequent example to describe the model.

After reviewing the literature on stress, we produced an integrated model, Stress Models Integration and Linkage Efforts (SMILE). We have taken the best ideas, added some of our own, and built them into a workable sequence. SMILE is a study of what occurs when a system experiences stress (Figure 3). Most stressors are identified and grouped as personal, family, occupational, organizational, and environmental sources. There are some transitional areas in which individual and occupational stress overlap. To address these transitional areas we have designed CF in three distinct phases: individual, work team, and organizational. Environmental stress permeates all of these areas.

Our approach to stress training focuses on the transformation of the organization. To study stress solely from the analysis of stressors or resulting behaviors is ineffective. Our objective is to study the system (Figure 3) and apply any lessons learned to the individual, the work-team, and the organizational scenarios. The content of the black box can be pictured as subsystems. Each system is drawn as a pyramid (Figure 4). There is no need to try matching subsystems across the pyramids. It is important, however, to know that a larger system may be divided into smaller, interactive subsystems. In each pyramid, the subsystems have a balanced relationship. This conforms to the concept of homeostasis, which leads to our definition of stress: Stress is

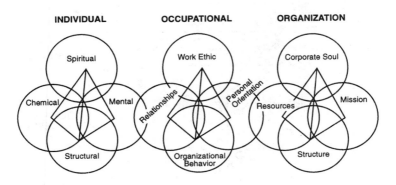

Figure 4. Subsystem Stress Pyramids

the disruption of homeostasis. Stress is neither the stressor that unbalances the subsystems, nor the resulting behaviors. Events and conditions often upset the balance of the system. In other words, too much or too little stress occurs. This is "system warp." A system will attempt to right itself or restore its balance when warp occurs. Imbalance must be effectively managed or the accumulated effect results in personal illness, impaired performance, and organizational dysfunction. These are parallel reactions to stress. The key to maintaining balance is in finding the appropriate level of stress to be productive, well, and happy.

Each system has a certain tolerance for stress. Both individuals and organizations exhibit idiosyncratic tolerances. Schafer[3] calls this the "comfort zone", and describes it as "the range of stimulation that is comfortable and healthy." The Tolerance for Stress scale in Figure 5 is hypothetical. Death occurs on each end of the scale. Too much or too little stress can kill both individuals and organizations. In Figure 5, appropriate or inappropriate levels of stress match one of the following states:

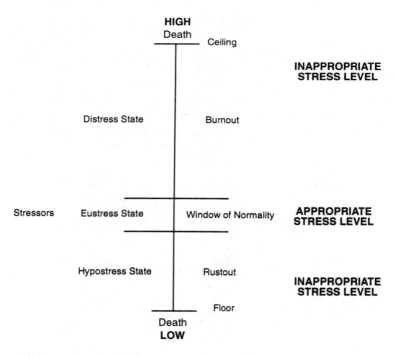

Figure 5. Tolerance for Stress Scale

1. *Distress* — a dysfunctional state, or "bad stress." Distress is what most people describe when they say "I'm under a lot of stress." This indicates there is excessive pressure, the condition is serious, and the situation is out of control. Such stress is the overload that produces illness and ineffective behavior within organizations. Distress is characterized as overwhelming.

2. *Eustress* — a functional state, or "good stress." Eustress comes from the Greek EU, meaning good. It implies the balance concept, where all things work in harmony. Further, it implies that one is experiencing enough stress to satisfy needs for challenges and opportunity. Eustress is therefore desirable.

3. *Hypostress* — a dysfunctional state, or "bad stress." Hypostress comes from the Greek hypo meaning "from under" or "beneath." If we move from too much stress to a state of less than enough stress, we have reached the other end of the spectrum. Hypostress is characterized as under-stimulation. In between the two extremes of high or low stress is the window of normality. That window is bounded by ceilings and floors, and is usually a narrow aperture; this represents the capability of a system to deal with stress. The window in Figure 5 is shown low on the scale to illustrate that some people operate from a pattern of routine, low-risk options. Stress management is confusing because the limits for people are unknown except when studied under laboratory conditions. Stress study is further complicated because tolerance levels vary for each person. This explains the phenomenon that what stresses one person may not stress another. It also explains why some organizations thrive at stress levels that would destroy others.

For practical applications, we use the tolerance for stress scale to describe a system's responses to stress. Four categories can be identified for either an individual, a work team, or an organization:

Type I — Reactive. This is a system that only reacts to its environment. It can never have time to do things in a planned way because it is always fighting fires. A reactive individual always reacts to someone else's control, whether it's a child's soccer schedule or a social calendar. A reactive organization never plans its future, because it operates on a crisis-management basis.

Type II — Responsive. A responsive system never gets caught with nothing to do. This is the one that crosses the t's and dots the i's. It is busy with form rather than content. A responsive person gives the illusion of being productively busy, but in reality avoids responsibility. Responsive organizations are busy looking good so they will not receive additional jobs.

Type III — Achieving. These are the average systems that accomplish the day-to-day tasks of life. They are the "good Joes" or the "dependable division." They are the workhorses of society. Occasionally, they have irregularities in their lives in the form of ineffective results. This is offset by occasional bursts of good ideas and duties above and beyond their normal range. Most people fall into this category.

Type IV — Supra-achieving. These are the rare, high-performing people and organizations of the world. They stand above their peers and competitors. Supra-achieving systems control themselves and their destinies. Vaill[4] has identified 47 hypotheses about these high-performing systems.

Given these distinct types of responses to stress, a person or an organization can realize that they have options. The technique we use in the basic training is to explain the other options so that managers and workers alike discover they don't have to be stuck with nonproductive, reactive results. Taking responsibility for life's choices is often very difficult for the stress student to accept. It is fundamental to make choices about one's life and to accept full responsibility for the consequences.

When given two high-strength, competing responses, or two equally unattractive consequences, it is easy to be an externally driven person and to blame others. Organizations and people that are externally driven never have to accept responsibility for their behavior and therefore can never be held accountable for their performance. A person suddenly becomes responsible for making his or her life work when he or she becomes internally focused. Organizations do the same when they gain control of their own management.

Supra-achieving persons and organizations have choices within the four types of behavior. The objective of training, then, is to make choices with full knowledge of the alternatives and the likely consequences. Our approach focuses on enriching life by making it appropriately stressful, while at the same time extending it to its fullest capacity. We are born with a stress "credit account" of unknown size. Every time we unbalance our systems, we make a "withdrawal" that results in a dwindling but unknown balance. Some people really do burn the candle at both ends by using up their credits too fast. We teach the principle of cutting the large withdrawals down to medium size, and the medium ones to small. This emphasizes the perspective that some creative tension in our lives is healthy and necessary.

Figure 6. Time Line Analysis

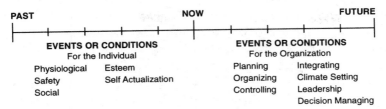

PAST   **NOW**   **FUTURE**

EVENTS OR CONDITIONS		EVENTS OR CONDITIONS	
For the Individual		For the Organization	
Physiological	Esteem	Planning	Integrating
Safety	Self Actualization	Organizing	Climate Setting
Social		Controlling	Leadership
			Decision Managing

Hooking Up

The grand finale of any stress-management program is changing unwanted behavior. We do this at two levels — one for the individual, and one for the organization. For both we construct a time line (Figure 6). Events and conditions from the past that produced unwanted effects are identified. These are traced back in a cause-effect-cause-effect sequence until the root cause is determined. This is then hooked up to the heirarchy of needs for the individual or a management principle for the organization. When enough of these events are analyzed, a pattern of behavior can be established.

The pattern of behavior is determined by looking at the pyramid appropriate for either the individual, the work team, or the organization. Consider which subsystem within the pyramidal system has been most violated. Since subsystems are interactive, altering one affects the other three. This knowledge guides the manager to the most troubled areas, where he or she must take specific action. After the past has been analyzed, the future side is developed. By predicting future events and conditions, comparisons can be made as to what type of stressors the organization is likely to encounter. Organizational transformation occurs now that the manager has a new choice. No longer does the process of organizational behavior send management down the same dysfunctional road. The knowledge that past events have not been as productive as desired stimulates new managerial behavior toward change.

Notes

[1] Meyer Friedman, "The Modification of Type A Behavior in Post-Infarction Patients," *American Heart Journal* 97:5 (1979), pp. 551-560.

[2] Suzanne Kobasa, "Stressful Life Events, Personality, and Health: An Inquiry into Hardiness," *Journal of Personality and Social Psychology* 37:1 (1979).

[3] W. Schafer, *Stress, Distress, and Growth* (Davis, California: Responsible Action, 1978).

[4] Peter B. Vaill, "Toward a Behavioral Description of High Performing Systems" in *Leadership: Where Else Can We Go?* eds. Morgan McCall and Michael Lombardo (Durham, North Carolina: Duke University Press, 1978).

Glossary

The explorers in every discipline find it necessary to invent language, or borrow it from other disciplines, to describe their experiences and discoveries at the edges of their fields. The pioneers of OT are no different. This glossary is an attempt to help the reader grasp the terms that are used repeatedly by the authors who have contributed to *Transforming Work*.

Alignment: The condition wherein people operate freely and fully as an intentional part of a larger whole. It is created when people see their organization's purpose as an extension of their personal purposes.

Attunement: A resonant, synergistic, and mutually nurturing relationship among the parts of a system; and between the parts and the whole.

Belief: A subjective judgment or proposition which is accepted as true by an individual without requiring supportive evidence. It is a statement of "fact" one makes to one's self. Although they are only our statements about reality, we usually consider our beliefs to be reality.

Consciousness: State of awareness in regard to some thing, sensation, emotion, or thought.

Dissipative Structure: All structures, including social systems, have been observed to absorb perturbations (fluctuations, stresses, etc.) up to a certain point, after which a wholly new, more complex structure rapidly arises. This notion is a challenge to the usual ideas about how evolution proceeds.

Empowerment: The creation of an environment in which individuals are encouraged to develop toward their full creative potential.

Evolution: Relatively gradual, smooth, uninterrupted change in a system.

Evolutionary Manager: A person or team which takes the lead responsibility for the process of transformation in an organization. They hold a metaperspective on the organization and the transformation process and serve a catalytic function. A special application of the fusion team concept.

Fast-tracking: The conscious acceleration and management of the transformational process in an organization.

Fear State Management: Chronically threatened by forces and events, acting to protect self and constrain others. (Contrast with Flow State and Solid State Management.)

Flow State Management: Being in harmony with the natural order of things. Working with the human and organizational factors present to accomplish one's larger purpose.

Fusion Team: A form of group management that looks after the creative process of large project groups, balancing the needs of members with the requirements of the project, budget, and timetable. Its membership may change at any time, and its leadership generally is shared and resource-oriented.

Hologram: A three-dimensional image created by laser photography. A unique and intriguing feature of a holographic plate is that every part of it contains all of the information needed to recreate the entire image. That is, the information is distribute generally throughout the plate. As a model and metaphor, the hologram is being used widely today in brain research, astronomy, physics, and organizational psychology.

Intervenor: An agent from outside a system, typically a manager in an organization or a staff advisor, who intercedes to solve problems or redirect efforts within the system in question.

Meta-: A higher-order perspective. Viewing the function and role of a system from the viewpoint of the next larger, encompassing system.

Metanoic: From the Greek word *metanoia* meaning "a fundamental shift of mind." Used to describe organizations where people operate from the viewpoint that, individually and collectively, they can create the future and shape their destiny. It was used by the early Christians to describe a reawakening of intuition and spirit.

Morphogenetic Fields: Fields of resonance, beyond space and time, which are hypothesized to organize the structure of reality into habitual or usual ways of being. If the hypothesis is valid, we may conclude that the reality of the universe is made up of habits (rather than of universal laws) which are subject to change through changed belief systems.

Myths: The stories we tell to explain the nature of our realities and indicate what is important. They are the "truths" to which we look in deciding how to conduct our lives. They reflect the collective or consensual beliefs of a group or society.

Node Points: Those critical points in an organization where knowledge, authority, and resources come together. Often good leverage points when facilitating transformational processes.

Norms: The expected, accepted, and supported behaviors of a group. The shared habits.

Organizational Energy: Human potential for action or the accomplishment of work. Also the outcome of tensions generated by polarities in organizations such as long-term/short-term needs or stability/change.

Organizational Form: Tangible aspects of organizations such as jobs, tasks, structures, policies, procedures, and results.

Paradigm: A prevailing worldview or collective belief system. The fundamental set of beliefs or organizing principles which are unquestioned and unexamined assumptions about the nature of reality. New paradigms generally do not replace old ones, but subsume them.

Performance: The execution and completion of required or desired functions.

Programming: The predictable, consistent patterns of perceiving and behaving arising from one's beliefs about the nature of reality.

Reframing: Changing the context or perspective from which one views the world. Whether reframing is conscious or unconscious, it indicates tile invocation of a new belief or attitude.

Ritual: The dramatic reenactment of a myth. An acting out of the central stories of the group. The regularized means by which groups get new members aligned with the old story.

Slough-Off Strategies: Preplanned ways to handle noncontributing operations or persons in an organization.

Solid State Management: Skillful at managing the formal aspects of organizational life: the structures, results, tasks, and numbers. Works within set boundaries and maintains set procedures. (Contrast with Fear State and Flow State Management.)

Synergy: The creative output of various inputs that is greater than any one or the sum of those inputs.

Transitions: Predictable cycles of change within the transformation process. Ideally, the transition cycle describes the change process as that which happens between two stable states. In reality, there are few if any stable states and we experience the cycle of transition on a continuing and multiple basis.

Transformation: Profound fundamental changes in thought and actions which create an irreversible discontinuity in the experience of a system. Generally the result of the emergence of radically new belief systems (paradigms).

Contributing Authors

Linda S. Ackerman Anderson is a consultant specializing in transformational change strategy in large private and public sector organizations. She has worked extensively to develop leaders' capacities to model, design and guide their organizations through profound change.
Being First, Inc., 1242 Oak Drive, DWII, Durango, Colorado 81301

John D. Adams, Ph.D., is presently involved in implementing innovative new work environments at Sun Microsystems, Inc., in Palo Alto, California. Prior to joining Sun, he had a 20-year international practice in organization and management development specializing in executive development, change management, and individual effectiveness in the workplace. He also serves as an adjunct professor in doctoral programs. He has been the author and co-author of several books, and is the general editor of the companion volume to this book, *Transforming Leadership.*
1360 4th Avenue, San Francisco, California 94122

Robert F. Allen, Ph.D., until his death in 1987, was president of the Human Resources Institute of Morristown, New Jersey, and professor of psychology and policy science at Kean College of New Jersey. His specialties included community and organizational change via a Normative Systems approach. His Lifegain program for health promotion continues to be used by a large number of organizations.

Karen Wilhelm Buckley has worked with a wide variety of clients for over twenty years in personal and organizational development. With Communicore, based in San Francisco, she is committed to strengthening underlying patterns of health.
425 Magee Avenue, Mill Valley, California 94941

Frank L. Burns is founder and president of Metasystems Design Group, Inc., of Arlington, Virginia. His work utilizes breakthroughs in mind research, cybernetics, and systems science relevant to executive development programs, strategic planning processes, and the transformation of organizations.
Metasystems Design Group, Inc., 2000 North 15th Street, Suite 103, Arlington, Virginia 22201

Alfred M. Coke, Ph.D., is an executive consultant with the Internal Transformation Group, IBM Global Services. Formerly, he was founder and principal of Al Coke and Associates, International, an organization development firm. He specializes in strategic visioning and planning, large systems change management, and practical business applications.
Al Coke & Associates, P.O. Box 483, Smithfield, Virginia 23431

Lawrence H. de Bivort, Ph.D., is president and director of Evolutionary Services Institute of Bethesda, Maryland. He is the developer of the Excel and BIOCOM programs and has developed specialized models and tools for the rapid development of private sector corporations.
Evolutionary Services Institute, 5504 Scioto Road, Bethesda, Maryland 20816

Saul Eisen, Ph.D., is director of the Organizational Development Program at Sonoma State University. He also consults with a variety of groups, communities, and organizations.
1623 West Sexton Road, Sebastopol, California 95472

Roger Harrison, Ph.D., is a pioneer practitioner in the field of Organization Development. He has participated in and contributed to nearly every phase of its growth — from survey research and team-building, to large systems change and organization transformation. He is a noted author of training programs, articles, and books, including *Consultant's Journey: A Dance of Work and Spirit.*
3646 East Redtail Lane, Clinton, Washington 98236

Charles F. Kiefer is founder and president of Innovation Associates, an Arthur D. Little company. He specializes in helping companies discover new business opportunities while simultaneously building the capacity for learning, innovation, and change.
Innovation Associates, Inc., 100 Fifth Avenue, Waltham, Massachusetts 02154

Charlotte Kraft, until her death in 1984, was a freelance writer, playwright, and writing consultant, and an editor for the Human Resources Institute in Morristown, New Jersey. She had been involved with many of the institute's community and organizational change projects.

Richard McKnight, Ph.D., is an organizational psychologist with extensive experience in management and executive development programs. He is exploring stress management and leadership education as pathways to the production of excellent goods and services.
Richard McKnight & Associates, 257 East Lancaster Avenue, Suite 204, Wynnewood, Pennsylvania 19096

Michael D. Mierau, a principal in The Millennium Group, Inc., is a consultant with over thirty years of experience in management, training and organization development, both as a military officer and as a civilian. A recognized authority in designing and building high performing teams, he has worked extensively with governments in Western Europe and Asia, as well as with managers in both large and small, public and private firms.
The Millennium Group, Inc., P.O. Box 12200, Newport News, Virginia 23612-2200

Dani Perkins Monroe is a consultant in Boston, Massachusetts, specializing in diversity and organization transitions. She has conducted research on transitional processes and worked with the dynamics of transitions in numerous Fortune 100 companies.
236 Huntington Avenue, Suite 404, Boston, Massachusetts 02115

Tyler Nelson, Ph.D., was formerly an organizational consultant for the U.S. Army, and is now an independent consultant. Her work focuses on executive development and on designing and implementing processes for helping organizational units work toward becoming high-performing systems.
847 North Temple, Salt Lake City, Utah 84103

David Nicoll, Ph.D., is president of Merlin Nicoll, Inc. His firm offers consulting services in business strategy, organizational design, human resources management, and executive leadership.
2013 South Selby Avenue, Los Angeles, California 90025

Harrison Owen, Ph.D., is president of H.H. Owen and Company in Potomac, Maryland. He has worked with a variety of organizations, including the Peace Corps, National Institutes of Health, and the Veterans Administration, where he discovered that his study of myth, ritual, and culture had direct application to these social systems. He convened the First International Symposium on Organization Transformation, and is the originator of Open Space Technology. Author of several books, his most recent is *Expanding Our Now: The Story of Open Space Technology.*
H. H. Owen & Company, 7808 River Falls Drive, Potomac, Maryland 20854

Peter M. Senge, Ph.D., is a Senior Lecturer at the Massachusetts Institute of Technology where he is part of the Organizational Learning and Change group. He is also Chairman of the Society of Organizational Learning (SoL), a global community of corporations, researchers, and consultants dedicated to the "interdependent development of people and their institutions." A noted author in the areas of learning organization theory and systems thinking in management, he wrote *The Fifth Discipline: The Art and Practice of the Learning Organization,* and he co-authored *The Fifth Discipline Fieldbook.*
MIT, E60-318, 30 Memorial Drive, Cambridge, Massachusetts 02142

Chandra Stephens, Ph.D., MFCC, is a psychotherapist in private practice in Sonoma County, California. She also is a trainer of therapists.
1623 West Sexton Road, Sebastopol, California 95472

Peter Stroh is a founding partner of Innovation Associates and a principal in its parent company, Arthur D. Little. He specializes in visionary planning, aligning diverse stakeholders around a common purpose, and systems thinking in service of organizational learning and change.
Innovation Associates, Inc., 100 Fifth Avenue, Waltham, Massachusetts 02154

Peter B. Vaill, is professor and holder of the Distinguished Chair in Management Education at the Graduate School of Business, University of St. Thomas in Minneapolis/St. Paul. He us widely known for his work on turbulence and rapid change which he calls "permanent white water."
Graduate School of Business, University of St. Thomas, 1000 LaSalle Avenue, Minneapolis, Minnesota 55403-2005

Diana K. Whitney, PhD., is a writer, speaker, and international consultant. She is a founder of The Taos Institute, where she teaches Appreciative Inquiry for global, social and organization change. Her consulting focuses on large-scale processes for organization change and the creation of global social change organizations.
P.O. Box 3257, 1010 Camino del Monte, Taos, New Mexico 87571

References

Ackerman, Linda S. *Managing Complex Change Guide.* McLean, Virginia: Linda S. Ackerman, Inc., 1982.

Ackoff, Russell. "Organizational Decision Making and Planning," Seminar Proceedings. Radnor, Pennsylvania: Sun Company, Inc., 1979.

Ackoff, Russell. *Creating the Corporate Future.* New York: John Wiley & Sons, 1981.

Adams, John D. *Understanding and Managing Stress.* San Diego: University Associates, 1980.

Adams, John D. "Health, Stress, and the Manager's Lifestyle." *Group and Organization Studies* 6:3 (1981): 291-301.

Adams, John D. "Planning for Comprehensive Stress Management." In J. Marshall and C.L. Cooper, eds., *Coping with Stress at Work.* Aldershot, United Kingdom: Gower, 1981.

Allen, Robert F., H.N. Dubin, S. Pilnick, and A. Youtz. *Collegefields from Delinquency to Freedom.* Seattle: Special Child Publications, 1970.

Allen, Robert F., and Charlotte Kraft. *Beat the System.* New York: McGraw-Hill, 1980.

Allen, Robert F., and S. Linde. *Lifegain.* New York: Appleton, Century, Crofts, 1981.

Argyris, Chris. "Double Look Learning in Organizations." *Harvard Business Review* 55:5 (1977).

Bandura, A. *Social Learning Theory.* Englewood Cliffs, New Jersey: Prentice-Hall, 1977.

Barfield, Owen. "The Rediscovery of Meaning." In R. Thruelsen and J. Kobler, eds. *Adventures of the Mind.* New York: Vintage Books, 1961.

Barrett, William. *Time Of Need.* New York: Harper & Row, 1972.

Barrett, William. *The Illusion of Technique.* New York: Anchor Books, 1978.

Beckhard, R., and R. Harris. *Organizational Transitions: Managing Complex Change.* Reading, Massachusetts: Addison-Wesley, 1977.

Beer, S. *Platform for Change.* Chichester, United Kingdom: John Wiley and Sons, 1975.

N. Belloc and L. Breslow. "Relationship of Physical Health Status and Health Practices." *Preventive Medicine* 1 (1972): 409-421.

Bennis, Warren. *Leading Edge Bulletin* (22 February 1982).

Berlew, D. "Leadership and Organization Excitement." *California Review* 17:2 (1974): 21-30.

Berry, Thomas. "Comments on the Origin, Identification and Transmission of Values."*Anima* (Winter 1978).

Burns, J.M. *Leadership.* New York: Harper & Row, 1978.

Capra, F. *The Turning Point.* New York: Simon and Schuster, 1982.

Capra, F. "The Turning Point: A New Vision of Reality." *The Futurist,* Vol. XVI; 6 (1982).

Connelly, Sharon L. "The Fusion Team: An Experimental Group Management Technology" in L.L. Franklin, ed., *An Army of Excellence: Visions of Our Future Force.* Carlisle Barracks, Pennsylvania: Delta Force, 1982.

Cox, S. *Indirections.* New York: Viking Press, Compass Books Edition, 1962.

Csikszentmihalyi, Mihalyi. *Beyond Boredom and Anxiety.* San Francisco: Jossey-Bass, 1975.

Dalven, R. *The Complete Poems of Cavafy.* Harcourt, Brace & Javanovich, 1976.

Davis, S.M. "Transforming Organizations: The Key to Strategy is Context." *Organizational Dynamics* 10:3 (1982).

DeLong, D. "Changing the Way We Think." *Boston Globe* (10 February 1981).

Drucker, P.F. *Management: Tasks, Responsibilities, Practices.* New York: Harper & Row, 1973.

Emerson, Ralph Waldo. "Literary Ethics." In R.E. Spiller, ed., *The Collected Works of Ralph Waldo Emerson,* Vol. 1. Cambridge, Massachusetts: Belknap Press of Harvard University Press, 1971.

Ferguson, Marilyn. *The Aquarian Conspiracy.* Los Angeles: J.P. Tarcher, 1980.

Forester, C.S. *The Indomitable Hornblower* [compendium of three novels, including *Lord Hornblower*]. Boston: Little, Brown and Co., undated.

Forrester, J.W. "Common Foundations Underlying Engineering and Management." *IEEE Spectrum,* Vol. I (1964): 66-77.

Forrester, J.W. "A New Corporate Design." *Industrial Management Review* [currently *Sloan Management Review*], Vol. 7 (1965).

Forrester, J.W. "Innovation in Economic Change," *Futures,* Vol. 13 (1981): 323-331.

Frankl, Victor E. *Man's Search for Meaning.* New York: Beacon Press, 1959.

Freeman, C., J. Clark, and L. Soete. *Unemployment and Technical Innovations.* Westport, Connecticut: Greenwood Press, 1982.

Friedman, Meyer, and R.H. Rosenman. *Type A Behavior and Your Heart.* New York: Knopf, 1974.

Friedman, Meyer. "The Modification of Type A Behavior in Post-Infarction Patients." *American Heart Journal* 97:5 (1979): 551-560.

Fromm, Erich. *Escape from Freedom.* New York: Farrar, Straus, Giroux, 1960.

Fromm, Erich. *To Have or To Be?* New York: Bantam Books, 1976.

Galbraith, J. *Designing Complex Organizations.* Reading, Massachusetts: Addison-Wesley, 1973.

Gelb, M. *Body Learning.* New York: Delilah Books, 1981.

Graham, A.K., and Peter M. Senge. "A Long Wave Hypothesis of Innovation." *Technological Forecasting and Social Change*, Vol. 17 (1980): 283-311

Graves, F. "Are These Men Soviet Dupes?" *Common Cause* 9:1 (1983).

Harman, Willis W. "Rationale of Good Choosing." *Journal of Humanistic Psychology* 21 (1981).

Harman, Willis W. "Visions of Tomorrow: The Transformation Ahead." *OD Practitioner* 13:1 (February 1981).

Harman, Willis W. *Institute of Noetic Sciences Newsletter* 9:2 (1981).

Harris, S., and R.F. Allen. *The Quiet Revolution: How Florida Migrants Changed Their Lives*. New York: Rawson Associates, 1978.

Heidegger, Martin. *Being and Time*. Trans. J. Macquarrie and E. Robinson. New York: Harper & Row, 1962; originally published 1927.

Hersey, Paul, and Ken Blanchard. *Management of Organizational Behavior: Utilizing Human Resources*, 4th Edition. Englewood Cliffs, New Jersey: Prentice-Hall, 1982.

Houston, Jean. *Life Force*. New York: Dell, 1980.

Houston, Jean. *The Possible Human*. Los Angeles: J.P. Tarcher, 1982.

Hubbard, B.M. *The Evolutionary Journey*. San Francisco: Evolutionary Press, 1982.

Ingalls, J.D. *Human Energy*. Reading, Massachusetts: Addison-Wesley, 1976.

Jayaram, G.K. "Creation of New Settings: A Dynamic Model" [unpublished monograph].

Johnson, R.A. *He: Understanding Masculine Psychology*. New York: Harper & Row, 1977.

Jones, R.S. *Physics as Metaphor*. New York: New American Library, 1983.

Kanter, Rosabeth Moss. *Men and Women of the Corporation*. New York: Basic Books, 1977.

Kobasa, Suzanne. "Stressful Life Events, Personality, and Health: An Inquiry into Hardiness." *Journal of Personality and Social Psychology* 37:1 (1979).

Koestler, Arthur. *Janus*. New York: Random House, 1978.

Kuhn, Thomas S. *The Structure of Scientific Revolutions*. Chicago: The University of Chicago Press, 1970.

Lao, Tsu. *Tao Te Ching*. Trans. Gia-Fu Feng and J. English. New York: Vintage Books, 1972; orginially published 6th century B.C..

Larsen, E. "Why Do Some People Outperform Others? *The Wall Street Journal* (21 January 1982).

Larsen, E. "Why Are Some Managers Top Performers? *The Wall Street Journal* (21 January 1982).

Lawrence, D.H. "Morality and the Novel." In E.D. McDonald, ed., *Phoenix: The Posthumous Papers of D.H. Lawrence*. New York: The Viking Press, 1968; originally published 1925.

Lewin, K. *Field Theory and Social Science*. New York: Harper & Row, 1951.

Maccoby, Michael. *The Gamesman: The New Corporate Leaders*. New York: Simon and Schuster, 1976.

Maccoby, Michael. *The Leader*. New York: Simon and Schuster, 1981.

Maiden, A.H. "Resonance." *Gaia* [quarterly publication of the Institute for the Study of Conscious Evolution], Vol. II; 2 (1980).

Markley, O.W., and W. Harman. *Changing Images of Man*. New York: Pergamon Press, 1982.

Marrow, A. *The Practical Theorist: The Life and Work of Kurt Lewin*. New York: Basic Books, 1969.

Maslow, Abraham H. "A Theory of Human Motivation." *Technological Review* 50 (1943): 370-396.

Maslow, Abraham H. *Motivation and Personality*. New York: Harper & Row, 1954.

Maslow, Abraham H. *Eupsycian Management*. Homewood, Illinois: Richard D. Irwin, Inc., and the Dorsey Press, 1965.

Mass, N.J., and Peter M. Senge. "Reindustrialization: Aiming at the Right Targets." *Technology Review* (August/September 1981): 56-65.

Matthews-Simonton, Stephanie. "Psychological Aspects of Healing," presented at "Healing in Our Time" Conference, Washington, D.C. (October 1982).

May, Rollo. *Love and Will*. New York: Norton, 1969.

Meadows, D.H., D.L. Meadows, J. Randers, and H. Behrens III. *The Limits to Growth*. New York: Universe Books, 1972.

Meadows, D.H. "Whole Earth Models and Systems." *CoEvolution Quarterly* (Summer 1982).

McCaskey, M.B. *The Executive Challenge: Managing Change and Ambiguity*. Marshfield, Massachusetts: Pitman, 1982.

McGregor, Douglas M. *The Human Side of Enterprise*. New York: McGraw-Hill, 1960.

McWaters, B. *Conscious Evolution: Personal and Planetary Transformation*. San Francisco: Evolutionary Press, 1982.

Mensch, G. *Stalemate in Technology*. Cambridge, Massachusetts: Ballinger, 1979.

Mintzberg, H. "The Manager's Job: Folklore and Fact." *Harvard Business Review* 53:4 (1975): 49-61.

Nadler, D.A., and M.L. Tushman. "A Model for Organizational Diagnosis." *Organizational Dynamics* (Autumn 1980).

Naisbitt, John. *Megatrends*. New York: Harper & Row, 1982.

Naisbitt, John. *Trend Letter* 2:4 (1983).

Nelson, R.F.W. *The Illusions of Urban Man*. Ottawa: The Ministry of State for Urban Affairs, 1978.

Nisbet, R. *The Quest for Community*. New York: Oxford University Press, 1953.

Ogilvy, Jay. *Many Dimensional Man: Decentralizing Self, Society, and the Sacred.* New York: Harper & Row, 1979.

Ouchi, W.G. *Theory Z: How American Business Can Meet the Japanese Challenge.* New York: Avon Books, 1981.

Pascale, Richard T. "Zen and the Art of Management." *Harvard Business Review* (March/April 1978).

Pascale, Richard T., and Anthony G. Athos. *The Art of Japanese Management.* New York: Simon and Schuster, 1981.

Peters, Thomas J., and R.H. Waterman, Jr. *In Search of Excellence: Lessons from America's Best-Run Companies.* New York: Harper & Row, 1982.

Pines, M. "Psychological Hardiness: The Role of Challenge in Health." *Psychology Today* (December 1980): 33-44.

Polak, F. *The Image of the Future.* Trans. Elise Boulding. San Francisco: Jossey-Bass, 1973.

Prigogine, I. *From Being to Becoming.* San Francisco: Freeman, 1980.

Quinn, J.B. "Managing Strategic Change." *Sloan Management Review* 23(1):55 (Fall 1981).

Roberts, J. *The Nature of Personal Reality.* Engelwood Cliffs, New Jersey: Prentice-Hall, 1974.

Roethlisberger, F.J. *Man in Organization.* Cambridge, Massachusetts: Belknap Press of Harvard University Press, 1968.

Rogers, Carl. *On Becoming a Person.* Boston: Houghton-Mifflin, 1961.

Rowan, R. "Those Business Hunches are More Than Blind Faith." *Fortune* 99:8 (1979): 110-114.

Russell, B. and T. Branc. *Second Wind: The Memories of an Opinionated Man.* New York: Random House, 1979.

Schafer, W. *Stress, Distress, and Growth.* Davis, California: Responsible Action, 1978.

Schein, Edgar H. "An Organizational Culture." Working paper. Cambridge, Massachusetts: Sloan School of Management, Massachusetts Institute of Technology, 1981.

Schein, E.H. "Does Japanese Management Style Have a Message for American Managers?" *Sloan Management Review* 23(1):55 (Fall 1981).

Schon, Donald A. *Beyond the Stable State.* New York: W.W. Norton and Co., 1971.

Schroeder, L., S. Ostrander, D. Dean and J. Mihalasky. *Executive ESP.* New York: Prentice-Hall, 1974.

Schwartz, Peter, and Jay Ogilvy. In "The Emergent Paradigm: Changing Patterns of Thought and Belief." *Analytical Report: Values and Lifestyles Program*, SRI International (April 1979).

Sheehy, Gail. *Pathfinders*. New York: Bantam Books, 1981.

Sheldrake, Rupert. *A New Science of Life: The Hypothesis of Formative Causation*. Los Angeles: J.P. Tarcher, 1982.

Siu, R.G.H. *The Master Manager*. Chichester, United Kingdom: John Wiley and Sons, 1980.

Sorokin, P. *The Basic Trends of Our Time*. New Haven: College and University Press, 1964.

Srivastva, S., and David L. Cooperrider, eds., *Organizational Wisdom and Executive Courage*. San Francisco: Jossey-Bass, 1997.

Steinbeck, J., and E.F. Ricketts. *Sea of Cortez*. Mamaroneck, New York: P.O. Appeal Press, 1971.

Trist, Eric L. "Urban North America: The Challenge of the Next Thirty Years." In W. Schmidt, ed., *OrganizationalFrontiers and Human Values*. Belmont, California: Wadsworth, 1970.

Vaill, Peter B. Commencement Address, George Washington University, Washington, D.C., unpublished (May 1974).

Vaill, Peter B. "Towards a Behavioral Description of High-Performing Systems." In Morgan McCall and Michael Lombardo, eds., *Leadership: Where Else Can We Go?* Durham, North Carolina: Duke University Press, 1978.

Vaill, Peter B. "Cookbooks, Auctions, and Claptrap Cocoons." *Exchange: The Organizational Behavior Teaching Journal* 4:1 (1979).

Vaill, Peter B. "The Purpose of High Performing Systems," *Organizational Dynamics* (Autumn 1982).

Vaill, Peter B. "OD as a Scientific Revolution." In D.D. Warrick, ed., *Current Developments in Organization Development*. New York: Scott, Foresman, 1984.

Wilber, Ken. *Eye to Eye: The Quest for the New Paradigm*. Boston: Shambhala Publications, 1982.

Woolfolk and Richardson. *Stress, Sanity and Survival*. New York: Sovereign, 1978.

Yankelovich, Daniel. "New Rules in American Life." *Psychology Today* (April 1981): 35-91.

Yankelovich, Daniel. "Toward an Ethic of Commitment." *Industry Week* 209:6 (1981).

Yankelovich, Daniel. *New Rules*. New York: Random House, 1981.

Yankelovich, Daniel. "The Work Ethic is Underemployed." *Psychology Today* 16:5 (1982).

Young, J.Z. *Doubt and Certainty in Science*. New York: Galaxy Books of Oxford University Press, 1960.